# GREEN FIRE

## Stories from the Wild

*Vis Medicatrix Naturae*

Earle F. Layser

*Frontispiece – Vis Medicatrix Naturae* is Latin meaning the
restorative, healing power of nature.

*To my parents, Earle Sr. and Elsie, to whom I'm forever grateful for their decision to move from the city and build a farm deep in the mountains near Cedar Run, Pennsylvania, providing me with the opportunity to enjoy a boyhood of exploring fields, forests, and streams, and meeting the wild inhabitants of those places.*

GREEN FIRE
Stories from the Wild
# CONTENTS

# I
## ACKNOWLEDGEMENTS

Writing a book of this kind necessarily requires researching and relying on the works of other authors and journalists. The attributions in the section on source materials are a testimony to that statement. To all the authors, naturalists, conservationists, scientists, biologists, and journalists upon whose coattails this book rides, my many thanks. I salute all who labored in the interests of wildlife and our last remaining wild places.

A number of people kindly gave their time and assistance by reviewing early drafts of particular stories, and others, the entire draft manuscript. Those who critically read and commented on individual stories included: Director of the Cougar Fund Sara Carlson; Arctic National Wildlife Refuge activist Vance Carruth; Teton Science School's pika project leader Embere Hall; and the Alta 4-H wolverine project participants Sue and Andy Heffron, and Mary Carol and Dick Staiger. The draft manuscript was read by filmmaker and author Charles Craighead, acclaimed wildlife photographer and author Thomas Mangelsen, and author and naturalist Bert Raynes. I greatly appreciate the time, helpful comments, and encouragement freely given by those folks.

I communicated with National Park biologists Steven Cain and Rick Wallen with questions regarding Grand Teton National Park's bison and Yellowstone National Park's bison genetics, I am grateful for their shared information and expertise.

Retired U.S. Forest Service biologist Timothy Layser contributed information about "caribou 109"and provided the image of 109. Retired forester John Joy provided a photograph of the north Idaho, Willow Creek bull caribou. Tetonia, Idaho, author and photographer Joe Smith volunteered a portrait of a bighorn sheep. Wildlife photographer Thomas Mangelsen kindly contributed an image of the Miller Butte cougar. The Bozeman, Montana, Wantulok Group provided several excellent photographs: the wolf portrait, the lopping wolf pack, a beaver, and the group of bighorn sheep rams. Dick Staiger and Andy Heffron came up with an image of Wolver-Dan obtained by their study's motion-sensory camera. The Yellowstone National Park on-line digital slide file was the source for the photo of Edgar Howell's grisly work with bison. The historical photo of bounty hunter Cleve Miller was obtained from the Denver Public Library Western History Collection, and that of the government hunters with wolf skins from the Arizona State Historical Society. The map image for the Jackson Hole Monument's Wildlife Park and photograph of bison being fed hay at the Wildlife Park were obtained from the Grand Teton National Park archives. I am indebted for the use of all the above images. They greatly contribute to the visual interest and credibility of the stories.

Yellowstone National Park Museum Curator Colleen Curry was very supportive in assisting with my research on Old Tex and directing me in the use of Yellowstone digital photographs on-line. Likewise, Grand Teton National Park archivists Alice Hurt and Laureen Lafrancois were very helpful in providing access to the Fabian Collection  records for the Jackson Hole Monument's Wildlife Park and assisting me in my search for historical photographs.

I want to make special mention of Jackson Hole historian Doris Platts, whose independent research and chronicling of early-day anti-predator activity in Jackson Hole and Sublette County, Wyoming, was most valuable in my crafting of the Pack's Memoirs and the Miller Butte cougar stories.

Journalist Jennifer Dorsey deserves special thanks for her freely given time and her initial line editing of the draft manuscript. Editor and naturalist guide Beverley Charette kindly did a "cold read" of each of the stories and provided editorial comments and criticisms; and, writer-editor Deb Baracato freely gave of her time and expertise to critically read and comment on a portion of the bison story.

I owe a great deal of thanks to Wendy Renner of the Wantulok Group for her professional skills and ideas in designing the cover, frontispiece, and the interior page lay out. Her technical abilities and skills turned the manuscript and materials into the physical reality of this book.

My wife, Pattie, has written and published many stories in periodicals and anthologies on western and wildlife art, outdoor activities, and nature, particularly related to Teton Valley and Jackson Hole, Wyoming. It's been my exceptionally good fortune in life to have a companion who is also engaged in writing and whose ideas and values are simpatico with mine when it comes to the subject matter presented in this book. We had many discussions over morning coffee on the book's content (as well as late night ones, too), and its production. Words are inadequate to express my gratitude for her patience, continuing support, constructive criticisms, editorial assistance, and enthusiastic sharing of ideas and life.

Finally, the stories in this book are the results of the author's research, interpretations, judgment, and chosen styles of presentation. If there are omissions, inaccuracies, or short-comings, those are solely his responsibility. Some of the material and presentations are non-traditional and perhaps even provocative. However, I have simply tried to communicate the stories in a non-technical manner consistent with my research, field observations, imagination, and life experiences. I am hopeful the tales will resonate in ways that are positive for both wildlife and my readers.

Earle F. Layser
Alta, Wyoming

# II
## INTRODUCTION

*A life of incomprehensible loneliness awaits a world where the wild things were, but are never to be again.*
—W. Stolzenburg, *Where the Wild Things Were*

This is a book for biophiles, people who love wild animals. It is an eclectic collection of original stories with interrelated themes about wildlife and wildlands. The narratives incorporate current issues, science, history, natural history, and folklore. They describe thirteen featured species' extraordinary adaptations and survival strategies and how they have directly and indirectly fared at the hands of man.

When I began writing these stories a few years ago, I started by chronicling compelling facets of the different species' natural history. The life histories of wild creatures are fascinating, but man's interaction with them adds layers of history and complexity, which also begs to be told. In researching and composing the narratives, I invariably found it unavoidable to also address recurring social and political issues and attitudes associated with contemporary wildlife management, conservation, and threats facing some of the species.

The end result is that while some of the stories are presented in a fictionalized and whimsical fashion that can be read on different levels, all have underlying serious messages, too. The stories are intended not only to be entertaining, but enlightening and informative. Interwoven or imbedded into each essay are unusual or generally little known, original, and often multilayered facets about the animal and its history. All the stories convey the value and need for conservation and the importance of protecting and restoring not only species, but entire ecosystems and wildland habitats. They also reveal some of the historic origins of the current problems, attitudes, and contentiousness surrounding the conservation and management of some species, particularly large carnivores.

In his 1944 essay "Thinking Like a Mountain," Aldo Leopold described how he witnessed the "fierce green fire" go out of a dying wolf's eyes. The story is an allegory of Leopold's intellectual journey that gives birth to a land ethic. It is steeped in symbolism. In that sense, the phrase green fire may serve as a simile for the environmental movement—from the dying wolf, enlightenment was born.

Nature program cinematographer and author Steve Nicholls, in *Paradise Found: Nature in America at the Time of Discovery,* equates green fire to "a vitality and abundance of nature that once existed and that we have forgotten."

Metaphorically, my title, *Green Fire,* is intended to include all those things. It is a flame that burns within wild creatures, a life force. Its glow is reflected in the indomitable and resilient spirit of untamed nature. What Nicholls maintains we have forgotten it is important for us to try to rediscover.

The early beginnings of many environmentalists, conservationists, and naturalists are as hunters or trappers, or through other outdoor recreation activities, or as ranchers and even as gardening urbanites. Those beginnings, as Leopold describes, can sometimes include "trigger itch." But over time, through innate curiosity, personal experiences, experiential discovery, and education, one builds an appreciation and sensitivity for the natural world.

For different individuals, the green fire may symbolically or experientially seem to burn more fiercely in some living things and places than in others, and in that way it also relates to sense of place, but it nevertheless radiates from all wild creatures, wild places, and untamed nature.

The heroes in these stories are the wild animals: the last of the plains bison, many of which near the end carried bullets embedded in their bodies from gun shots they had managed to survive; the last of the wolves in the early twentieth century, who had missing toes, paws, teeth, and tails from having escaped leghold traps, escaped death by disgorging poisons, or survived being shot, but still continued to elude their pursuers; and the beavers that were trapped and hunted to near extinction, but in a demonstration of resilience, have repopulated former habitats throughout the Rockies.

In recent years, a Yellowstone wolf journeyed to Colorado and back; a wolverine that showed up in California's Sierras had its origins traced by DNA analysis to the Rockies; another wolverine, tracked by telemetry, trekked from Yellowstone to Rocky Mountain National Park in Colorado; a mountain lion collared in South Dakota showed up in Oklahoma; a remnant band of antelope seasonally moves between Jackson Hole and the Green River Basin; and annually, the Porcupine caribou herd in the Arctic National Wildlife Refuge migrates a greater distance than Africa's famed Serengeti wildebeest. These are epic odysseys, not only in terms of distances, but from the standpoint of both the man-made and natural obstacles the animals must overcome. Measured by any human standard, which is perhaps to say anthropomorphically, they represent courageously bold and intrepid journeys.

Scientists use the terms "dispersal" and "migration" to describe such movements. But the terms alone fail to adequately describe the daunting challenges facing animals nowadays in circumnavigating fences, highways, towns, farms, river crossings, and mountain ranges, and in avoiding dogs, livestock, hunters, and people in general. Those wild animals display an indomitable spirit. If people were to travel those same amazing distances on foot, unaided, and under similarly hazardous circumstances, they would be celebrated for bravery and heroism. They would be lauded in history books. Wild animals that make those journeys display a life force or vitality that is an intrinsic part of untamed nature.

One can hardly mention the Rocky Mountains without the mental association of iconographic wildlife: beavers, bison, grizzly bears, mountain lions, wolves, mountain sheep, mountain goats, pika, and even whitebark pine trees, all emblematic of the American West, all survivors in their own rightful world.

The word survivor is from the Latin *supervivere*, meaning "to live a super life." But wild animals are born to live their lives fully until the end, no matter when and how that may come. They know no other way. They play out their roles as the creator or evolution intended. Their lives are all, in fact, "super lives." The animals that are the subjects of this book, among others, can be said to represent the wild or untamed nature in our Western lands; to the extent they exist, the land retains its wilderness character.

A common theme runs through each story: considering the adversities wild animals face, their lives transcend the ordinary. They reside in unique worlds parallel to our own and in an anthropomorphic sense, many live legendary lives. The lives of these wild creatures frequently and lamentably end in tragedy, often from travesties perpetuated by mankind. Fatalism is pervasive, perhaps unavoidable. It's also an important contemporary ethical question of wildlife management just how much wild animal's lives should be determined by man's technology, control, and intervention.

Is wildlife really free and wild when it is under man's continual electronic surveillance? Should some limits be placed on the extent of control and management of natural systems, wildlife, and wildlands, as per the 1964 Wilderness Act, if they are to be considered wild and functioning ecosystems? What should regulated hunting's role be in the twenty-first century? And to what extent can government agencies' and organizations' contribute to resolving the growing dichotomy between contemporary society and the natural world? These are just some of today's wildlife management issues.

Native Americans have long recognized the symbolic and talismanic power of particular wild animals. These stories demonstrate how, even today, wild animals represent symbols that contemporary society has adopted and utilizes in characterizing our lives, places, and livelihoods. The naming of state animals is just one example: Colorado, the Rocky Mountain bighorn sheep; Montana, the grizzly bear; Wyoming, the bison; and Utah, the Rocky Mountain elk. In the northern Rockies, only Idaho has named a domestic animal, the horse, as its state animal.

Regardless that much of contemporary society is ensconced in urban areas and the virtual world, and that they are detached from nature and the natural world, the spirit and legendary power of wild animals still stimulates people's imaginations and often contributes symbolically to defining modern culture, sense of place, and purpose. This speaks loudly for both the real and symbolic power wild animals convey.

A majority of the narratives center on or are related to the Greater Yellowstone region. One might argue the Greater Yellowstone has become a center for leading-edge interaction and attempts at synchronicity with wilderness species within the conterminous United States. It is a region that is constantly serving to redefine our relationship with the land and wildlife. The continuing evolvement of people's coexistence with grizzly bears, the celebrated 1995 reintroduction of wolves, and events such as the Teton Science School's 2010 pika conference held in Jackson, Wyoming, are wide-reaching examples.

Additionally, only in Teton National Park is there a "Wildlife Brigade" comprised of employees, volunteers, and interns that functions to reduce potential wildlife conflicts along roadsides, particularly "bear jams," in order to allow park visitors to view the animals. And, as Howard Quigley, senior research biologist for Berigia South's cougar project, recently exclaimed to journalist Cory Hatch, in "A Lion's Tale," *Jackson Hole* magazine, winter 2009-10, "For forty years, we [biologists] have been studying wildlife biology without a full complement of predators. Now we have one place we can do it: the Greater Yellowstone Ecosystem."

The Northern Rockies' Greater Yellowstone Ecosystem, and also the Crown of the Continent centered on Glacier National Park might, in fact, be considered evolving prototypes for Caroline Fraser's *Rewilding the World* (2009). "Rewilding" means biological restoration. Fraser identifies three things that are necessary: "cores, corridors, and carnivores." The concepts are incorporated into the Yellowstone to the Yukon Biodiversity Strategy (Y2Y), which focuses on core areas connected by corridors and retaining an interconnected landscape from Yellowstone to the Yukon. Likewise, the Northern Rockies Ecosystem Protection Act before Congress proposes to designate 23 million acres of wilderness that would similarly protect biological corridors and connecting ecosystems.

In the Greater Yellowstone landscape, the core areas are the national parks, wildlife refuges, and national forest backcountry and Wildernesses; the corridors are the north-south mountain ranges and island ranges that provide connectivity for dispersal; and the carnivores are grizzly bear, mountain lions, wolverines, and wolves—"flagship species" that symbolize entire conservation programs. According to Fraser and others, carnivores play a crucial role in regulating one another, other predators, and their prey. This was graphically illustrated in a March 2010 *National Geographic* story entitled "Wolf Wars" by Douglas H. Chadwick.

A recent poll analysis by journalist Jonathan Schechter asked the citizens of two resort communities—Aspen, Colorado, and Jackson Hole, Wyoming—what they considered the most important environmental element contributing to quality of life. Wildlife ranked number one for residents of the Hole; not one Aspen respondent mentioned the natural world. Significantly, the National Museum of Wildlife Art, the only museum of its kind anywhere, is located in Jackson Hole. For both Jackson Hole's residents and visitors alike, wildlife plays a major role in the mountain enclave's popularity, grandeur, economy, and sense of place. Its wildlife is more than just locally or regionally important, it is of national and international significance. The resident's of the Hole's deep sense of place is something that derives from their association with wild animals and a corresponding empathic response for wildlife.

The way a society treats wildlife says a lot about the enlightenment of its culture. Certainly the contributions wild animals make to our lives are more significant than the 2008 vice presidential candidate Sarah Palin's flippant comment in

*Going Rogue*: "There's plenty of room for animals—right next to the mashed potatoes." The historical vignettes presented as part of the stories in this book go deeper, providing insights into how we as a society have related to, dealt with, and valued particular species over time. The origins of present day attitudes towards certain species are revealed in the histories of our interactions with them.

Few things more rapidly disclose basic philosophical differences between individuals or cultures than their attitudes towards wildlife, particularly the large predators—the fanged creatures. The irrational and insane hatred of predators appears to be almost genetically linked within certain elements of our society. It is often passed on from generation to generation. It is a dubious heritage. One unfortunate result is that certain animals have become recognized more as symbols of contentiousness, rather than appreciated as the awe-inspiring and singularly unique creatures they represent.

The human population in the Rockies is expected to double in the next twenty to forty years. A 2010 study by University of Wisconsin scientist's Volker Radeloff, et al., "Housing growth in and near United States protected areas limits their conservation value," *Proceedings of the National Academy of Sciences*, predicted a preponderance of future residential development will be located less than fifty kilometers from national parks, national forests and Wildernesses. We are competing directly with wild animals for space. Wildlife, a singularly vital part of our national heritage, is being forced to make the most of the diminishing space and habitat.

While sapien—as in *Homo sapiens*—means "to know," a relatively small percentage of our overall population actually seems "to know" or to care about wildlands and wildlife. Are we destined to live in a world, as author Robert James Waller writes, that "is too small and too selfish and too beset upon the trivial and transitory" to share it with wild creatures? Some see this question as a dilemma wherein we must chose between either people or wildlife, but an alternative is a progressively planned and decided coexistence.

Not long ago, I proposed a wildlife drive to a highly-successful couple from Chicago's corporate world that were visiting us. I explained how magnificent it was to view bison within the natural setting of Grand Teton National Park: The shaggy beasts spread out across Antelope Flats, I said, belly deep in wildflowers, with the dramatic snowcapped peaks rising skyward behind them. Our Chicago friends politely, but casually dismissed the idea, "Oh, we've seen buffalo before on a farm in Michigan."

On another occasion, I suggested to a couple visiting from New York—again successful and sophisticated people when measured by our culture's standards—that they might enjoy the close-up viewing of wintering elk afforded by Jackson Hole's National Elk Refuge. They were amused, as if I were a well-meaning simpleton. "If you've seen one elk, you've seen 'em all," they replied."

Those attitudes are not uncommon within modern-day society. In some people's minds, if one looks at an animal's pelt, a taxidermy specimen, or a caged animal in a zoo or on a farm that is all there is to it. Been there, done that. Everything about the animal and what it represents is then apparently known and understood. Wild animals become no more than objects, or at best, no different than barnyard animals. The way of thinking is pervasively common, and it has been around a long while, too. It was reflected in the Smithsonian's nineteenth century practice of sending out hunters to acquire specimens for exhibits before the particular animal went extinct from over hunting.

This is not to deny the great importance of zoos and museums for species restoration, preservation, education and science, but museums can be deadly dull in comparison to observing the live animals and their behaviors in their natural habitat. The person that is satisfied by simply observing a caged animal or taxidermy specimen denies appreciation for the fact that every species represents a singular and sentient creature that ecologically occupies a distinct niche. It is my hope the stories in this book will stir a reader's imagination and curiosity and help convey the idea that each wild animal is a unique creature, and that their habitat is part of a world we share, or need to share, if wild creatures and nature are going to continue to be a part of our lives.

Obviously, because people in our culture are successful in terms of their specialty, career, or politics it does not automatically translate that they are cognizant or sympathetic to the needs of wild animals or to preserving wildland habitats. Success in our postmodern society is not defined in the Renaissance sense. It does not necessarily translate to being broadly educated, intellectually curious, nor universally informed. The unfortunate result of over specialization, monomania, or just plain ignorance, can be religious, political or corporate indifference to the persecution of wildlife and the destruction of habitat. It is one reason environmental education and experiencing nature is vitally important for balance and well-being in our urbanized society and corporate world today, especially for young people as described by author Richard Louv in *Last Child in the Woods* (2005). Contrary to some homocentric beliefs, humans are not totally separate and apart from nature; history, biology, the theory of evolution, and DNA science prove otherwise.

Most people today will never observe a grizzly bear, cougar, wolverine or wolf in the wild. Where these animals are found, they occur in low densities over wide geographic areas often in rugged terrain. Generally, they are very wary and avoid people, so chance sightings or encounters are infrequent. Sure, viewing the relentless head-down pacing of an animal at the zoo or seeing a specimen prepared by a taxidermist is readily possible. But coming upon the animal in the wild and interacting with it in its natural habitat ah, now that is something else. It can be a moment or event that becomes a lifelong memory.

In the case of powerfully talismanic animals, such interactions can be life altering. For young people, as my Wolveranne story reveals, it can be an experience that gives direction to their lives and the selection of careers. Our society and people's lives will be greatly impoverished if the quests and opportunities for those kinds of experiences should no longer exist.

People are drawn to live in the Rockies to be close to nature. Many act as if they believe their proximity to wildlands and wildlife conveys status. As mentioned earlier, Radeloff, et al., reported that in 2000, 38 million residential units existed within fifty kilometers (30 miles) of protected lands (national parks, national forests, Wildernesses) in the United States. The development in close proximity to protected lands is projected to continue to grow 45-50 percent in the next twenty years. Unfortunately, those people often end up sanitizing and destroying the very thing they sought. The living symbols of wilderness, especially the fanged ones, are rarely tolerated in their own backyards.

The results of biophobia are little changed today from when our forefathers acted upon similar feelings. As the bison, cougar, grizzly bear and wolf stories in this book illustrate, control and manipulation of wildlife, for the most part, still remains a war with nature. Only today, the numbers of people and technology give mankind an even greater edge and potentially even greater destructive capability than in the past.

Scientists tend to narrowly focus on metrics, statistical proofs and facts, meanwhile ongoing undesirable outcomes are sometimes overlooked or ignored. Field scientists avoid giving names to radio-collared animals and instead assign numbers. A name might provoke sentimentalism or empathy with the animal; the public might emotionally identify with it, which might interfere with study methods, management decisions, or encourage controversy. And, we do not hunt and kill animals, but rather "harvest" or "regulate" them. But too much detachment can be deleterious to understanding and appreciation and the willingness to protect certain wildlife and natural habitat.

I sympathize with the biologists who are required to be wing walkers; master jugglers, conducting balancing acts. For reasons of career and self-preservation, they sometimes practice keeping their cards close to their chest and avoid publicly or passionately expressing their professional opinions in order to minimize controversy or getting cross-wise with warring factions. Only a fortunate few, mostly in research or programs popular with sport hunters, are in positions to publicly identify with and champion the animals that originally attracted them into their profession.

The stories in this book illustrate not only the historical complexities of wildlife resource issues and the origins of public attitudes towards certain species, but also touch on the sensitive, multifaceted, bureaucratic, and political attitudes confronting biologists and resource managers today. And they also reveal that some public and resource officials are not above letting their own political maneuvering, biases, and contrary mindsets actively interfere with objective decision-making and scientific management of wildlife.

While I recognize the value and efficacy of science and science-based wildlife management, and gratefully acknowledge the importance of the contributions of dedicated professional game biologists and scientists—such as those Harold Picton and Terry Lonner have documented in *Montana's Wildlife: Decimation to Restoration*—I also believe that science sometimes fails to fully communicate or translate to the broader general public. A general example is a 2009 Gallup poll that showed only 39 percent of Americans accept the theory of evolution; the remaining 61 percent either had no opinion, remained unconvinced, or were hostile toward the theory. This is despite the fact that science has explained the mechanism by which evolution operates through the study of DNA. What might that potentially warn about the local official's or general populace's opinion when the theory of evolution is the foundation upon which modern biology is built?

The management application of scientific findings often lags behind their discovery by decades. For researchers, it's sometimes easier to bury one's self in science, while remaining divorced from the social and political trench warfare of application.

Adding to the general populace's confusion, resource agency administrators are sometimes driven by secular agendas and local politics. Agency administrators sometimes selectively apply their own personal interpretations, influence, biases, and spin to science's findings. In short, scientific management and wildlife conservation can over the short-term be trumped by local politics and agendas as some of the stories herein illustrate.

In my experience, the general public rarely distinguishes between applied science and pure science. Typically, an agency's resource management actions and decisions are not based on science alone: economics, local politics, interpretations of laws, and institutional traditions enter into it. The results are that the needs of the wildlife species or their ecology are rarely a foremost priority. Considering all the above, perhaps it would be wise as a rule to purposefully err on the conservative side when determining harvest quotas and management practices and give the benefit of doubt to wildlife and wildland in making conservation decisions.

Most wildlife and wildland protection decisions are reversible, but those harming or destroying the resource are frequently and tragically slow to be corrected or are irreversible.

Invariably, natural resource management decisions are compromises. Moreover, compromises are further compromised if push comes to shove. Overtime, a gradual erosion of our wildlands and wildlife resources can result. In short, in the bureaucratic and political tug-of-war that characterizes agency decision making, who is it that speaks for wildlife, especially for non-game and predator species? As my stories demonstrate, it is often *not* the agencies we've entrusted with those responsibilities but, rather, it ends up being self-appointed watchdog entities, non-profit organizations, and individuals outside of government agencies that assume the responsibility.

In the end, the biggest challenge conservationists and resource managers face today is understanding and resolving anachronistic mindsets, particularly indifference, fear, or blind hatred for particular wild animals and wildlands; mindsets that appear to be passed down through generations within some segments of our society. As these stories demonstrate, those attitudes frequently surface within local politics and the officials and citizens whose ancestors were involved in settlement and agricultural production on our Western lands. One wonders also if a lingering influence of the federal government's Animal Damage and Pest Control Agency's (now called Wildlife Services) propaganda and money for agriculturalists from a past era, as chronicled by Michael J. Robinson in *Predatory Bureaucracy* (2005), still plays a role, too.

Some of the essays in this book also touch on man's quiet but insidious interference with what has been called "the pageant of evolution." Humans are capable of exerting a selective force on the genetics and evolution of animal populations within relatively short time. For example, the larger, more threatening and aggressive grizzly bears are the ones removed from the population; the social bonds of wolf packs are destroyed, resulting in lone wolves potentially mating with feral dogs and creating hybrids with less fear of humans; the largest, most fit and dominant male wild sheep are selectively taken out by trophy hunting; bison with migratory or aggressive tendencies are destroyed, and what may phenotypically appear to be a bison may in fact have a genome polluted with cattle genes from cross-breeding experiments over a century ago. What do practices that select in favor of individuals that are smaller and less aggressive, or more furtive, passive, sedentary and non-migratory, portend for the ecological fitness of the species overtime?

My narratives are not intended to be academic treatises, nor has a consistent format been used for each story. Each tale has been approached differently. The specialized language of science has mostly been put aside. Instead, I've employed an anecdotal approach akin to traditional nature writing intended for a general audience. Imbedded in the narratives are current issues related to the species. The stories are a marriage between science and imagination. I have incorporated history, contemporary issues, romance, myth, folklore, fantasy, conjecture, animism, sentimentalism, and mysticism into the essays. I have used a range of techniques to convey information in an easily understood and entertaining manner, including anthropomorphizing, presenting animals as sentient beings, and even having animals verbally expressing themselves (not in a fantasy manner, however). On some topics, I have undoubtedly expressed what for some maybe controversial and unpopular points of view or opinions; and, I have been told, "grisly" (graphic) ones, too. The material has been subjected to my interpretation and viewpoint, which not too surprisingly, may have potential to generate some disagreement. But all this does not mean that the subject stories are not built upon professional experience, detailed research, and facts; they are.

Throughout the narratives I refer to backcountry, wildlands, wilderness and Wilderness. These are places that have their natural features and ecosystems, including wildlife diversity and populations, relatively intact. Generally, they are places without roads or motorized access, or where road density is very low and motorized use is seasonally restricted. I have used Wilderness, with a capital W, when referring to congressionally designated wilderness. Wildernesses, backcountry and undeveloped or roadless areas on public lands—national forests, national parks, wildlife refuges, Bureau of Land Management—make up most of our remaining Western wildlands. Such places potentially comprise Fraser's core areas for rewilding and the Y2Y initiative.

My stories are frequently and inescapably about loss. There are many losses in the natural world that we can lament—vanished original forest and prairie vegetation, the loss of wilderness, the reduction in numbers of once-abundant species and the extinction of others as author Steve Nicholls has documented. But my work also acknowledges and is grateful for the many positive contributions to conservation that citizens, sportsmen, scientists, conservationists and lawmakers alike have made and are making.

In that sense, these stories are also about restoration and conservation. Examples are the rescue of animals driven to the edge of extinction, such as the beaver's resiliency and widespread return, the bison's resolute recovery, the grizzly bear's dogged persistence, the wolf's reintroduction and spunky recovery, and the true grit of wolverines—all flagship species representing important wildlife conservation successes. Other major achievements we are all familiar with include: the national park idea itself; public lands—the national parks, national forests, and national wildlife refuge system; the congressional designation of Wildernesses; endangered species critical habitat identification and protection; restoration of game animals, game management regulations and enforcement; and, clean water requirements. It all represents, as Bozeman, Montana, writer Todd Wilkinson identifies, "a beacon of wildlife conservation for the world and a source of pride, inspiration, and wonder for American citizens."

In the Discussion and Source Material section, I have provided background on what inspired each story, an accounting of the source materials I researched and utilized in crafting each narrative, and also in some cases, additional commentary or asides related to other contemporary issues facing particular species that were not included within the essay. A section with a listing of general questions has been provided after the Discussion and Sources to stimulate or assist reader group discussions.

I do not expect everyone will agree with all my presentations or points of view, but it is my hope these essays will nonetheless help educate and assist in developing public awareness, stimulate insights and interest, and perhaps contribute to informed and compassionate public responses on behalf of the conservation of wildlife and wildlands. If the stories remotely accomplish any of those things, then this work will have achieved a worthwhile purpose. If a reader's knowledge or insights are enhanced, if a curiosity to learn is excited, and if educational value is gleaned from these stories—which ultimately translates into greater appreciation, tolerance, and an understanding for the importance of wildlife and wildlands—then I will have succeeded at a level far beyond simply authoring historical, entertaining, and informative tales.

A final disclaimer, should anyone want to interpret these tales as "anti-hunting," let me say, I have been a hunter all my life. My narratives nevertheless unabashedly advocate a need for consciously coexisting with the featured animals and the natural world in an age of rapidly diminishing habitat. The true sportsmen I know are inclined to support this idea; if not totally, at least for the most part. They recognize fair chase hunting ethics, properly regulated hunting, transparency in management, and a reexamination of some long-standing game management traditions and attitudes, are being called for in the twenty-first century.

Conservationist and Montana author Rick Bass writes, "We do what we do—spend long hours writing or teaching or working—to preserve or create that which we [love and] find beautiful." His statement explains what is behind this book: my love and respect for wildlands and wildlife, and a lifetime of finding beauty in them. I am hopeful this work may contribute in some small way toward preserving opportunities for others to discover and experience the beauty, wonder, and benefit to be found in the natural world.

Grizzly bear with two cubs, Yellowstone National Park (photo by the author).

# III
## STORIES FROM THE WILD
# 1
## The Spirit of Tosi

❧    ❧    ❧

*He [the bear] was the predominant thing in that country, and for him to be in it at all meant that there had to be more country like it in every direction and more of the same country around that...He was an affirmation to the rest of the Earth that his kind of place was [still] extant.*
　　– John McPhee, *The Encircled River*

Tosi was a Shoshone brave and medicine man who once served as a hunting guide for Owen Wister, author of the western classic *The Virginian*. Tosi didn't like being confined to the reservation. He preferred the solitude and freedom of the mountains and frequently spent his summers in a remote, high-elevation, glaciated basin at the south-end of Wyoming's Gros Ventre Mountains.

The vast basin is hydrographically confusing because it drains into the Green River at the north-end of the Wind River Mountains, not the Gros Ventre. This hidden, out-of-the-way place eventually became known as Tosi's Basin. The 11,380-foot crest forming the divide at the head of the drainage is the most prominent summit in the Gros Ventre Mountains; it is named Tosi Peak.

More than a century after Tosi had roamed the basin, and white people living near there had forgotten about him, a grumpy old grizzly bear wandered into this lonely place, making it his home. Historically, the bear's ancestors had ranged throughout the watershed, but they all had been trapped and shot off decades earlier. Grump did not know he was living outside the area people had designated "grizzly bear recovery zone." But like Tosi, he wasn't one to stick to his officially assigned place.

The basin is mostly glacier-scoured limestone supporting scattered whitebark pine and alpine fir krummholz—trees huddled together in clumps to protect themselves from the unremitting wind—and mountain meadows. Snow often persists there until mid-July and mosquitoes torment unmercifully. As the raven flies, it wasn't all that far from town, but still it was off the beaten path and people seldom visited there.

Occasionally, a horseback rider or hiker would come across a large bear track or mound of scat in the basin and tell his friends about it in the Stockman's Bar downtown. The locals would all hoot and poke fun at the person for making up tall tales: "Hey, thar ain't no griz up thar; *my* Granddaddy cleaned 'em all out years ago."

Over the years, the owner of a guest ranch located along the upper Gros Ventre River had observed chillingly large bear tracks in the soft dirt of the trail while riding the divide. Seeing the nearly foot-long fresh tracks in some ways made the guest ranch operator more edgy than if he had spotted the bear itself—the great bear had been there very recently; he imagined it lurking somewhere nearby, but unseen, at that very moment. The hairs on the back of guest ranch owner's neck tingled; but he never told anyone, he didn't want to frighten his guests away.

Otherwise, Grump's solitary presence far up in the mountains mostly went unnoticed and ignored, and that's the way the old bear liked it. One thing was for certain, though: Grump was not a cute and cuddly teddy bear. He was, in fact, a large, powerful and potentially dangerous grizzly bear.

When he was little more than an overgrown cub, Grump had a number of harrowing encounters with people. Always he managed to survive by ignominiously fleeing.

Once, in Yellowstone National Park, he caused a traffic jam; what people nowadays call a "bear jam." Hundreds of people swarmed about with car doors slamming and cameras clicking before he could retreat into a lodgepole pine thicket. Another frightening experience was when he attempted a nighttime highway crossing; blinding, fast moving lights flashed past him, and automobile horns blared.

Finally, he was driven from his habitat by human activity everywhere he went. As a result of these unpleasant and frightening encounters, Grump became both elusive and reclusive, avoiding people, dogs and livestock. This learned behavior was the secret to his longevity.

Some summers a rancher brought sheep accompanied by dogs and a herder into the basin. The grazing season was short, and the sheep had to be trucked long distances. As a consequence, it didn't always pay for the stockman to use his Wilderness grazing allotment. But running sheep in the high country was a long-standing family tradition, so the rancher stubbornly held onto his national forest permit, despite it generally being a marginal economic enterprise.

Although grizzlies are sometimes attracted to prey on domestic sheep, Grump steered clear of them. He did not like the irritatingly-noisy bleating and baaing woolies; they smelled strange, excreted endlessly, and stripped the mountain meadows of vegetation that normally he and other wild animals would have utilized.

Tosi Basin was not an easy place for a bear to make a living. Grump was mostly a vegetarian, focusing on sedges, alpine bistort, biscuit root, spring beauty, cow parsnip, and other plants, as well as whitebark pine seeds and berries when he could get them. He was living testimony of the Kutenai Indian belief that the grizzly bear spirit was in charge of all roots and berries.

Occasionally, Grump supplemented his omnivorous diet with a ground squirrel or marmot when he could catch them or dig them out of their dens; his mighty forequarters and three-inch long claws displacing impressive amounts of rock and earth. He even ate ants, grasshoppers, and army cutworm moths, which in some years emerged in copious quantities in the high country.

It took a lot of foraging for Grump to maintain his one-quarter ton bulk. He was always hungry. But every year, by the time autumn winds moaned through the krummholz and snow arrived, he supported a lustrous thick coat of silver-tipped hair and was thoroughly fattened.

One summer, Grump was surprised to discover he was no longer alone. Three other grizzly bears were occupying the basin with him—a six-year-old female, with unusual blond pelage, and her two semi-grown cubs, the equivalent of bear teenagers. Their scent was everywhere. Grump resented their presence. It was his territory and there was barely enough food for him, especially after sheep left parts of the basin trampled and grazed.

He grumbled and grouched to himself as he shambled about his customary haunts.

Like Grump years before them, the three displaced bears had traveled south along the mountains, searching for a new home after humans had encroached upon their habitat with logging, livestock grazing, residential subdivisions, golf course developments, roads, and always ever increasing numbers of people.

Scientists call such movement "dispersal." Normally, dispersal is important for a species' long-term survival, preventing inbreeding and allowing expansion into new territory or reoccupation of old. However, as more and more people moved into what historically had been grizzly bear range, the bears were kicked out of everywhere they went outside of Yellowstone National Park, including public lands around Paradise Valley, Gallatin Valley, Meeteetse, Sunlight Basin, Togwotee Pass, the West Slope of the Tetons, the upper Gros Ventre, West Yellowstone and Big Sky. Dispersal is risky business for grizzly bears.

Some of those places were once even designated as "Situation 1 Habitat" by federal agencies, meaning that public land and resource management decisions were supposed to favor the needs of the bears over other land uses. Instead, the dispersing bears were captured, marked and relocated back into the park or adjacent Wildernesses, rotating them around the ecosystem as if in a game of musical chairs. The bears couldn't know they were expected to stay within Yellowstone National Park; the park had become a zoo without bars.

Along the way, Blondie and her adolescent cubs had acquired two of what federal and state biologists call "strikes," having twice been caught causing mischief. In actuality, they were just doing what bears sometimes do: raiding garbage cans left on porches, scrounging in compost piles, breaking down fruit trees, stealing coolers out of the backs of pickups, harassing livestock, and once even mock charging some tourists who approached too close. Another run-in with people or livestock—a third strike—and they would be recaptured and either sent to a real zoo or euthanized.

Blondie also was not aware that the collar she was wearing transmitted radio signals that allowed biologists to spy upon her movements and location. Technology is the means by which agencies are constantly monitoring and managing wild bears. "Management" is a euphemism for controlling; too often control results in the destruction of the animal. More than one out of five Yellowstone bears at the time was equipped with a radio telemetry collar. This time, though, the three bears had traveled so far from the place where Blondie was originally collared that biologists had temporarily lost track of them.

The three were ravenously hungry; the nearly grown cubs were bottomless pits anyway.

In their search for food in the basin, they came upon the sheep herd and quickly developed a taste for mutton, killing nearly a dozen in short time and mauling a few others in a "surplus-killing" spree. In the predator-prey interaction, the sheep had failed to communicate anything at all to the bears—neither resistance, nor mutual respect or appropriateness—only panic. Lamb was an easy meal.

The sheep's terrified nightly bawling and bleating, a spooked horse, cowering dogs, and in the morning, scattered and missing sheep, along with partially eaten carcasses buried under scraped-together litter mounds, sent the horrified herder running for town, fearfully looking back over his shoulder. The old beat-up .22-250 rifle the sheep owner had loaned him to shoot coyotes was left behind, forgotten in the tent.

The herder's immigration status had been an issue. Similar to other fugitives roaming outside their designated place, the herder had liked the basin for its solitude. He figured no authorities would bother him there, but he had not anticipated the bears from hell.

When the word got out in town that rampaging griz were killing sheep up in Tosi Basin near panic ensued. Meanwhile, the sheep had been left to fend for themselves, and the teenage bruins, which by now had learned to clumsily catch their own bleating and panicked prey, enjoyed a field day. Rack of lamb became their favorite; they killed and partially ate nineteen more sheep in no time.

Back in town, the tempo of rumors and calls for bear management reached near-frenetic proportions. Stories about bear depredation appeared in newspapers throughout the region; the boys down at the Stockman's Bar boasted "if only they was allowed, they'd take care of the problem"; mothers kept their children home; ranchers claiming to resent government interference called their congressman demanding immediate action; and a platoon of federal and state agency biologists and administrators descended upon the little town.

Grump heard the "whop, whop, whop" of the game officials' helicopter, which was sling-transporting a large culvert trap into the site, before he saw it. He bolted across the open rocky terrain as fast as he could go, but before he could find hiding cover they spotted him. The chopper circled back, and the biologist riding next to the pilot in the jump seat exclaimed: "There's our sheep killer, a big ol' boar!"

The chopper went back and forth several times transporting men and traps into the area where the sheep had been killed. The culvert traps were baited with lamb carcass smeared with honey. The traps were then covered with brush and tree limbs, while dirt was spread on the inside to make them appear more natural. Foot snares were also set around recent kills.

Meanwhile, the sheep owner moved his wooly ruminants down the mountain out of the area, having been given permission by the U.S. Forest Service district ranger to temporarily graze them outside his permitted area within the Wilderness. The state administered depredation fund also wrote out a check, generously compensating him for the full amount he reckoned he was owed for his losses.

The next morning the echoing "whop, whop" of the returning chopper could be heard. Grump hid out near 11,000 feet elevation, high amid rocks and boulders. The biologists expected to find the ol' boar in the trap. Instead they were surprised to discover an enraged and snarling sow, Blondie. They quickly anesthetized her with a dose of Telezol administered using a seven-foot-long "jab stick."

One of the sub-adults was crashing about in a second trap. Then they noticed yet another bear watching from nearby. A biologist, backed up by an assistant with a high-powered rifle, approached it and from a respectable distance shot a tranquilizer dart into its haunch. The darted bear staggered around and finally collapsed. "This place is swarming with grizzlies!" the biologist shouted excitedly.

Using Blondie's ear tag number, a rap sheet for the three sedated bears was found in the data base. They were judged to be "problem bears" that somehow had wandered far outside their normal range. The incriminating records showed they had already racked up two "strikes" before cultivating their taste for lamb chops. Sheep killing was a big number three.

Naturalist Ernest Thompson Seton fatalistically believed "the lives of all wild animals end in tragedy," and so it was with this grizzly family. Blondie's impressive light-colored hide now decorates a wall in a State Game and Fish office. And when you are in Denver, you can visit her progeny and watch their endless head-down pacing at the zoo. The two juveniles were consigned to a life sentence with no chance of parole. The three were grizzly bears doing the wrong thing in the wrong place, neither one of which modern society tolerates.

Meanwhile, Grump had returned to his old habits and was hungrily engrossed in grazing on alpine vegetation. The traps sat empty for a week because Grump wisely avoided the spot where the scent of man and the commotion of helicopters coming and going were centered. However, the biologists had spotted him earlier. They knew "another big ol' griz was still up there," somewhere.

The pros and cons of leaving a grizzly bear to prowl Tosi Basin were debated in an emotionally charged public meeting. There was little "pro." A top federal biologist, intent upon demonstrating the responsiveness of his agency's bear management program, assumed near-heroic stature with the town officials and ranching community when he lurched to his feet, puffed up and loudly proclaimed: "We can't leave a big boar grizzly out there next to a herd of sheep." The town hall crowd cheered him.

This time when the tell-tale "whop, whop" of the rotors approached, Grump was caught out in open country. Alarmed, he ran, but there was nowhere to hide. The copter zoomed in from above and behind him. There was a pneumatic "pop" sound, and he felt the stinging smack of a tranquilizer dart in his rump.

Unlike sows and cubs, male grizzlies in their prime are allowed only one strike. It was puzzling to the biologists, though, because Grump had neither a record nor any strikes; at least none they could determine. He was not in their data base. After considerable and heated debate, it was finally decided to relocate Grump. But one cynical biologist strongly argued against it, saying, "He'll only kill livestock somewhere else."

After getting a protocol approval from the Interagency Grizzly Bear Committee for the relocation decision and consulting with the National Park Service, park administrators unenthusiastically agreed to take Grump. Dangling semi-unconscious from a sling under the chopper, he was ignominiously transported deep into the Yellowstone National Park backcountry, somewhere near Heart Lake.

When Grump awoke, he didn't know where he was. He sat on his haunches and looked around. He felt very woozy. Nothing looked familiar. He vaguely remembered the state game department workers gathered around him. And he recalled the startling sting of the tranquillizer dart striking him while he was running. His ear hurt where an annoying shiny metal tag had been attached, and his mouth ached painfully; he had been tattooed on the inside of his lip, and one big tooth was missing. Why had they pulled his tooth? It was a traumatizing experience, even for a grizzly bear.

What Grump didn't know was that he had been captured, measured, weighed, aged (using the tooth that was pulled), and tattooed. His ear was tagged with an identification number, M293. Some of the biologists even had their photographs taken posing with Grump, lifting his enormous head up while his tongue lolled out. His photograph would decorate their office walls. He was now officially included in the Interagency Committee's statistics and database; he had a rap sheet. By some fluke, however, he was not fitted with a telemetry collar or implanted with a transmitter.

When nighttime came, Grump oriented himself by the night sky and began a beeline south along the interconnected mountainous landscape. He slipped past outfitter camps in the Thorofare, crossed the Togwotee Pass highway late the next night, navigated the Gros Ventre Wilderness, avoided all people, and several days later arrived back home in Tosi Basin. He was very hungry and tired from his ordeal, not to mention cranky.

Following the sheep-killing incident, the county commissioners wrathfully passed a resolution stating, "wolves and grizzly bears were economically and socially unacceptable species" in their county. The inane posturing reassured residents that locally elected officials—and the ideology they represented—were in control; not biologists, the federal government, environmentalists, or any other outsiders. However, it was of no consequence to the bears or wolves, which were unaware that they had been officially ostracized; they went about their accustomed business as usual.

Afterward, when nightfall came to Tosi Basin, the stockmen in a show of bravado would build up their fire, pass a whiskey bottle around, and recite a chilling story of a time not so long ago when a whole swarm of blood-thirsty grizzly bears invaded a herder's camp, ran the herder off scared for his life, and wantonly slaughtered and ate dozens of sheep night after night. The ranchers kept a semi-automatic 12-guage shotgun loaded with rifled slugs leaning against a tree close at hand. And they cursed all grizzly bears, the federal government, and damn environmentalists. What they unconsciously feared was the wild America they thought their forbearers had destroyed.

Afterwards, they slept fitfully, startled awake by any night sounds, including even the customary baaing of their sheep. Even hardened hearts and minds can not escape being stirred in some way by the great bear.

In 1996, the Wyoming Stock Growers Association passed a resolution calling for removal of the grizzly bear from protection under the Endangered Species Act, and also saying: "Problem bears should be removed in an expedient manner and not returned to the wild." In April 2007, a sympathetic administration responded, and the U.S. Fish and Wildlife Service officially de-listed Grump and his kind from protection under the Act.

In 2008, a year after delisting, a record seventy-nine grizzly deaths, including eight cubs, took place within the Greater Yellowstone region—a 15 percent decrease in the population. Twenty of the bears were killed by hunters who claimed to have shot in "self-defense." Considering prevailing state and local attitudes, what delisting continues to portend for the grizzly bear's future isn't totally known yet. We can only guess based on what the past tells us.

Today, legend has it that a big ol' griz still inhabits Tosi Basin. Picture him lumbering about, rooting in the alpine meadows, the wind roughening his thick coat of silver-tipped fur, craggy, snow-capped mountains in the background—a scene emblematic of all lost wild American.

Lately, no one sees the bear anymore, but some claim to have spotted his tracks along the divide. If he's there yet, and some of us like to believe he is, Grump is now a very old bear. Others insist it's not a bear at all but, rather, it's the spirit of Tosi, the Shoshone medicine man, which keeps returning to prowl the basin in the form of a grizzly bear.

Nature's habitat restoration engineer, the beaver (photo by Judy Wantulok).

# 2
## Castor the Snake River Beaver

*Should you ask where Nawadaha*

*Found these songs, so wild and wayward,*

*Found these legends and traditions,*

*I should answer, I should tell you,*

*In the bird's nests of the forest,*

*In the lodges of the beaver...*

—Henry Wadsworth Longfellow, *Song of Hiawatha*

If I told you a quirky rodent fueled the exploration of North America and was a reason for wars being fought, and that the rodent powered lucrative economic enterprise, international trade and the building of fortunes, would you believe it? Sounds silly and farfetched, I know, but it is true. Few other wild animals have had as great an influence on world history as the affable beaver.

Of course, it wasn't actually the beavers themselves that brought about all those things.   Rather, it was man's inexhaustible pursuit of the large rodent for its lustrous fur; not unlike greed for gold.  The New World's real El Dorado was not precious stones nor metals, but fur.

In 1638, the beaver had the misfortune to have King Charles II decree the compulsory use of its fur in the manufacture of hats. As a result beavers were mostly exterminated in Europe by the late seventeenth century. But demand for the animal's fur continued to grow. In the New World, the economic craving for beaver pelts (called plews) resulted in hunting the once abundant animal to extinction in eastern North America and the expansion of the fur trade deep into uncharted regions of the West and Canada. The French called those who sought furs and trade in the far regions, *coureurs de bois*—"the runners of the woods."

It is estimated North America had at least sixty million beaver before European settlement. In the Rockies, historical trapping records indicate that at places there were up to "sixty to eighty beaver per mile of stream." Explorer David Thompson, who walked across a great deal of North America from 1784 to 1812, even crossing the Rockies in 1807, commented that the land was "in the possession of two distinct races of beings, men and the beaver."  And in his report to President Jefferson, Meriwether Lewis declared, the American Rockies were "richer in the beaver than any country on Earth."

British explorer and fur trader Samuel Hearne was the first to describe the natural history of beaver in his journals, *A Journey from Prince of Wale's Fort in Hudson's Bay to the Northern Ocean,* published posthumously three years after his death in 1795. Until then, the life history of the beaver was little known and consisted mostly of outlandish tales.

The principal product derived from the beaver was felt. The rich under fur, called fur-felt, beaver-wool, or *muffoon* was used for making clothing, most of all, hats. Beginning in the seventeenth century, it became fashionable for men to wear felt hats. London dandies fancied beaver top hats. The type of hat one wore also identified a person's occupation, status and wealth. A fine beaver-felt, broad-brimmed, stove-pipe top hat was a prized possession—a symbol. It's estimated that by 1700, England alone had a potential market for five million hats. It took the fur from one beaver to make a hat.

From beaver to hat, however, was a difficult and lengthy process with many interrelated steps. It began with trapping or hunting the animal along faraway streamside habitats in the mountains, often under threat of hostile attack; the laborious task of skinning, made even more oncrous by stiffened carcasses found frozen in traps; the time-consuming and disagreeable work of fleshing pelts; long and arduous overland transport of pelts to the traders; storage and then shipment to buyers in distant cities and to Europe; and finally, the involved and complicated process of manufacturing the furs into clothing. Hatters used mercury in their work. As a result, their careers were frequently short-lived and fraught with suffering from mercury poisoning. The mercury affected their central nervous system, hence the expression: "mad as a hatter." Truly, a felt hat deserved to be prized.

At the fur-trade peak, beaver plews sold for three to four dollars a pound. Increasing scarcity meant increasing value. The rule was to trap out and then get out. The fur trade prospered until the furbearer became scarce and silk hats became more popular than felt. The beaver era was generally thought to have been mostly over by 1840. Prices for a beaver skin dwindled to a dollar or less. Still, Hudson Bay Company records show three million plews sold in London between 1853 and 1873. Demand for the beaver's dense, luxuriant pelage was never totally stilled.

Long after the fur-trade era had ended, in the later part of the nineteenth century, when riffraff on the American frontier were pressed to state their occupation, their invariable reply was "trappin'." Still, the semi-aquatic rodent managed to survive, albeit in reduced numbers, in remote locations throughout the mountainous West. Artist Thomas Moran, accompanying the 1872 Hayden Expedition exploring Pierre's Hole—today's Teton Valley located in what is now southeastern Idaho, a place where mountain men and the fur trade had been active earlier— recorded that large beaver dams stretched across Teton Canyon. One can hardly imagine such a scene in Teton Canyon today. However, the longest beaver dam ever recorded was in Montana: 2,000 feet!

When settlers arrived throughout the West, they also trapped furbearers to raise cash money, a rare item in those times. By the twentieth century, some states adopted laws protecting the beaver. But illegal beaver trapping, even in Yellowstone, the nation's first national park, posed a serious problem. Poachers, such as Thomas Garfield, at the south end of the park, and William James, on the Madison River, were apprehended with illegal beaver pelts in the late 1880s. Nevertheless, a 1920s survey in Yellowstone National Park reported nine beaver colonies had managed to survive in the northern range.

In Jackson Hole, Wyoming, in the early twentieth century, one notorious poacher was Charles "Beaver Tooth" Neal. Legend has it that every year after trapping season, Beaver Tooth and his wife pretended to have a disagreement, after which she'd drive away in a wagon with all her considerable baggage. The game wardens along the route out of the valley were said to be too "gentlemanly" to ask her to unpack the wagon for inspection. However, she always came back, and the Neals would once again have money. Charles was cunning and crafty. Catching him with illegal beaver pelts became the ambition of every game warden in the area; none ever did, though.

The beaver proved to be resilient. When the demand for beaver fur declined, the prolific rodent gradually repopulated its historic range in many areas, spreading back across much of its former wilderness habitat.

Beavers are a great deal more important in nature's ecological scheme, however, than just pelts and hats. They are "ecosystem engineers" renowned for their ability to change the landscape by gnawing down trees and damming streams. Historically, their dams and impounded waters were often extensive in size and area. The flooded areas became wetlands, which served to slow floodwaters, prevent erosion, raise the water table, and purify water by filtering it through collected silt.

In the past, streamside meadows and willow bottoms were called "beaver meadows." These places are frequently taken for granted in our mountain valleys and riverscapes today, but they actually originated by silt deposition behind beaver dams centuries ago. Beaver-created wetlands and meadows provide rich habitat for other mammals, fish, amphibians, and waterfowl. Early settlers frequently took advantage of the slough-grass or sedge meadows for grazing and harvesting "wild hay" for livestock.

Native Americans referred to the beaver as "the sacred center," because it created habitat for so many other species, although, the American Indian persecuted the beaver for its

valuable fur, too. Similarly, ecologists today consider the beaver to
be a "keystone species," a species upon which a web of ecological
relationships depends and that has a disproportional role in
maintaining or creating an environment fostering biodiversity.

In recent time, a beaver, who we'll call Castor, was born,
along with his sibling, in a mud burrow dug by his mother beneath
the willow-covered banks of the Buffalo Fork of the Snake River.
Normally there would have been a pair of adults, since beavers
practice long-term monogamy, but on a moonlighted night, her
mate was caught on the uplands away from the river by a pair
of hunger-emboldened coyotes. Her mate succumbed only after
a ferocious battle.

The entrance to their burrow was below the water surface,
but engineered to be well above water line at the end of the
slick and muddy tunnel. There a chamber had been scooped
out, and a nest of wood fibers and bark was fashioned. It was a
humble lodge compared to those traditionally made from piles of
interwoven sticks, branches and mud.

The kits, as young beaver are called, were born with their
eyes open and within twenty-four hours were able to swim. It
was of little avail, though, since the burrow chamber was pitch
dark and the dive through the underwater tunnel into the river
currents was much too daunting for them at first.

Outside the den along the river bank, green sedges were
peeking through last season's matted brown leaves, and pairs
of merganser ducks were busily occupied along the shallows.
It was May, and riparian willows and cottonwoods stood ready,
awaiting a final vernal verdict before their bud scales would
cautiously release the new pastel-green foliage.

For days, the kits only awareness of the world outside
the burrow chamber was the coming and going of their mother.
Strange scents clung to her cold wetness. The rapidly growing
youngsters began to follow their mother down the burrow to the

water. Shortly after that, they all emerged on the river together. It was mid-June, and the Buffalo Fork was swollen with snow melt rushing down from the Continental Divide.

At dusk and in the crisp early mornings, with their mother serving as a crepuscular guide, they quickly discovered how to search for solid foods. They grazed on willow and cottonwood twiglets, sprouting sedges and grasses, and the tuberous roots of wetland plants growing along low ground bordering the river. It was an odd sight to see beaver shambling along, grazing on shore.

It became a great game to climb the muddy banks of the receding river and toboggan back down, plunging into the water. Afterward, they would rest in the shallows. And using their hand-like forepaws and the unique split nail on their hind feet, adapted for that purpose, they would caress and groom each other.

One morning, while playing on the mud slide, after Castor had splashed into the water, they were startled by the loud slap of their mother's tail as she dove for deep water. The sound was followed by a rush of air as a bald eagle with a six-foot wing span swept past. The raptor snatched Castor's sibling from the mud slide, and with powerful wings flopping and beating, it managed to half-drag and half-carry the pitifully squealing kit away. A tail slap on water normally warns beavers on land to flee to the water, but the kit had little time to react.

Thereafter, Castor closely followed his mother's cues, and they were more cautious about venturing out in the daytime. They generally lived a nocturnal or diurnal life, venturing from the burrow only in the shadows of dusk or before dawn to graze onshore. Their summer diet included a surprising variety of herbaceous vegetation, including willow and aspen leaves, ferns, berries, mushrooms and even algae that grew along the water's edge.

Castor learned about gnawing down cottonwood trees and eating the woody cambium beneath the bark, too. Physiologically, beavers have a special adaptation. They employ microbial fermentation in their digestive process, allowing them to effectively extract nutrients from woody materials.

His mother had a propensity to spend hours at night gnawing on cottonwoods, returning again and again until she had felled even the largest trees. Beavers' incisors continue always growing. Gnawing was necessary to keep them worn down. With their sharp, chisel-shaped incisors, they were able to drop a small six-inch tree in less than an hour.

Nights grew colder, the river became lower, and Castor was surprised early one morning by the sheen of ice on the water surface. As he paddled along, it shattered noisily before him. In response to the changing season, the cottonwood tree's leaves had turned a golden-yellow hue.

The two beaver became busier with the onset of autumn, following worn trails inland to gnaw on large trees. When a tree began to crackle and waver, they would stop cutting and hurry back down the trail in a clumsy galloping manner. After the tree crashed to the ground they would linger in concealment along the river, fearful the noise may have attracted a predator.

The limbs of felled trees were cut into convenient lengths, and both of them worked industriously to drag the severed pieces to the river. There they would bury one end in the muddy bottom, weighting branches and limbs down in front of the burrow. This was their winter larder. The Navajo Indians claim their people learned to store and ration food from the beaver.

The two beavers amassed a large, loose pile of freshly cut material. It soon became locked in ice when the river froze. They would search for other kinds of food during the winter, too. But mostly, when they weren't sleeping in the wood fiber nest inside the burrow chamber, they would spend time stripping bark from the branches they had cached and eating it.

Afterwards, they'd carry the peeled pieces back out of the burrow and release them in the current under the ice. In summer, fisherman would come across the smooth cleanly-peeled sticks lying along the river and marvel at the artful manner in which the bark had been removed.

Castor grew rapidly. He now weighed twenty-two pounds. He was a powerful swimmer. His torpedo-shaped body was wrapped in a thick coat of waterproof fur; he used his broad tail for propulsion and steering while simultaneously thrusting with his webbed feet. He was what scientists called "hydrodynamically efficient." He was capable of traveling a quarter mile or more under the ice for five minutes and then retracing his route back to the burrow waterline for air. Sometimes he would expel his breath under the surface of the ice, where it would form a wide, flat bubble. After the bubble of air purified, he would breathe it in again. This trick allowed him to stay under the ice even longer.

It's an alien world below the ground and under snow-covered ice. Light levels are constantly low. Presumably life beneath the ice and in a burrow becomes rather routine, maybe even monotonous. Under these conditions, beavers lose track of normal day length and adopt their own circadian rhythms. But when the first openings in the ice appeared in mid-March, Castor and his mother were quick to discover them and breathe the mountain zephyr's promise of spring.

Once again they were able to cruise along on the surface, look for roots amid the shallows, and hear the passing waterfowl. On one of those early spring days, while decaying snow still covered the riverbank, when his mother paddled through the burrow entrance, a steel object jumped up and fastened itself to her foreleg. She dove for deep water but was abruptly restrained by a long-weighted chain. She rolled and thrashed and gnashed her teeth on the unyielding steel jaws. For the rest of the night, Castor hid trembling in the burrow chamber while she fought against the thing that held her. In the morning there were some noises, then quiet.

Before dawn the next day, Castor cautiously crept down the burrow, paused at the waterline and, with a powerful dive, glided toward the entrance. As he cleared the burrow opening, he gave a hard thrust with his webbed hind feet. Simultaneously, there was a metallic snap and something painfully seized the toes of his hind foot.

Castor lunged for open water, but it held onto him. In mortal fear, he desperately tried to bite the thing that gripped him. In his frantic efforts, his sharp incisors slipped off the smooth steel and severed one of his caught toes. Blood colored the water crimson. He struggled blindly, painfully twisting and rolling around and around, winding the chain up tightly, until by chance it provided him leverage. Instinctively wrenching with all his strength, he suddenly broke free. When the trapper arrived to check his sets the next day, he was disgusted to discover his catch consisted of just two toes from a beaver.

When Castor tore free, instead of diving back into the burrow, he plunged into the river current. He didn't surface again until he was nearly a half-mile downstream. And he continued to travel downstream the rest of the morning. Finally, he hid beneath a large log jam that had been created by a hydraulic in the river. After dark, he explored along the jutting ledges and banks, until by accident he came upon an old lodge. It was set tightly behind a large boulder to protect it from the current. Castor dove and entered the den through a large entrance beneath the waterline. Inside, the deserted musky chamber was more than five feet across.

During the night, the bad-tempered old beaver who sometimes inhabited the lodge returned. He had been out on one of his springtime scent-marking forays. Immediately, without hesitation, he attacked his uninvited guest. Castor attempted to escape from the teeth-chattering and hissing menace by rushing for the lodge's exit. The churlish old rodent was more than twice Castor's size. He powerfully latched onto Castor's tail with his long teeth; his incisors gnashed through the thick scaly-hide and coarse flesh. Once again, Castor struggled in a terrified panic to free himself from vise-like jaws, this time of a different kind. In desperation he wrenched himself free and, scrambling from the lodge, he escaped into the river currents.

Driven by his painful wounds, Castor rode the swift currents downstream. The river was flowing forcefully, swollen and muddy from snowmelt. During the daytime, he hid under log jams or the river bank. At nights he cautiously fed on cottonwood suckers near the water's edge. Gradually, his lacerations and severed toes healed, but he would bear the scars and a maimed foot for the rest of his life.

It was during high water that Castor discovered and explored the slough. At high flows it was fed by a channel from the main stem of the river, but for the rest of the year it was spring fed. The backwater rarely flooded, and it flowed reliably during periods of low water. Grasses and sedges covered the low ground around the slough, behind which were riparian thickets of alder and willow intergrading into groves of cottonwood. Castor instinctively gravitated to the unoccupied favorable habitat and made it his home.

Life was good for a beaver on the isolated Snake River slough. Over a period of several years, Castor built a series of dams. He worked at night piling up and interlacing sticks, anchoring them with rocks weighing up to five pounds, and cementing the rocks in place with mud. The blocked channels flooded adjacent low ground. This in turn called for expanding the dam system. Getting muck and rocks from the bottom just

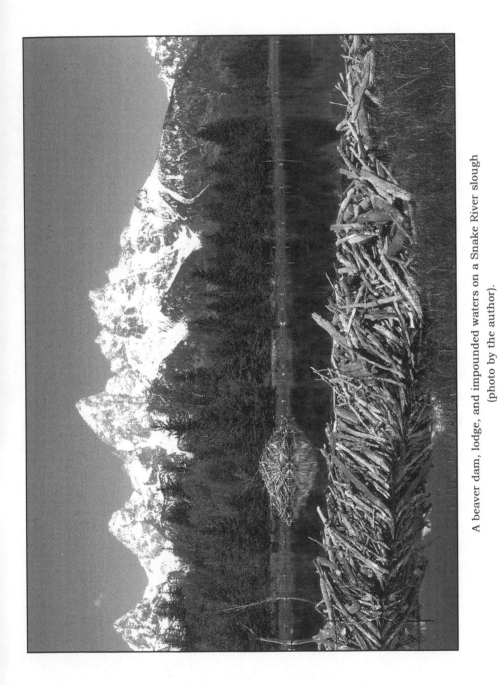

A beaver dam, lodge, and impounded waters on a Snake River slough (photo by the author).

above the dam deepened the pond. Every gob of mud, stick and stone in the dam was moved by his hand-like forepaws. Long, heavy sticks were carried in his teeth, sometimes with one end appearing to ride across his back, and strategically placed. After each spring, he repaired the freshets in his dams.

His system of ponds and channels grew. Lengthy canals were dug across shallows and low ground to reach favorite food sources. In winter, the canals were used to mine for willow roots beneath the icy banks, which further extended the canal system. Other short ditches that served as landings for feeding and transport of material from surrounding uplands were created. The canal system also served as a defense. It provided means for a quick escape when predators threatened. Indeed, wolves sometimes patrolled the area, hoping to catch Castor foraging on shore. And mountain lions that are known to prey upon beaver sometimes stalked the river banks.

Over time, Castor's den grew from a bank burrow to a large conical-shaped lodge, the beaver equivalent of a log cabin. He periodically added peeled sticks, large trimmed limbs, and the unused accumulations from his winter food cache. On top of each layer of sticks, he plastered heavy coatings of mud. The lodge was surrounded, moat-like, by water. Several times, ravenous grizzly bears had waded out to the lodge and attempted to dig through the sturdy structure. Even their powerful exertions could not penetrate it.

In early spring, Castor would sometimes leave his lodge and explore along the main stem of the river and its tributaries, doing a kind of beaver walkabout. He would build mud pies along the banks and dash them with castoreum—a complex substance, chemically similar to salicylic acid or aspirin, produced in a glandular sac at the base of his tail. It was a way of scent marking his territory. These wildly perfumed mud pies deposited along the shore also served to advertise for a mate, too. And early one summer, he returned to his lodge on the spring creek slough accompanied by a young female.

The following spring there were five beavers occupying the backwater lodge, two adults and three kits. While Castor scent marked family territory, his mate was occupied with the care of the kits. The colony grew, and the extent of dams, pond flooding, and canals they engineered was truly remarkable. Sometimes they'd engaged in mud-pie games. After one had deposited his castoreum, another would come along and make a deposit on top of it. This continued until the mud pile got quite large. It was a family scent pie.

For years, in the twilight and on starlit nights, the splashing and tail-slapping noises of the very large colony of working beavers could be heard along the slough and ponds. The downstream height of some of the dams now exceeded twelve feet. And some measured eighteen feet or more across the base. The surface area of impounded water was equally impressive. The well-maintained dams kept the water level at the lodge entrance ten-to-twelve-feet deep, even during low-water periods. "Busy as beavers" is trite, but true; their lives were filled with purpose.

As time passed, aquatic plants anchored themselves in the silt and sandy-loam pond bottoms, aquatic vegetation emerged from the shallows and wetland plants lined the shores, trout inhabited the ponds and spawned in the clean gravel of the spring inlets, boreal chorus frogs proclaimed it as their home, all kinds of waterfowl as well as other birds fed and nested there, dragon flies and a host of other insects flitted about, and moose commonly foraged along the bank and in the pond shallows.

Eighteen years had passed since Castor first found and dammed the backwater. During that time there had been little demand for beaver pelts. But now a global resurgence for fur, driven by the fashion industry, took place. The "wild look," as it was called, had become the vogue. In 2001, U.S. fur sales totaled 1.35 billion dollars, down slightly from a record 1.69 billion in 2000. Felt-fur hats were once again in style, commanding over two-hundred dollars for a hat.

Still, modern-day beaver trapping was not really a moneymaking proposition. But it attracted some for the "sport;" and also, the nostalgia of reliving the Mountain Man era. The cost of a resident trapping license was thirty dollars. In 2002, the Wyoming State Game and Fish Department sold 1,206 furbearer trapping licenses. A strict limit was set on the number of beaver that trappers were allowed to take. And each pelt was required to be tagged by a state game officer before it could be marketed.

Castor's colony inhabited a section of the Snake that was difficult to access. However, in winter, it could be reached by a snow machine. And so one day in March, a trapper arrived at the still mostly frozen ponds by snowmobile. He untied his snowshoes from the snow machine and, strapping them on, scouted the perimeter of the impressive engineering works of Castor and his clan.

The trapper was amazed at the size of one lodge. It was eighteen feet or more across the base and piled high with years of accumulated chunks of wood, branches, sticks, rocks and tightly-packed mud. While snow blanketed the rest of the area, the top of this structure was snow-free, melted off by the escaping animal heat. While several colonies of beavers inhabited the backwater in an upstream series of dams, ponds and lodges, this lodge was the granddaddy of them all. It was the most remarkable the trapper had ever witnessed.

Next to the big lodge there was an ice-free landing littered with cleanly peeled sticks. It was Castor's favorite idling spot. Along the water's edge at this landing, the trapper placed a small bundle of aspen branchlets that he had cut. Then, taking a bottle from inside his jacket, where he kept it to prevent it from freezing, he sprinkled some castoreum over the sticks. In the shallow water below the sticks, he set his favorite trap, a No. 4 Newhouse, powered by double-long springs. He secured the trap by noosing a stout number nine wire over the end of a sunken log deep at the bottom of the pond, and then also attached a sizeable weight to the chain close to the trap. Finally, guide sticks were placed so that any investigating beaver was led into the trap.

The heavy Newhouse trap was an antique. The trapper's grandfather had once owned and used it. It was solidly built from good steel. The passage of years had done nothing to weaken its powerful springs. Getting into the trapping business at one time involved considerable investment. Nowadays, however, the market is flooded with inexpensive traps, cheaply made from weapons-grade metal by China; another benefit of the global economy.

Imported inexpensive traps still effectively serve their purpose. Using those, the trapper made additional sets in the canals and runways, where the frequent coming and going of beaver had kept the water relatively open and ice-free.

Castor fought a valiant battle with the thing that grasped and bit into him high on his forelegs. The old flat-tailed warrior dove for deep water, taking the heavy weight and trap with him. He shattered his teeth on the unyielding object, the steel jaws becoming permanently nicked and gouged from his fierce efforts. Gradually the weight of the trap and its fastenings exhausted him and bore him to the pond bottom. For an animal that can hold its breath under water for twenty minutes, drowning is an ignominious death.

The next morning the trapper unceremoniously hauled the drowned animal up from the pond bottom by the wire attached to the trap chain. He didn't fully appreciate his catch until the weight of it was brought to the surface. Then he gave a low whistle of surprise. The beaver was huge! From the tip of his massive expressionless rodent face to the end of his tail, he measured nearly five feet; the hind feet, when the webbing was spread, were larger than a man's hand; his tail was ten inches across. At three different places the tail had pieces missing from its margin, and a deep six-inch-long scar occurred near its base. A piece of one ear was gone. And the left hind foot was missing two toes; it was obvious he had escaped from a leghold trap years ago. It all spoke of past combat, narrow escapes, and a long, but challenging life in the wild.

The old beaver topped the scales at seventy-eight pounds. Not a record—the biggest beaver ever recorded from Wyoming was a 115 pound goliath—but still the biggest the trapper and his cronies had ever seen. The large rodent's hide was thick and heavy. The fibers of his flesh and gristly-fat beneath the hide were so coarse the trapper had difficulty penetrating their toughness with his sharp skinning knife.

Beaver pelts are classified by size. In trapper's jargon, a "blanket beaver" generally weighs fifty to sixty pounds (or the hide width and length combined totals at least seventy inches). This beaver was larger. It fit the heavyweight category of a "super-blanket"—greater than sixty pounds. The trapper sold the impressive pelt for sixty-five dollars. It didn't cover the combined cost of operating his 4x4 vehicle and snow machine and his trapping license.

Today, the number of beavers in the United States is estimated to be less than 5 percent of that occurring before the early European trappers and settlement. Gone, perhaps forever, are the large beaver colonies that centuries ago altered landscapes and created streamside meadows and willow bottoms, sedimentary landforms which today we generally take for granted.

The confluence of Horse Creek with the Green River in Wyoming was the site of the Mountain Man rendezvous' in 1833, '35,'36,'37,'39 and 1840. It's a place that represents hallowed ground in the history of American fur trapping. The last gathering of trappers was held there by the American Fur Company in 1840. It was attended by such luminaries of the fur-trade era as Andrew Drips, Jim Bridger and Henry Fraeb. You may smile, though, upon learning that beavers have dared to reoccupy their ancient habitat on the Green River tributaries in that area—streams coming off the east slope of the Wyoming Range and the west slope of the Wind River Mountains—once the epicenter for the pursuit of beaver fur and the gathering of trappers during the Mountain Man era.

It's a tribute to nature's resilience that Castor's kin have returned to the headwaters of the Green, Snake and upper Missouri Rivers, and elsewhere. And, too, as author Steve Nicholls has pointed out, all the ecological restoration work the beaver is doing doesn't cost us, nor government agencies or conservation organizations, a single penny.

"Caribou 109" at Summit Creek on the Salmo-Creston highway,
British Columbia, c 2007 (photo by biologist Leo De Groot, B.C. Ministries of
Environment, courtesy Timothy Layser ).

# 3

## Ghosts of the Forest

*We grieve only for what we know.*
—Aldo Leopold

Large, dark-colored deer with collars of grayish-white pelage silently appear in the ancient cedar-hemlock forest. They move phantomlike through the shadowy, snow-laden groves, loosely abreast of one another, alternately pausing in stop-start manner to browse the long strands of arboreal lichens festooning the tree branches or to paw through the snow for cured herbaceous material. Their dewclaws click curiously. The animals' long, stilt-like legs and large spreading hooves appear uniquely adapted to the deep snow. Both the cows and bulls have antlers, but the males are much larger, palmate and massive.

In pursuit stalk Native Americans on snowshoes, armed with lances and bow and arrows. The deadening of sound by the

heavy snow cover contributes to the surrealistic scene— predator
and prey frozen in space and time. The Kutenai (Kootenai) Indians
called this forest deer *naxane* (pronounced nookanee).

Long ago, when the Kutenai hunted this unusual ungulate
in the snowy forests of the Selkirk, Purcell and Cabinet
mountains, in what today is northeastern Washington, northern
Idaho, northwestern Montana and adjacent Canada, the existing
wilderness would have scaled or measured in terms of thousands
of square miles.

The Indians felt they could always depend on this unwary
cervid for subsistence. The forest deer were plentiful even
when other game was scarce. Naxane were an integral part of
their culture. The lives of the Kutenai and the forest deer were
interwoven. In the Indian village, the deer's flesh could be seen
drying on racks, while women sat working its tough hide into
moccasins, leggings and blankets; it was not unlike the integral
use of bison by Native Americans on the plains to the south and
east of there.

At times, Kutenai braves followed ancient paths through
the heavily forested mountains to Sineaqueteen, the old crossing
place on the Pend Oreille River, where they traded furs and
the hides of naxane. The white man's name for the forest deer
was caribo or caribou. Today, the mountain caribou, a race of
woodland caribou, is considered the most endangered animal in
the contiguous United States.

The name caribou is a corruption of the northeastern
Canada Micmac (Miq'mac) Indian word *xalibu*, meaning the
pawer or shoveler. It describes the deer's characteristic of digging
through snow for food.

The caribou of the northern forests are distinct from their
tundra-dwelling relatives to the far north. The latter occupied
the ice-free area in northwestern Alaska during the Ice Age,
whereas those evolving into woodland or forest-inhabiting

caribou dispersed south during a warming interval and became distributed along the southern fringes of the northern or boreal forests, named after *Boreas*, the Greek god of the north wind. When climate changed and the ice returned once again, they were isolated from their tundra relatives.

Tundra-dwelling or barren-ground caribou are known for their vast migrations. Their woodland cousins generally reside within definable home ranges. In mountainous terrain, they are apt to display some seasonal elevation movements. In the United States as recently as a few centuries ago, woodland caribou were widely distributed across the New England states, the northern part of the Lake states, and the northern Rocky Mountains.

Woodland caribou have adapted to living along the edges of habitat in flux. Over long periods of time they have shifted their geographic distribution in response to climatic changes and the subsequent advance and retreat of ice and boreal forest. The caribou's genetic memory has evolved in concert with shifting habitat: glaciations and interglacial periods, cycles within cycles, expansions and contractions, the little climatic optimum and little ice age. In short, the distribution of woodland caribou over periods of time has not been static, but, rather, has shifted geographically in response to climatic fluctuations and habitat conditions.

Palaeontological records show that during the Ice Age, caribou were distributed as far south as New Jersey, Nevada and New Mexico. They followed the retreating ice and boreal habitat northward. One wonders, what the comparative southern limit of their range may have been during the hypsithermal, the apogee of a warming period 7,000 years ago. Stasis, it seems, is an illusion of man's construction, particularly for some types of ecosystems.

Glaciers in the Rocky Mountains have been shrinking— up to 70 percent or more since 1850— in response to warming climate. In 1900, Glacier National Park appeared aptly named, it had 150 glaciers. But in 2003, a study revealed only twenty-five glaciers, twenty-five acres or larger, remained. And, while glaciers everywhere have been gradually decreasing over the past century, they are now reportedly shrinking at three to four times the rate that they were in the 1950s and 1960s. Concurrently, the distribution of woodland caribou appears to have been shrinking northward from previous southern limits of their ranges, too.

Climate change can be a precursor to habitat alterations or shifts, but another ecological mechanism adds a layer of complexity in terms of man's time frame. Alteration within some habitats does not necessarily follow in lockstep with climate change. In some situations it sets the stage, but there is lag time involved in adjustment. In those cases, disturbance or perturbation events precipitate habitat adjustments following climatic change.

Some habitats may persist out of sync with climatic conditions for an indeterminate time. An example might be a centuries old relict forest. Without catastrophic disturbance, the attrition or changes in the forest's biota may be very gradual, at least in terms of man's timeframe. However, the biota occupying relict or remnant habitats are at risk and are highly vulnerable to disturbances, such as forest destruction or fragmentation resulting from wildfire, logging, roads, or insect infestations; or additionally, attrition of individuals from the population through predation, road kill, hunting, or disease. Species existing in those situations are vulnerable, balanced precariously on the edge of decline or local extinction.

When habitats and populations under stress from changing climate are catastrophically impacted, it is unlikely they will ever re-establish themselves in the short term. Succession by more adaptable, aggressive, or invasive species is more likely to occur. For example, what may have once been cool, moist, western red-cedar forest might be succeeded by Douglas fir and other species associated with the warmer and dryer conditions and, all too often nowadays, weedy species, too. Where woodland caribou once occurred, white-tail deer and their attendant predators replace them. The ecosystem reaches a tipping point and flips into an entirely different state, frustrating any attempts to restore it to the former conditions. Reestablishment of the biota, representative of the original cooler, moister ecosystem, is not likely to occur within man's time frame.

Some species may disperse to more favorable habitat, if and where it may exist. In other cases, where biota have become isolated in island-like situations and connectivity between natural habitats does not exist, localized extinctions may result. In the above manner, species living on the edges of marginalized habitat or within relict habitats may dramatically disappear in relatively short time from where they once occurred. They may exist in man's recent memory, but are now rare or no longer extant. Only Grandpa, oral tradition, or passages in historical or scientific literature recall them. The above accounting appears to be—or to have been— the situation for woodland caribou in the contiguous United States.

Restoring biological communities once parts of the system go missing, even with modern scientific and technological methods, has proven to be elusive in this situation. All the king's horses and all the king's men—bureaucrats, officials, managers, and biologists alike—cannot put it back together again.

In the nineteenth century, when prospectors, miners and settlers first penetrated the rugged mountains and thickets of northern Idaho's towering interior rainforest in the Priest Lake country—a forest pervaded by dark shadows and mystery—they found caribou in good numbers. Pioneers subsisted on resources at hand; caribou became a menu item.

During this era, prospector Billy Houston discovered precious metal in the mountains north of Priest Lake. His find later became the Continental Mine. Understandably, Billy didn't want to leave his rich claim, but he unwisely became snowbound in the remote and rugged Selkirk wilderness.

Billy was in big trouble: he had insufficient supplies to last out the winter. When he was down to his last bean, without substantial shelter, and up to his vest pockets in snow, caribou began mercifully drifting through the forest about his camp. He apparently had plenty of rifle cartridges and matches. When spring finally arrived, Billy, whom everyone had given up as dead, came down out of the mountains. He was soot covered, scruffy and a bit long in the tooth, but still very much alive. He became a Priest Lake legend for having survived the winter on caribou meat and an improvised shelter made from their hides. Something the Kutenai Indians had successfully done for centuries.

In the late-nineteenth to early-twentieth century, outfitters were putting hunters into the mountains of north Idaho for the purpose of taking trophy caribou. Locally known as king caribou, Selkirk caribou and mountain caribou, they were larger than their barren-ground cousins and had darker pelage. Mountain caribou still occurred in relatively good numbers back then; relatively vast areas of habitat still existed.

It has been said that where cultural constraints on humans are the weakest, devastation on wildlife and habitat proceeds the most swiftly. The caribou, as the Kutenai Indians earlier attested, were unwary and easily killed. Caribou were not protected by state game laws, if any game laws existed at all. In the late nineteenth and the beginning of twentieth century, shooting with impunity was the custom. Hunters did not stop with killing just one or even a few animals; when a herd was discovered, it was annihilated.

Caribou head mounts, which still hang in establishments in north Idaho, and Spokane, Washington, and elsewhere in that area today, frequently came from this time period. Rumor has it that a timeworn and dusty head mount in Jack's Bar in Bonners Ferry, Idaho, was killed by Theodore Roosevelt. A grove of old-growth western red-cedar in north Idaho, where Roosevelt camped on his caribou hunt, is today named after him: The Roosevelt Grove of Ancient Cedars.

After the early exploitation, reports of caribou encounters still continued to filter in from woodsmen and marten trappers like Pete Chance, Rex McCracken and Harry Yerbury in north Idaho, and Bob Gray and James Monroe in northeastern Washington, and from early-day forest rangers, such as Art Pauley, who constructed some of the area's first trail systems.

The prospectors, loggers, trappers, forest rangers and sportsmen who frequented northeastern Washington's and north Idaho's wilderness in the early to mid-twentieth century, encountered caribou, but perhaps in lesser numbers than in the past. The earlier hunting and a massive reduction in the amount of habitat from large wildfires around that time period took a toll. In those years, the wilderness, although diminished from aboriginal times, could still be scaled in millions of acres or hundreds of square miles.

Settlers attempting to build homesteads in this area in the late 1800s and early 1900s, found the work required to beat back the wilderness and clear the primeval forests paralleled that encountered by pioneers in the forests of eastern North America two centuries earlier. The deep volcanic-ash soils on low-lying sites frequently supported stands of huge western red-cedar that required felling and burning. Farming around stumps was a common practice. It was derisively referred to as "stump farming." The productive forestlands bordering low elevations and valleys were the first to be cleared and settled.

Original western-red cedar forest at Sullivan Lake in northeastern
Washington, c 1920s
(photo courtesy Metaline Falls Historical Society, Washington).

For the people who did not stray from the lowland valleys, stories about caribou were nothing more than tall tales. One forest worker in the Yaak River country of northwest Montana claimed to have had a surprise encounter with caribou at such a close range, that he could "see 'em blink." He was ridiculed and the drainage named "Wink-um Creek." Washington's Senator Hall (for whom Hall Mountain is named) had a hunting lodge near Sullivan Lake. He put up with a great deal of ridicule after he declared that caribou occurred there. Nevertheless, thirteen place names in the northwestern United States contain the word "caribou," referring to the past occurrence of the animals. Today, it is safe to say the people residing in those locales have never seen a caribou. The name means nothing more than a place.

In the years before snowmobiles and when there were only a few primitive roads, relatively few Euro-Americans entered this region's wilderness with its forcboding forests and understory thickets of Devil's club, deciduous rhododendron, and fool's huckleberry; and with its intolerable mist and rain, and deep winter snow, all set within rugged-glaciated mountains.

Scientists labeled the region "interior rainforest," because of its dense coastal-like vegetation and the cool-moist climate (read: foggy, rainy and snowy). The eco-region supported incomparable forests: red cedars over eight feet in diameter, western white pine towering over two-hundred feet, huge hemlocks, massive and aged larch and Douglas fir. Nowhere else in the Rockies did forests achieve such splendor.

The region also supported a unique assemblage of North Country animals—lynx, grizzly bear, wolf, mountain caribou, wolverine, bog lemming—many of which are rare or endangered in the conterminous United States today. Scientists correlated the presence of these animals to the areas "wet to very-wet climate"—most of which arrives in the form of snow and fog—and "the existence and distribution of [the once] extensive old growth cedar-hemlock and subalpine forest" habitat.

In the early twentieth century, a number of back-to-back unusually warm, dry years occurred, which, when combined with dry lightning storms and centuries of fuel accumulation, resulted in catastrophic forest fires. Author Timothy Egan chronicles the destructiveness of the epic 1910 north Idaho conflagrations in *The Big Burn*. The huge wildfires burned incredibly hot. At places entire forested watersheds within the caribou's range were slicked clean during 1910, and again in the unburned areas by wildfires in the 1930s, 1940s and 1960s, effectively wiping out large areas of old-growth forest potentially comprising the mountain caribou's habitat.

Meanwhile, woodland caribou had mostly disappeared from Maine, Minnesota and Wisconsin by the early twentieth century. In spite of heroic research efforts to save the last woodland caribou at Red Lake, Minnesota, they were largely gone by the 1930s.

As far as is known, they had existed there for centuries; suddenly they were gone—disappeared.

Transplanting woodland caribou back into their historic habitat at Red Lake in 1938 and 1940 failed. Attempts to restore caribou into their former habitat in Wisconsin in 1973 had similar results. Efforts to reestablish caribou in their historic habitat on Mt. Katadin, Maine in 1963, and as recently as 1989 and 1990, also failed. Reasons given: brainworm (transmitted by white-tail deer), predation, and poaching. But, more simply, "the animals dispersed and disappeared." The attempts to restore a piece in the ecosystem gave real meaning to the Humpty Dumpty metaphor.

After woodland caribou had disappeared from the Lake States and northeastern United States, caribou still persisted in the remote regions of north Idaho, northeastern Washington, northwestern Montana and adjacent Canada. However, already in 1929, zoologists had begun reporting that the caribou in the northwestern United States were also extirpated. But, reports and sightings by local outdoorsman and forest workers continued, contradicting academic and government agency skepticism.

Still, few outside the local area knew or believed caribou occurred in the northwestern United States. State game departments at that time made little effort to inform otherwise. Presumably, game official's feared publicizing the existence of mountain caribou would have resulted in unnecessary hullabaloo. It could have complicated or even jeopardized traditional deer and elk hunting. After all, caribou were not classified as a game animal by any of the western states.

Likewise, acknowledging the presence of grizzly bears in the southern Selkirks at that time was also controversial for the same reason. It would have made the game and forestland managers' jobs more difficult, more political, and might possibly have even diverted attention and revenues from traditional black bear hunting.

As a result, although they hardly resemble a white-tail or mule deer, caribou were mistakenly shot by inexperienced sport hunters, such as two killed in the South Fork of the Salmo River in northeastern Washington in 1937. The hides of those two animals were accessioned into the National Museum as specimen numbers 264164 and 264165. And three more killed on Shedroof Divide in Washington by deer hunters in 1952; and another in the Pack River drainage in north Idaho in 1953. These were, of course, the ones that were recorded, how many went unreported isn't known. But the kills confirm the caribou's presence in those years.

In the post-war boom in the 1950s and 1960s, road building and logging accelerated on the national forests. By then, the remaining occupied caribou habitat in the Northwest occurred only on national forest lands. What had once been expansive National Forest roadless area was rapidly being opened up through road building and logging, making more country accessible by motorized vehicles. With more people in the woods—recreationists, hunters, U.S. Forest Service personnel, logging crews—during all seasons, there was suddenly a spate of caribou sightings.

The caribou continued to be treated mostly as a local curiosity. State game departments at that time continued to remain low-key on the fact that the caribou existed. Most people automatically associated caribou with long migrations. The U.S. Fish and Wildlife Service labeled them "transitory and peripheral" in the United States. Contrary to historical distribution information, the U.S. Fish and Wildlife Service declared that the caribou were *not* resident but, rather, "occasional migrants from Canada." Other agencies chimed in with "you can't manage for occasional migrants or peripheral species."

In the late 1950s, Paul Flinn, a state game department employee in north Idaho, took it upon himself to photograph the caribou and document observations in an attempt to bring attention to this unique animal. He found caribou in the Monk Creek, Rock Creek, Lime Creek, Spread Creek, Continental Creek, Malcom Creek drainages and elsewhere in north Idaho. In one herd alone, he counted twenty-three.

But the potential for resource management conflicts and controversy, if attention were to be spotlighted on these unusual animals, was unpopular with so-called commodity interests. Flinn's job went away as a result. But his black-and-white photographs demonstrate the mountain caribou's relatively common occurrence in north Idaho from that time period.

Meanwhile, sightings by U.S. Forest Service employees and others continued to be reported and dutifully filed, such as: J. Frank Meneely's "fifteen to twenty at the head of Boundary

Caribou herd at Rock Creek in north Idaho in 1956
(photo by Paul Finn from the author's 1973 caribou monograph).

Creek," and others at Priest River and Pack River. Idaho biologist Ray Rogers recorded "fifty caribou using a section where logging was underway;" and Washington state biologist Stan Guenther spotted two different bands—nine in one, three in the other—in northeastern Washington. Filing sighting observations was the benign management attention generally accorded non-game species in those days.

In 1961, the Salmo-Creston Highway was completed. The highway bisected the heart of the southern Selkirk caribou's range across the international border in British Columbia. It turned out to be a major contributor to mortality. Salt used to de-ice the mountain road attracted the caribou, resulting in numerous road kills. Signs were posted warning motorists of the hazard of caribou on the highway. Roadside poaching followed. British Columbia Conservation Officer Dave Gray reported *no less* than ten caribou killed in the first two years the highway was open.

Meanwhile, timber harvest, with its accompanying roads and improved public access, continued to eat away at the animal's habitat in the U.S. The Forest Service in those days operated with a clear mandate: "bring old-growth, decadent forest under management by converting it into young, thrifty, fast-growing stands." A secondary goal was creating and improving motorized public access.

"Intensive management" and "benefit to the local economy" were slogans used to justify management actions. Budget, career advancement, and the agency's local regard were tied to "getting the cut out." The most efficient manner for the agency to achieve its timber goals was to clear-cut old-growth forest and burn the huge amount of unmerchantable residue. Sawmills in those days were generally inefficient and trees that couldn't be economically utilized were felled and left to be disposed of by broadcast burning. It was all accomplished under the auspices of the 1960 Multiple Use Sustained Yield Act as "multiple use."

Forest Service personnel believed in their mission, and they skillfully carried it out with efficiency uncommon for a government agency. They spoke of it as "applied science." Local communities also equated it to good forestry practice and multiple-use. The communities profited directly from road-building contracts and logging and sawmill jobs. Timber was the local communities' bread and butter, right up there with apple pie and motherhood; the more, the better. The U.S. Forest Service was a different organization back then compared to today; in some ways, a fact not all bad.

The rapid conversion and fragmentation of old-growth forest by logging was detrimental to the caribou and other forest habitat-specific species. It figures into the earlier discussion on animals occupying relict habitat on the margin of their ranges, where lag effects due to climate change may be in play. The concept of maintaining connectivity between habitats to allow dispersal of biota did not exist in those years. In retrospect, it's safe to say, long-term impacts from the extensive destruction and fragmentation of old-growth habitat in the Northwest had significantly more biological effects than were directly observable or recognizable at the time. The biological effects are continuing to be felt yet today.

In the 1960s, the U.S. Forest Service planned to build roads and conduct timber harvest in one of the last remaining large roadless tracts in northeastern Washington and northern Idaho—the Salmo-Priest. The Salmo Basin was tucked into the far northeast corner of Washington, bordering up against British Columbia and north Idaho. It was an out-of-the-way place, little known or visited by the general public. It included some of the last habitat occupied by mountain caribou in the lower forty-eight.

A mini-drama played out within the local Forest Service organization. In an impromptu meeting at the Sullivan Lake Ranger District, the forest supervisor invited discussion among personnel by asking: "How should the Forest Service manage the Salmo Basin?" The national forest's programs at that time, as mentioned earlier, were driven by budgets based on proposed timber harvest levels, local politics and economics, and a perceived congressional mandate. The forest supervisor, after a career of having witnessed wildlands vanish, may have had some second thoughts.

The half-dozen foresters present took turns expressing their professional opinion on what they believed was the "best management" for the Salmo. Invariably each cited statistics on the amount of board feet of timber, the forest's decadent condition, the need for silvicultural management, and the benefits to the local economy that road building and timber harvest would provide. It wasn't a question of whether to road and clear-cut the drainage basin; it was how to do it most efficiently and when and where to get started.

When it was a junior forester's—called a JF—turn to speak, he expressed an outrageously contrary opinion: "I think the area should be designated Wilderness, especially considering the assemblage of northern species—caribou, marten, lynx, moose, grizzly bear, wolverine, bog lemming, and maybe even gray wolf—that occur there. Many of those species are becoming rare in the lower forty-eight states. They are what Aldo Leopold called 'wilderness species'... and the mountain caribou occur nowhere else in the conterminous U.S."

Had the ghost of Leopold walked into the room, the meeting would not have been more stunned to silence. The Wilderness Act had been legislated only three years earlier. Many in the agency grumped about it and did not endorse it. And, while wildlife habitat was supposed to be one of the national forest's "multiple uses," in those years, timber-producing national forests employed no biologists.

In the uneasy silence that followed, cynical grins appeared on some faces. The foresters assumed they had just witnessed career suicide. A directed reassignment would soon follow, sending the JF to a grazing resource job in the grasslands of eastern Montana, where there were no trees.

The district ranger appeared red-faced and embarrassed. He attempted to apologize for the young forester's audacity, mumbling, "He's research oriented." Surprisingly, however, the forest supervisor legitimized the JF's comments by noting, "There's obviously a wide range of views on what should be done with the Salmo." And the meeting lurched uncomfortably on to another topic.

Afterwards, the derisiveness began. The young forester was asked, "If there are caribou there, where do they go in winter and what do they eat?" The JF was surprisingly informed. He had read all the literature he could get his hands on, believing it was part of his job to know those things. "They have a 'reverse migration,'" he explained. "In winter they move into subalpine forest at high elevation, where they feed on the lichens growing on trees—arboreal lichens, *Alectoria spp.*"

"Oh," smirked a staff man, "I guess they just burrow through the six or seven feet of snow that's up there, right?"

"Lichens, eh?" snickered another forester, "The stuff growing on rocks?"

"No, arboreal lichens; it's an epiphyte hanging from tree branches. In late winter, the snow settles and becomes more stable. The caribou have broad, snowshoe-like hooves, and stilt-like legs, adapted for getting around in deep snow. They're the ultimate backcountry snowshoers. And, actually, the deeper the snow gets, once it firms up, the better it is for them. They can reach higher into the trees to get the lichens."

Arboreal lichens (*Alectoria spp.*) within snow-covered subalpine spruce-fir forest along the Salmo-Sullivan Divide, Selkirk Mountains, northeastern Washington (photo by the author).

Someone hooted, "You gotta be kidding." Another ridiculed, "Yeah, pigs fly, too." The JF's boss counseled: "Look, we've got a job to do. There are tens-of-millions of board feet of timber that need harvesting in the basin. The local community is dependent on us. Let's not complicate things by bringing up caribou in the multiple-use assessment report. Wildlife is not our responsibility, it belongs to the state."

The JF started to say, "The state is the public's trustee; the wildlife actually belong to all of us, and the Forest Service is entrusted to manage the habitat." But he stopped short, not wanting to contradict his boss.

Sometime afterward, at the University of Idaho, when the JF mentioned caribou, a senior professor of mammalogy snidely asked the young forester if he thought the Yeti or Bigfoot also existed in the mountains of north Idaho. "What is needed is a cryptozoologist, a person who studies 'hidden animals'," he said with a sarcastic smirk.

For the next several months, on his own time in the evenings and on weekends, the fledgling forester took it upon himself to interview and talk with longtime local residents—old marten trappers and forest workers—sift through Forest Service and Game Department files; pick the minds of other agency biologists, particularly the Canadians; and obtain published material on caribou biology, behavior, habitat requirements, and historical records.

After studying the literature and the anecdotal information he had accumulated—amounting to hundreds of caribou sighting locations and incidents—it occurred to him to plot the records on a map. The results showed the mountain caribou's historic and recent distribution within the northwestern United States and adjacent Canada. It was the first time such a map had been compiled for the caribou in that area.

In those days, wildlife management and administrative coordination with state biologists was the grazing management staff's function. The position also included administration of the domestic livestock grazing programs on the forest. The young forester showed the grazing management staff officer his map and data, expecting to find a professional ally. Instead, the staff man became agitated. He felt the JF had trespassed on his turf.

But the range staff officer would never have bucked the system nor done anything proactive for wildlife, especially not a non-game species. His career was characterized by not rocking the boat, safely rising in the bureaucracy over time by never sticking his neck out. The range specialist reached for the young forester's chart, asking him to hand it over: "I'm in charge of wildlife; I'll take care of it." The JF was taken back. Shaking his head, he refused: "It's my data and chart; I compiled it on my own time."

In the months following, a contract was awarded to survey a location for a road into the Salmo Basin. The contractor cut out and constructed a helicopter landing pad in the forest near the Salmo Guard Station, a remote Forest Service cabin that existed deep in the basin. The cabin was a vestige from an earlier era. The growling of chainsaws, motorized trail-bikes, helicopters and shouting men invaded the deep silence of the basin's ancient forest. In spite of the commotion, when the work first began, crew members remarked on seeing caribou on several occasions.

The contractor's crew set up a work camp at the guard station site. In the unenlightened carelessness of the time, they disposed of their garbage and refuse in an open-pit dump they excavated in the forest a short distance from their camp.

Word got out that the contractor's crew was experiencing bear problems. Nonetheless, the workers continued to dispose of their garbage in the open pit, seemingly oblivious to the reason why bruins kept showing up in camp. The crew did not distinguish between grizzly bears and black bears; they were just bears. In fact, at that time, it wasn't a generally known or an accepted fact that grizzly bears even occurred there. The frequent emergence of bears out of the deep forest and their wandering into camp spooked the engineering crew and kept them on edge.

Because of the difficulty of access, the typography, dense vegetation, and inclement weather, the surveying for eight miles of road into the basin went on for three seasons. It was said thirteen bear were shot and killed by the engineering crew over the course of the field work.

Meanwhile, the JF was patronized as a well-intended and capable sort, but few really took the caribou issue serious. That changed, however, after the JF took a big risk by requesting the use of the national forest's contract aircraft to conduct an aerial survey. From what he had learned in his research, if any caribou existed, they might be spotted from the air in the open subalpine forest in late winter. The places he had identified where caribou had historically been reported to occur.

In early February 1971, the young forester and his boss made a deal. He could use the contract airplane and pilot for a few hours. But if he did not find any caribou, he would shut up once-and-for-all about them and the impacts of road development and harvesting timber in the Salmo Basin might have on them.

It snowed the night before he was to fly, but the morning brought clear and sunny skies. Conditions for aerial observation were excellent. As soon as they flew across Pass Creek Pass, north along the Shedroof Divide, there were caribou, just as he had been predicting. Numerous fresh tracks could be seen trailing through the open subalpine forest along the west slope of the divide in Washington. There were no other large animals but caribou that could have made the tracks at that time of year in the deep snow at that elevation.

North of Thunder Mountain four caribou were spotted in open subalpine-fir forest. The pilot circled around at near treetop height, while the JF obtained photographs. They spotted more tracks and caribou north of the Continental Mine and on Kaniksu Mountain in adjacent Idaho.

Observing and photographing the caribou changed the dynamics of the issue: caribou were, in fact, extant in the United States! The predictability of their locations gave credibility to the young forester's argument that caribou were resident, not "wide-ranging, peripheral or transitory animals." Their range was definable. It also gave legitimacy to the idea that the caribou's habitat—lichen-rich, old-growth forest—should be considered for protection in forest management and planning.

Concurrently, around those years, a time of change ushered in for the Forest Service. The early 1970s saw the emergence of citizen advocacy and strengthening of the environmental movement. The National Environmental Policy Act of 1969, roadless area inventories, public involvement, public scrutiny of resource management practices, requirements for land use planning, the Endangered Species Act of 1973, internal directives calling for "ecological management," and the agency having to deal with administrative appeals and court actions; all of it happening in relatively short time. About that time, too, the JF received recognition for his work and was promoted and transferred to another national forest.

The competing congressional and management directives and their conflicting goals produced a type of organizational schizophrenia within the Forest Service. On one hand, need for a land ethic and ecological management was espoused. But, pragmatically, on-the-other-hand, road building, opening up new country, and harvesting timber—"bringing the forest under management"—was still the basis for congressional budget appropriations. Timber was still the big ticket item in the Forest

One of three bull caribou observed in a timber sale area on Willow Creek, a tributary of Granite Creek that flows into Priest Lake, on November 25, 1969 (photo by John Joy).

Service budget, not non-commodity resources, not protecting old-growth forest habitat, certainly not caribou.

Contracts were awarded and the Sullivan Creek road in northeastern Washington was reconstructed to accommodate log hauling up to the crest of the Sullivan-Salmo Divide. The next road contract, which was written and sitting on the shelf ready to go to bid, was for the Salmo Basin itself. Today, however, the road still terminates at the divide. The caribou, their habitat, and the Salmo-Priest roadless area had become controversial issues; some even wanted the roadless area studied for Wilderness classification.

The Forest Service's newly adopted environmental review process required public involvement to be a part of the decision-making process. The Spokane Chapter of the Sierra Club, the Spokane Mountaineers, and other local activists took a proprietary interest in the Salmo. Studies on the grizzly bears and caribou were proposed by University of Idaho faculty. For the caribou, it grew into an International Mountain Caribou Technical Committee composed of state, federal agency, university, and Canadian biologists.

Portions of the Salmo-Priest roadless area became elevated to a wilderness study area. The mountain caribou readily became a wilderness surrogate, attracting the attention of journalists. They became a local conservation *cause celebre*. But while the caribou were reported to be out there somewhere, frustratingly, they were rarely seen. Journalists dubbed them: "the ghosts of the forest."

In 1983, the U.S. Fish and Wildlife Service, after years of foot-dragging, finally classified the southern-Selkirk caribou population "endangered." A "Recovery Plan" was prepared in 1985. It was revised and updated in 1994 (critical habitat for the caribou has never been determined, but a recovery zone was mapped). By then, only thirty or fewer caribou were believed to exist in the southern-most Selkirk population. The small numbers of caribou in the Purcell and Cabinet Mountain in northwestern Montana, which may have still occurred up until a decade earlier, by then, had vanished.

In 1984, a 41,335 acre Salmo-Priest Wilderness was legislatively declared, all of it in Washington. Today, it boasts the largest remaining growth of virgin forest in that state; truly, a relict forest. There is also an additional 17,505 acres of contiguous terrain along Crowell Ridge, as well as 20,000 adjacent acres in Idaho, that is roadless. Idaho's congressional delegation, however, which some have criticized as "perennially brown," resisted taking any legislative action on adjoining roadless area within their state. The state's motto *Esto Perpetua*—let it be perpetual or in perpetuity—does not necessarily apply to the perpetuation of Idaho's wilderness resources.

Today, the Forest Service manages the Idaho roadless portion in the Upper Priest for backcountry and wildland recreation, administratively termed "roadless themes." The roadless theme area is also secondarily intended to provide wildlife habitat. Other places in north Idaho that in past decades were occupied caribou habitat have pretty much been fragmented by roading and logging, "brought under management." In contrast to earlier times, the remaining wilderness can be scaled in terms of tens of square miles or less.

Gone also are the days when adjacent Canada could be counted on to provide wilderness habitat, travel corridors, and connectivity for the dispersal of rare animals. Forests there have also been heavily roaded and logged, and the habitat fragmented. In recent years, mountain caribou have been extirpated from over 43 percent of their historic range in adjacent British Columbia and the Provincial Government reports caribou numbers have declined 30 percent.

A great deal of study of the caribou has been accomplished since the 1970s by expert biologists using modern scientific methods. In the late 1980s, the first attempts were made to augment or restore the herd by adding individuals to the faltering population in north Idaho. Sixty animals were net captured over a period of years in British Columbia and transplanted to predetermined sites in the Ball Creek drainage. The adequacy of habitat at the release site had been studied beforehand, and it was determined to meet all the necessary criteria. The augmentation site was also a place that had historically supported caribou. Nevertheless, the radio-collared transplanted animals apparently were unimpressed. They quickly dispersed back north, assimilating with other existing herds or returning to their original herd in Canada.

The southern Selkirk mountain caribou population numbers remained perilously low, but prospects appeared hopeful once again, when, in the mid-late 1990s, another attempt at augmentation was made by wildlife professionals. Over a three-year period, forty-three radio-collared mountain caribou were transplanted into three previously occupied habitat sites in northeastern Washington. Some of the transplanted animals dispersed from the area; among those who remained, mortality was unusually high. Around half of the released caribou never survived their first summer—predation, poaching, unknown causes, and even accidental falls contributed to the high mortality.  As a result, the British Columbia Wildlife Ministry suspended its participation in the project.

In 2001, the British Columbia government officially recognized that its own mountain caribou populations were imperiled. The primary battlefield to protect the caribou and their habitat had moved northward into Canada. The Canadians defined the problem as a "continuous range contraction and increasing separation of caribou into smaller, isolated subpopulations, leaving islands or remnants of occupied habitat surrounded by warmer ecosystems." As climate warms and areas are logged, or habitat is otherwise disrupted, the remaining islands of habitat are shrinking and viable habitat keeps shifting northward; not unlike what occurred over the past century within the United States along the southern margins of the caribou's range.

A recent Canadian research report states, "Recovery efforts should be directed at factors contributing to the fragmentation and isolation of populations." Not surprisingly, it is an extremely unpopular program with the province's timber industry.

Over recent decades, heroic efforts administered and carried out by dedicated wildlife professionals to save the caribou in the United States have cost millions of dollars. What price can one put on extinction? In spite of the best efforts, the southern Selkirk caribou population has remained at or less than thirty animals. Fifty-two animals were reported after herd augmentation in 1995; but five years later, the number was back down to thirty-five. In 2005, surveys located only three caribou on the United States side of the border.

One of the transplanted animals, a two year old bull, who became know as "Caribou 109" (109 were the last three digits of his radio collar frequency), was captured in the Hart Range near Prince George, B.C. in 1998 and relocated to Pass Creek Pass in northeastern Washington. Unlike many of the other transplants, Caribou 109 settled into his new home. He was a magnificent animal. He would generally winter in the vicinity of Little Snowy Top Mountain at the headwaters of the Salmo River in Washington. Sometimes he was accompanied by other caribou, and they'd range south from Little Snowy Top along the Shedroof Divide. And each year in April or May, 109 would move back north along the mountain corridors to join other caribou in Canada.

The caribou have a consistent crossing place on the Salmo-Creston highway near Summit Creek in British Columbia. In 2007, Caribou 109 was struck by a vehicle at the crossing spot and killed. In 2008, three more caribou, two bulls and a cow, were also killed there. It's the same place caribou were annually being reported road killed already beginning in the late 1960s. The road kills have been allowed to continue unabated over the years, while at the same time there has been continuing investment, work, and talk about recovery of this small caribou population.

Not everyone cares. The late-season snow conditions that characteristically allow caribou to travel along the north-south high-elevation ridges and interconnected forested basins are also ideal for backcountry snowmobiling. Canada reached agreements with snowmobile clubs to stay out of caribou habitat. But in the United States, a thriving snowmobile business was allowed to develop on the national forest within the caribou recovery zone.

A lawsuit filed in 2005-06 against the U.S. Forest Service in north Idaho by the Selkirk Conservation Alliance and a federal judge's ruling finally stopped the activity. A local snowmobile proponent publicly denounced the ruling, calling it "domestic terrorism that will bring about local financial pain." An attitude not progressed beyond the earlier era's "shooting with impunity."

The mountain caribou are Pleistocene relicts genetically programmed to travel a singular evolutionary path. Manipulation or management of the caribou and caribou populations themselves has not proven to be the key to their survival, at least not along the southern fringes of their ranges. Conservation success means relieving *all* the factors detrimentally impinging upon the animal and its specific habitat needs. In modern times, for a wilderness species like the caribou, that presents no small challenge.

Today, mountain caribou are considered the most endangered animal in the United States. The human population in the Rockies is predicted to double in the next twenty to forty years, and demands on wildlands and natural resources will only increase. And, if climate warming continues, it further leaves little of this rare animal's habitat within the United States.

If current trends continue, the odds are that caribou will be completely gone from the lower forty-eight states within a decade. Who will grieve for the mountain caribou? In America today, when 75 percent of our population live in urban areas, how many will know or care? Woodland caribou are already gone from Maine, Minnesota, Wisconsin and northwestern Montana in relatively recent time. Soon only the ghosts of the Selkirk caribou, like those of the Kutenai Indians, may haunt what remains of the once wild, deep-and-dank cedar-hemlock and subalpine forests along the connecting high-elevation divides and basins in northeastern Washington and north Idaho.

A water ouzel on a mid-stream boulder in Teton Canyon, Wyoming
(photo by the author).

# 4
## The Undine and the Merle:
## Why the Ouzel Curtsies

*Little gray surf-bather of the mountains!*
*Spirit of foam, lover of cataracts, shaking your wings*
*    in falling waters!*
*Have you no fear of the roar and rush,*
*Must you fly through mad waters,*
*Must you batter your wings in the torrent?*
*Must you plunge for life and death through the foam?*
"The Water Ouzel"
—Harriet Monroe (1860-1936)

This whimsical tale is about the enchantment of flowing
waters and a small merle. The wren-like bird is happily at home
balancing and bobbing on mossy rocks, while all around it
torrents rush. You can find this small feathered creature along

misty mountain streams within rugged and lonely canyons, amid the vortex and cascades. As you watch, the small bluish gray-black bird dives into and swims about in the rushing currents. And somehow it even appears to glide and wing its way along the bottom, withstanding the force of the rushing stream! Naturalist John Muir called it "the hummingbird of flowing waters."

When the bird magically surfaces, it hops onto a boulder and hyperactively dips and bobs —up and down, up and down— doing a curtsy, as if it is bestowing respect or acknowledging applause, perhaps. It is a bird that neither Audubon nor Wilson ever met.

The feathered creature is named a dipper, water thrush or river crow by some. But most folks call it the water ouzel. How is it, you may wonder, that this little, stub-tailed bird has learned to live and swim amid the dancing cold waters of mountain streams? And why is it forever bobbing or curtsying?

To answer those questions, we must go back in time. Originally, we may speculate, the bird lived an ordinary lowland life. While it resembled an outlandishly plump wren, it was no gifted songster. And compared to its thrush relatives—bluebirds, robins, and the varied thrush—it was quite drab. And we might also guess it didn't know how to swim either, because unlike most aquatic birds, it is hatched without webbed feet.

A very long time ago, Earth experienced great change. A warm, dry climate followed a glacial epoch. Vast glaciers occupying the mountains and valleys reluctantly relinquished their crushing icy grip, begrudgingly releasing water in response to the warming clime. Mountain rivulets grew to great glacier-fed rivers.

Cataclysmic, powerful, pounding torrents eroded deep canyons and sent thunderous cataracts hurtling off high ledges, plunging and roiling into vaporous froths below. A marvelous drapery of flowing waters tumbled off the backbone of North

America. It was a primordial time when fierce mountain gods sculpted and fashioned the land with awesome forces. The torrents within the dark gorges rushed in channels eroded by the dissipating glaciers.

In time, Earth healed herself. And when sunlight illuminated the spray about the plunging rapids, waterfalls and cascades, rainbows were revealed and layers of polished canyon rocks glowed colorfully. In time, mosses and ferns flocked the rocky debris and shone with a resplendent deep-green hue behind the mists.

The drumming reverberations of flowing waters resembled a living heartbeat. Millraces twisted and sparkled, splashing joyously, leaping and surging; and in the water's boundless rush, oxygen ions disassociated into rarified mists of negative ions that were exhilarating to breathe.

Within the netherworld of the roaring and rushing waters— deep within chasms, defiles and glens—waterfalls pounded and cascades sparkled, and vaporous mists rose within these hidden and mystical places. Mountain gods and spirits abided, and still do, in those wild, awe-inspiring and beautiful spots. Back then, the gods also spoke to mere mortal creatures.

Over millennia, the retreating glacier's outpouring buried vast areas of lowland beneath stony rubble. The dramatic alterations to mountains and valleys brought forth new landscapes and habitats. Our merle's original home was forever transformed. The little bird tried to appeal to Mother Nature. However, she was too involved with the larger cosmos to give much attention to a little bird's plight of homelessness. Its pleas got short shrift in the larger scheme of things. Mother Nature's sagacious response was to say, "It's not the biggest or strongest that survives, but rather those that best meet the challenges of adapting to change."

Desperate and angry, the little gray bird decided to journey to the source of the changes—the beginning of the waters—to confront Earth's forces. The merle was a courageous little bird; perhaps a bit naïve, too. From the fluvial plains it began making its way upstream, flying and hopping from boulder to boulder along river bottoms and ascending secluded canyons.

Its nestlings and their offspring's offspring for uncountable generations continued the journey, higher and higher into the mountains. Millennia passed, with the little gray bird successfully meeting challenges and adapting to changes along the way.

It was an inner journey as well as physical one. The determined bird developed the adaptability, fortitude and disposition to make its living in the new and changing environments it encountered.

There was one constant in the bird's quest amid the canyons: the surging waters. The water was endless and eternal, never sleeping, always moving. It moved merrily in brooks, it sang in rapids, and shouted in cascades and waterfalls. Journeying through time along the mountain streams, the little gray bird became intimately familiar with the god of motion's eternal ballad. Sometimes it was slow and melodic and at other times rapid and thunderous, but always, forever flowing and moving. The realm of mountain streams displayed a power gifted from sky-piercing mountains and the force of Earth's gravity.

The bird was unaware of it, but the god of motion had been imprinting on it for a long time. Over time, it was imbued with the spirit of motion. It gradually found itself continually bobbing up and down, and ever since it has continued to bob and dance to the endless rhythms of flowing waters.

Sometime later, while performing their endless graceful waltz with gravity, water nymphs and sprites revealed themselves to the bird. The spirits sang and laughed aloud in the currents.

They invited the gray bird to freestyle the rapids and riffles with them. And from the sprites and water nymphs, the bird received the magnificent skill of its fearless swimming ability.

Regardless of ice, frost or currents, clad in its waterproof suit of feathers, the bird learned to fearlessly and unhesitatingly plunge into intimidating waters, where it skillfully navigated and snorkeled along gravel stream bottoms hunting food—aquatic insects, larvae, and small minnows. The swift mountain streams had indeed become the bird's home. The waterways became so imprinted on the bird that it always followed the meandering stream courses in flight, never cutting across or over ground.

One day along the Falling Fork, the little gray bird heard a distant siren drumming. As the bird continued journeying towards the source, the sounds swelled to an awe-inspiring, crashing crescendo. The cacophony reverberated among the canyon walls as the stream roared down a chasm and leaped off a high precipice. Long tresses of green water corkscrewed downward, crashing and shattering into mist and spray, interwoven with rainbows. It was a magical place, filled with mystery. Few mortal creatures had ever dared venture into it before.

As the gray bird approached the formidable waterfall, a beautiful undine took form within the fall. She sparkled radiantly, while long emerald tresses flowed and twisted about her like a watery gown, and rainbows played about her misty hem. Mere mortal creatures were easily entranced into spells by the undine.

Suddenly, the undine foamed in wraith and tumultuously rumbled: "I am the spirit of falling waters, and since before the morning of time, I have been consigned by the mountain gods to wait for a suitable mate to be attracted by my eternal drumming. I demand to know why a little, plain-feathered biped is trespassing into my mystical realm; you are certainly not a 'suitable mate.'"

Located deep in the park's backcountry, Union Falls has a 250-foot drop and is
the second highest waterfall in Yellowstone National Park
(photo by the author).

Seeing the little bird shrink in trepidation, the undine's mood shifted, and she poured forth conciliatory murmurs: "I rarely reveal myself to mere mortal creatures, and I suppose I have behaved badly. The water spirits have sung to me about your long and admirable journey. I have been expecting you to someday discover my ethereal sanctuary."

In its quest, the gray bird had learned that regardless how independent and capable it liked to believe it was, and regardless what it had accomplished, much was owed to the help of others: the mountain gods, the god of motion, the nymphs and sprites, all came to mind. As the bird bobbed up and down curtsying, it wisely listened carefully and respectfully to the moist melodic whispers emanating from the undine's falling waters.

"Long ago," the undine bubbled, "the gods gave your relative, the desert canyon wren, a marvelous song, but I have an equally wondrous and enchanting gift for you, a reward for your long and marvelous journey. Hereafter, you are granted the power to pass through falling waters and to make your nest and home within the refuge of the inaccessible cliffs hidden behind my watery veil.

"There is no other bird or creature blessed with this ability. The cliff swallow perhaps comes the closest. Moreover, I have asked the canyon shadows and reflective swift waters to create the illusion that you are sometimes a dramatically jet-black bird and at other times bluish-gray. No longer will you appear as just an ordinary gray bird. Most people will call you 'water ouzel,' and scientists will dub you *Cinclus*; referring to your waterproof toga, a bold name for a little feathered creature, I dare say."

Realizing it was no common gray bird, the water ouzel spontaneously and energetically bobbed up and down, up and down, on a midstream boulder and sang a clear and ringing wren-like song: "keet, keet, keet." It sang its melodious notes and trills in chorus with the sounds of the flowing waters. In its courageous journey through time and ever-changing habitat, it had evolved and become adapted to a singularly unique ecological niche.

After flitting tentatively about in the spray, it deliberately flew into and through the cataract to the mossy rock ledges behind the veil of falling water. The visual effect behind the waterfall was kaleidoscopic; the ouzel's home was truly a place of enchantment. There it fashioned a "moss hut" for a nest from the greenery that covered the rocks. Its hatchlings reared in this magical place would answer to the siren's wilderness song all their lives, knowing the comforting sound of falling water even before they hatched.

"One more thing," gurgled the undine pleasantly. "You were blessed by the spirit of motion from the flowing waters, but you must consent to give meaning to your constant bobbing."

"Yes, what might that be?" chirped the ouzel from behind the falls.

"Your bobbing resembles a curtsy, and in that manner you will acknowledge your gratitude and respect to the water spirits for all eternity," murmured the undine with everlasting finality.

Today, when you visit the fast-flowing mountain streams high in the Rockies and happen upon a slate-gray, stub-tailed bird perched on a midstream rock, watch as turns it head from side to side as if listening and then bobs up and down in the fashion of a curtsy. Then you will know you have met the water ouzel. You will also recognize it is still happily and gratefully acknowledging Nature's gifts. The bird's presence signifies a pristine mountain stream. And because the ouzel is there, you will further know that you are at a wondrous spot, a place of enchantment, where water spirits and sprites reside, and a place possessing the restorative powers of nature. The ouzel assumes unspoiled mountain streams will continue to sing to it forever. We can only hope what it believes is true.

Wind-deformed whitebark pine tree in the Wind River Mountains, Wyoming
(photo by Pattie Layser).

# 5

## The Nutcracker and
## Whitebark Pine's Covenant

*A tree stands motionless. It is nerveless and silent, its trunk seems solid and it contains no organs in the usual sense. Yet a tree is alive from the cap of its deepest root to the tip of its highest twig.*
—Rutherford Platt, *The Great American Forest*

On the alpine crags in the northern Rocky Mountains, there is a pine tree that grows very slowly and to great age. It is a remarkable species that captures the imagination of everyone who ventures into its magical mountain realm. Many of those growing today were already more than a century old when the Pilgrims landed at Plymouth. It is an important conifer, but not for its lumber. The tree's name is quite ordinary—whitebark pine; but its rugged existence is extraordinary.

Whitebark pine, known scientifically as *Pinus albicaulis*, grows on harsh sites, frequently at timberline. It often appears to be rooted in bare rock; at other places, it clings to precipitous slopes high in the mountains. The lofty rock outcrops and frost-fractured rock rubble it inhabits provides refuge from wildfire. In winter it often becomes encased in rime, forming what are known as "snow ghosts." Its evergreen and long, willowy branches are extremely tough, allowing it to withstand heavy snow loads and cyclonic winds without breakage. The branches are so flexible and resistant to breakage that they can be tied into knots, like whip cord. And, its needles are heavily waxed and insulated with resin to protect it against drying and the elements. Like other members of its family, it diffuses a scent of pine, which it dissipates into the rarefied mountain air.

The Lakota Indians have a saying that the strength of a tree comes not from its growth in favorable years, but from survival under challenging and difficult times. Whitebark pine epitomizes the Lakota metaphor: it demonstrates great strength under the most challenging of conditions. In old age the tree can appear weather-beaten, wind-deformed, lightning-scarred, twisted, and knobby and gnarly. It is a stoic old man of the mountains; often a lone summit sentinel, a survivor against all odds. Long after it dies, until fire returns its ashes to Earth, its indurate, bleached-white skeleton persists.

Long ago, this tree evolved a unique complication. Unlike most pines, it produces very large and wingless seeds. But its purple cone scales, even after loosening, will not open far enough to allow the oversized, nut-like seeds to escape. Also, it bears its cones at the very tips of its uppermost branches, and the cones are not easily detachable. While those morphological characteristics serve to protect its seeds in the icy cold and wind-blasted alpine environment, they also hamper regeneration of new trees. Its cones do not open or detach until the seeds are no longer viable.

After much time had passed without any of its seeds taking root or producing a single scion, an ancient whitebark pine became distraught. It waved its cone laden branches in the wind at other forest creatures, beckoning their attention. The pine had noted that more than twenty animals and birds relished eating its seeds, which are rich in fat and protein. Surely one of them would help find a solution to its unique dilemma if it appealed for help.

A passing deer that paused to daintily nibble on alpine forbs responded by snorting, "Your cones are much higher than I can reach, and besides, I generally do not eat pine tree seeds."

A chubby marmot sat up on a boulder and listened attentively to the pine's plight, but confessed, "I can sometimes climb trees, but not to the very top branches."

A goshawk looking for grouse in the whortleberry bushes below swayed on its perch in the tree's topmost branches. Preening itself indifferently, it admitted, "I have neither the interest nor the time for your pitchy cones that might foul my flight feathers."

Sometime afterward, a porcupine shuffled past while grazing on the flowers of the herb spring beauty, the plant Longfellow's Hiawatha called *miskodeed*. It shook its quills and rasped, "The branches bearing your cones are too flexible, they will not bear my weight."

Each summer a gray-crowned rosy finch built its nest in nearby rock crevices. The finch confessed it did use its short, stout beak for cracking open seeds, but it was not able to open pine cones.

Next a curious red-crossbill alighted and appeared to take a keen interest, but finally acknowledged, "It's true my bill has evolved to open conifer cones by levering the scales apart, but I must admit, your scales are too thick for me to undo."

Later, a bear wandered by. It eagerly offered to help! Actually, the bear was always famished and angling for another meal; it was a hopeless plunderer. However, this particular bruin was not able to hoist his considerable bulk very far up the tree. And, secretly, he did not relish the tree's sticky resin getting all over his fur either. Frustrated, he growled at the tree, "If I was able to climb higher, I could break off or maybe bend the branches down that bear your cones. Younger and more agile bears sometimes do that." The tree was alarmed and not happy with that potentially destructive prospect.

After grumbling around at the base of the tree for awhile, the bear had another idea. He slyly confided to the tree, "Maybe I can get red squirrel to scurry up your furthermost limbs and gnaw the cones free, while I stay down here on the ground and chew the seeds out of them for you." Bear inadvertently salivated at the thought.

The tree noticed the drooling; it really could not trust the bear. The tree fretted about what scientists termed its "seed fate." If the bear got its cones, there would be no seeds left to sprout. It would chew the cones apart and eat every last seed.

Bruin went lumbering off on his mission to recruit a squirrel to help him. Along the way, he searched for anything else he could eat. While bear was looking for the rodent, a gray bird, built like a small crow with a powerful beak, flew over the tree. He was attracted by the beckoning branches that were heavily weighted with cones.

The bird, which called itself a nutcracker, perched on a high branch and listened while the gnarly old tree confessed its predicament: "My cone scales are hard and very strong, I keep them tightly closed to protect my seeds from the cold and ice-blasting wind. But I may have overdone it. Now I'm not able to open them far enough to allow my seeds to escape. Can you do anything to help?"

Clark's nutcracker (photo by the author).

"Kraak khraa," the nutcracker croaked, "I resemble a bird called a "nutjobber," I can use my beak as a chisel to peck apart your cones and get the seeds out, but I am going to eat them for my trouble." The nutcracker proceeded to demonstrate, splitting apart the hard indehiscent cones with his powerful beak. It got a few seeds free and promptly swallowed them. The pine tree did not enjoy watching its seeds being consumed, but it was impressed with the bird's deft ability.

The bird's proficiency evoked a latent memory in the tree. It recalled that a cousin of the nutcracker, the western scrub jay, collected acorns from the California black oak and hid them in the soil. The scrub jay played a crucial role in maintaining oak savannas. Perhaps, the pine thought, the nutcracker might be enlisted in a similar arrangement.

The ancient tree sighed in the blustery wind, and then shrewdly proposed a compromise to the nutcracker, one which would be mutually beneficial: "I will produce cone crops as often as possible if, in exchange, you will agree not to eat all the seeds but, rather, store some for later use."

Attentive and amused by the proposal, the nutcracker chortled "And why should I do that?"

"Because," the shrewd old tree replied, "if you cache some seeds, you will have food during the cold of winter. Think about the squirrel, the beaver and the pika: they each store a winter food supply. It could make your life in the mountains less difficult."

The nutcracker had indeed endured a very tough winter; the possibility that he might avoid that in the future got his attention. The tree was wise. It was counting on the industrious nutcracker to not only get the seeds out of its cones, but also to cache more than it would ever eat; hopefully, then forgetting where it had hidden them all.

If the bird secreted them in the soil or duff, they stood a chance of growing. The tree rationalized future generations of nutcrackers might also benefit from new trees growing and from the seeds those trees would eventually produce, too.

An agreement was reached. Both thought they had gotten the better deal, so each was eager to honor the compact. Their contract has, in fact, been honored by both of them for millennia. Scientists refer to it as a "mutualistic partnership."

Meanwhile, bear waddled about in the forest and finally found the squirrel, but not before he had consumed some grasshoppers, ants and berries, and had also rubbed himself on nearly every rough tree stob he encountered.

The red squirrel was busy collecting mushrooms and storing them in forks of trees to dry.

Bear grunted, "Urghh," to get squirrel's attention and then told the rodent about the tree's predicament; bear's version was rather self-serving: "The whitebark pine needs your help to get its cones down from its high branches onto the ground."

"Is that all? Why should I bother," chattered the impatient and hyperactive squirrel?

Bear paused and stood upright, reaching as far up an aspen tree as he could, deeply engraving the smooth bark with his claws, while trying to appear casual and indifferent,

"I think it's so the whitebark pine's, ah, ample and delectable seeds might produce more trees for squirrels like you to frolic in." Playing to the squirrel's ego, bear crooned, "Of all the forest animals I know, you are the most fearless and talented climber, able to reach the highest of tree tops. That is why the tree sent me to recruit your help."

By then the squirrel barely heard the bear, she was thinking instead of the pine's cone crop and how good the plump nut-like seeds tasted, especially in the cold darkness of winter, when she'd dig them up from her cache deep beneath the snow.

Squirrel knew better than to come down the tree while the bear was close by, so she began running along limbs, jumping from tree to tree, scampering along downed logs, scurrying across boulders, and climbing far up the mountain to reach the place where whitebark pine grew. It was a weather-beaten place she would normally only visit temporarily and that was when the whitebark pine produced a cone crop.

When squirrel finally arrived at the old pine tree, she found there was a profusion of oversized cones glistening in the trees uppermost canopy. The rodent chattered excitedly to the tree, "I've come to help you get your cones down; I can climb your highest branches. My jaws are strong, and my teeth are sharp for cutting cones loose. I'm the right animal for the job; neither the chipmunk, deer mouse nor the vole has strong enough jaws."

In a whispered zephyr, the tree replied, "Nutcracker has already agreed to assist me, thank you. We do not need an overly eager rodent's help."

But there was little the tree could do; squirrel was not to be deterred. She quickly scampered up the tree and began rapidly gnawing off cones, dropping them to the ground. Nutcracker, seeing what he considered *its* cones being taken by the rodent, gratingly croaked and cawed, "Khraa, go away squirrel. Stay away."

The squirrel barked back, "The tree needs my expert climbing and gnawing skills to get its cones loose and on the ground, not picked to pieces by you."

Squirrel furiously scampered around in the tree's canopy, snipping off cones with its strong sharp teeth, letting them fall to the ground. Squirrel was capable of cutting hundreds of cones loose in an hour. Nutcracker and squirrel squabbled back and forth as they competed for the fat strobili.

After red squirrel had industriously gnawed off several dozen cones, she raced back down the tree. One at a time she gathered them up and carried them off, stashing them under a nearby log. After accumulating a large cache, a "larder hoard," she decided to rest. Sitting on a limb she favored as a feeding perch, she chewed open a cone and feasted on the seeds.

Meanwhile, the nutcracker was busily flying back and forth—chiseling cones apart in the top of the tree, getting the seeds out, and carrying them off in his throat. Over time the nutcracker evolved a specialized sublingual pouch just to carry seeds. The throat pouch was able to hold over a hundred whitebark pine seeds. The bird hid the seeds in widely scattered locations in the soil, beneath duff, and in rock crevices; it practiced "scatter hoarding," as compared to the squirrel's "larder hoarding."

Incredibly, the nutcracker buried tens of thousands of seeds in a single autumn. In a remarkable display of spatial memory, it eventually recovered and ate three-quarters of them. But the forgotten ones, just as the pine had trusted, offered the potential to germinate into new trees.

Meanwhile, a golden-mantle squirrel, which resembled an overgrown chipmunk, was attracted by all the activity. It scurried around beneath the tree, and with its keen nose it was able to locate a few seeds that the nutcracker accidentally dropped. It ate one and carried the other off to store in its own larder.

During this time, bear was preoccupied by his discovery of a patch of huckleberries. After gleaning the berry bushes clean, he remembered the pine cones and wandered his way back up the mountain to the tree. He had purple stains comically smeared all over his muzzle and fur.

The bear grinned, showing his purple-stained teeth, and grunted, "I've come back to rescue your cones and seeds. I sent squirrel, ahead of me. Did she show up? Is she helping you?"

The pine tree knew its earlier suspicions were correct: bear's only interest was another meal. Since this bear was not very successful in climbing and breaking off cone-laden

Whitebark pine cones chiseled open and seeds removed by Clark's nutcracker (photo by the author).

branches, he had cleverly encouraged the squirrel to serve as his intermediary.

The ancient tree stoically ignored the bear. After not getting a response, the bruin began circling, nose-to-ground and sniffing, round and round he went in an ever-widening search. Finally, he came upon the squirrel's cache hidden beneath a decaying old log. "Aha," he snorted. Moving the timber aside with a powerful swipe of his paw, he began digging furiously, unearthing the squirrel's entire stockpile.

Seeing the bear digging in her midden, squirrel became very distressed. She chattered and barked: "Stop it, stop it! How did you find it? I hid it so well." Squirrel was additionally agitated because she instinctively understood that if she built a substantial cache—eventually containing thousands of cones—the larder could possibly carry over to support several generations of her kind through hard years.

Just out of reach on a limb above bear the squirrel chattered angrily: "Stop it, stop, go away bear! You're nothing but a klepto-parasite." It was true, but bear was too busy pilfering the cache, chewing cones to pieces and lapping up the seeds, to pay any attention. Later, that night, a timid deer mouse furtively visited squirrel's cache site. The mouse scurried away, carrying off the last edible remains.

Every autumn in the high country, the drama between the whitebark pine tree, nutcracker, red squirrel, and bear is replayed. The nutcracker soars over a sea of tree tops, chortling and looking for ripe cones to expertly pick apart for seeds. Then, carrying more than a hundred seeds at a time, it hides them across scattered locations. The whitebark pine relies on the nutcracker to disseminate its seeds. Groves of nutcracker-planted pines in the high country attest to the longstanding and successful partnership between the bird and the tree.

When you are hiking in the high country, it's possible to identify the pine trees that were planted by nutcrackers. The birds frequently bury several seeds together, resulting in trees that are multi-stemmed or growing in clumps, while others sprout from odd places, such as in the middle of a mountain meadow, tightly up against a boulder, or out of a rock crevice somewhere on a lonely alpine ridge. All were likely planted by nutcrackers.

While the nutcracker honors its long-standing contract, the red squirrel also remains busy, year after year, opportunistically gathering and storing cones. Occasionally, trees sprout from its caches, but frequently bears also dig up the cones and eat them. The squirrel unwittingly serves as a go-between for the bears to access an otherwise mostly unattainable food source. Still, lucky for squirrels, bears don't discover all their larders. Meanwhile, golden-mantle squirrels, chipmunks, mice, voles, Canada jays, and others opportunistically participate in pine seed harvest, too, however they can.

The lives of whitebark pine, nutcrackers, red squirrels and bears in the northern Rockies are interrelated in a cooperative, mutually beneficial relationship, a loose type of symbiosis. It is just that bear, snoring contentedly in his winter den, fattened by a squirrel's larder of cones obtained from trees planted by the nutcracker, hasn't figured out how to reciprocate just yet.

Ecologists call whitebark pine a "keystone species." Like the single stone in the arch that holds the entire surrounding structure together, the whitebark pine plays a singular role in northern Rockies high-elevation ecosystems. In recent time, however, the pine, and therefore the web-of-life relationships that have existed for millennia between it and other species, is threatened by an imported disease and insect infestations. In fact, some conservationists have recently petitioned to have whitebark pine listed under the Endangered Species Act since the tree has sadly undergone severe decline throughout its range in recent decades.

The whitebark pine tree is highly susceptible to blister rust, *Cronartium ribicola*, an infectious fungus, brought to North America from Europe about one hundred years ago. It first attacked eastern white pine, then western white pine, and now its spread to whitebark pine, infecting and killing them, too. The fungus's microscopic spores are transported by wind, insects, and the feet of birds. Whitebark pine mortality in northern Idaho, northeastern Washington and Montana, since the pathogen's arrival, has been catastrophic. In Glacier National Park alone, scientists estimate blister rust has killed over 90 percent or more of the whitebark pine.

In a double jeopardy, trees weakened and stressed from warming climate, drought, and blister-rust disease are then assailed by bark beetles and killed. Because of the normally cold climate where whitebark pine grows, bark beetles were generally not a factor in the past. The insects were not able to complete their life cycle in the wintry environment. But with the advent of back-to-back unseasonably warm years, the altitude at which the pine grows no longer assures protection from the beetles. This is particularly evident, for example, in the Absaroka Mountains in Wyoming and Montana, where, in recent years, bark beetles have destroyed whitebark pines over extensive areas.

The blister rust and beetles have infested whitebark pine throughout much of the Greater Yellowstone ecosystem, where, up until recently, it was believed the cold, dry climate would protect the trees. In a 1997 computer modeling study, scientists direly predicted that over time this keystone species, whitebark pine, could disappear entirely from the Greater Yellowstone region as a result of factors related to climate change. Whitebark pine provided an important source of food for the grizzly bear, which is federally listed as a threatened species.

At present, Wyoming's Wind River Mountains appear to be one place where the blister rust pathogen and bark beetles have not severely impacted the whitebark pine, at least not yet.

Some argue a rust-resistant tree could theoretically evolve or be developed in the laboratory. But, in practice, artificial reforestation of whitebark pine throughout the vast, high-elevations of the northern Rockies is not a practical prospect. Even if rust-resistant seedlings were successfully propagated, the trees grow very slowly. And, since where they naturally occur is in inaccessible high-mountain locations, it's not a species that lends itself to large-scale artificial reforestation.

The potential loss of whitebark pine throughout the northern Rocky Mountain high-elevation ecosystem has grievous and unsettling biological and aesthetic consequences, not unlike those experienced in eastern North America, when the great American chestnut tree was destroyed across its entire range by an imported blight disease.

Long-term the outcome is still uncertain. But we can count on the help of the nutcracker and other birds and animals to industriously do their part to assure the tree's survival. That buoys my hope more than any laboratory studies or proposed forestry projects. As long as gnarly veterans survive on lonely, isolated, and windswept alpine crags, and nutcrackers continue to gather and plant their seeds year-after-year, there is hope for the tree's survival.

Pika in Alaska Basin, Teton Mountains, Wyoming
(photo by the author).

# 6

## The Bellwether in the Rock Pile

*The high hills are a refuge for the wild goats; and the rocks for the conies.*
    – Psalms 104:18

Examine the high-elevation boulder fields, rock slides, talus, and scree closely, there could be more there among the rocks than you first realize. If you're lucky, you'll spot a salt-and-peppery-brown, hamster-size animal. It's typically perched on a jutting rock beneath an overhanging boulder. The small animal positions itself to command a strategic view, while being hidden from soaring raptors above. It basks in the sun, even as it keeps a vigilant lookout. It's a diminutive icon of alpine environments and untamed nature.

Notice, a short distance away, within the talus, its sibling is busily eating a dried marmot pellet, while another member of the colony scampers through a narrow rock passage, carrying a large wad of vegetation crossways in its mouth. Suddenly a movement catches the self-appointed lookout's attention and it sounds a warning:

"Eenk... eenk."

The hiker paused and scanned the boulders trying to determine the source of the odd high-pitched bleat or squeak, or maybe it was a barking sound?

"Eenk."

There it was again?

The novice backcountry hiker, frustrated at not being able to locate the source of the sound coming from somewhere in the boulders, first here and then there, finally moved on. The camouflaged little rodent was able to "throw its voice," warning its relatives without revealing its location to what it considered a potential threat.

When the hiker returned to camp, he told his comrades, experienced mountaineers, about a "squeaking-bleating sound" coming from nowhere. One of them asked, "Did the sound appear to come from a talus slope or rock slide?" "Yeah, it did," replied the neophyte. "Then you probably heard a rock rabbit," said the mountaineer.

"Hey, how about a pack rat?" someone else joked. "They hang out in rock slides.

They're called wood rats or trade rats, too. Once I had one carry off a spoon from camp; it left me a stick in its place, but I never heard of one bleating."

Another quipped, "It could also have been a boulder bunny, whistling hare, mountain rabbit, mouse rabbit, little chief hare, pica, pika, cony, or if you prefer, a coney. They are all names for the same animal, *Ochotona princeps*. However, not to add confusion, but early European explorers called gophers and rabbits "conies," too. That's how the name Coney Island originated—I guess there were once lots of rabbits there."

Experienced mountaineers are frequently erudite people. There is something about the mountains and wilderness that attracts widely read and knowledgeable people; or perhaps it's the mountains induce humility, encouraging a desire to learn more about one's surroundings. In any case, one of the mountaineers outdid the others by explaining that the name "coney" originated from ancient Hebrew, meaning "the hider;" and that there is a closely related species to the American pika which lives among the rocks in the Holy Land.

Seeing the disbelieving expression on the novice's face, the mountaineers laughed. "We're not spoofing you." Your squeaking animal goes by a variety of names, most call it a *pie-ka*. But the correct pronunciation is really *pee-ka,* which is also sort of like the sound they make.

Long ago, the American pika—a small but stocky, roman-nosed, tailless, rabbit-like creature, with rather large rounded ears and a bush of long whiskers—scurried through time and across the land bridge, called Beringia, which once connected North America to Asia. It was the Ice Age, and this little silky-furred lagomorph had evolved an affinity for cool climates.

The Rocky Mountains at that time were mostly buried beneath ice. As the glaciers receded, pikas followed their retreat higher and higher into the mountains, making their homes in the jumble of rock rubble left behind.

In spring, as snow recedes from high-elevation talus and scree in the Rocky Mountains, pikas timidly emerge from a long winter spent in a subniveous environment, deeply buried beneath snow and ice. Deep snowpack is important for them; it protects them from the extreme cold.

They were active under the snow all winter, constructing tunnels between rocks and crevices, and protecting their larders of stored food from bushy-tailed wood rats. Except for their vocalizations, winter for them was a silent, dark world. Their long, bushy-whiskers provided them the tactile means to navigate their opaque and, to us, mysterious habitation. When they first venture out into the bright daylight of spring, they do so very cautiously.

At the same time in spring, a host of other denizens within the rocky habitat also become active. Ground squirrels, golden-mantled squirrels, chipmunks and marmots awaken from their profound sleep; wood rats begin rustling around at night, adding more sticks and objects to their nests, and voles and white-footed mice search through the crevices for winter's leftovers.

All the rodent activity creates small pathways, tunnels and burrows within the boulder fields. These do not go unnoticed. The bustle of the small mammals attracts predators, such as pine martens, coyotes, hawks, and pound for pound, the most vicious of all predators: weasels or ermine. The pikas are wise to be extra cautious.

The pika's need for watchfulness was reinforced by a frightening experience during the winter. An ermine was able to burrow through the snow and squeeze into one of their tunnels. Mountain rabbits rarely survive an encounter with an ermine hunting for a meal.

Pikas live in colonies and members of the colony are invariably all related to one another. The average-sized colony consists of five rock rabbits spread out over up to an acre, each one with its own territory. Each marks its neighborhood with secretions from their cheek glands rubbed onto rocks. And each adopts its own boulder to urinate on, until the rock becomes encrusted and white from all the many markings.

While every individual defends its territory, they generally range over a larger area. This causes endless squabbles and chases. First an occupant chases the intruder back into its own territory; then comically, the chase reverses and the original intruder chases the other. Males do not tolerate each other, nor do females get along with other females.

Cony was the name of a rock rabbit born into an average litter of three. Within eight days, he and his siblings could walk on their short legs and imitate adult vocalizations. They grew rapidly. Within a month, their mother kicked them out of the nest into a severe and hostile environment to fend for themselves.

Right away, Cony was aggressively chased across and around the rock slide from one territory into another. It was the season when colony members were extra intent on defending their space from any intruders. They were instinctively driven to defend their territory because of their competition for vital food which had to be harvested and stockpiled for winter.

Year-round living in the Rocky Mountains at high elevation requires extraordinary survival strategies. Beginning in mid-summer, members of the colony devote their time to the critical gathering and storing vegetative material. Much time and energy is spent collecting plant material—cutting and caching bouquets of vegetation—and then guarding those larders. They construct haystacks beneath rock overhangs, in crevices, and alongside boulders and ledges. Pikas rely solely on the hay piles they build for their winter food supply.

Cony didn't have a lot of time to establish his territory and set up housekeeping before severe weather would arrive. What he settled for wasn't the best spot in the rock pile. Foraging areas and meadow edges were a greater distance away for him than for other colony members, but it was workable. Finding a favorable place to live within the colony, where he could gather and store food before winter arrived, while not infringing on neighboring territories, was absolutely critical to his survival. The severity of the alpine climate afforded him precious little time. Somehow, without being taught, he instinctively did the things that constitute what is to be a pika.

He began industriously gnawing off pieces of thimbleberry, twinflower, Indian paintbrush, raspberry, whortleberry, aspen, fireweed, stonecrop, bluebell, sedges and grasses. Then he would scamper across the rocks carrying or dragging the cuttings, some up to two-foot long. His favorites were the colorful flowering stalks of mountain bluebells, fireweed, and Indian paintbrush.

Next he spread his richly-colored cuttings on rocks to dry. Then he carried the cured plant material that resembled dried flower bouquets to his pre-selected larder sites. As his piles of dried plant material increased in size, he would stand on his hind legs to add more to the top, making conical-shaped haystacks. Some of his piles reached two feet in height. It was an amazing feat for such a little animal. No wonder people call pikas "the little haymakers."

Like other colony members, Cony aggressively protected his hay mounds. To assure that there was no doubt of ownership, after he built a haystack, he would stand on his hind legs and urinate on it. He also always defecated at the same places in the rocks next to his haystacks, too, until there was an accumulated pile of his pellets next to each hay mound.

If he found a dried marmot pellet, he would add it to a haystack for a special winter treat. The scoop on eating poop— which has a fancy term: coprophagia—is that the pika's high-fiber diet is difficult to digest. Reingesting their droppings helps to capture vital nutrients and minerals. Marmots practice coprophagia, too.

When Cony needed a break from haymaking and protecting his territory, he would sit under an overhanging rock and eat the scented flowers and fresh green plants that he had harvested.

By early autumn, bushel-size piles of cured vegetation had magically appeared here and there within the rock rubble and talus. Besides the occasional alarm vocalizations, another curious sound began emanating from the rocks: males began making noises, described as "singing," to attract a mate.

But when an alert marmot living next to the pika colony whistled a warning call, they suddenly all became quiet. A weasel was seen slithering across a boulder on the edge of the colony. It was the one enemy that pikas avoided voicing a vocal alarm about for fear of giving away their location.

Once on the trail of a pika, weasels and ermines are not easily distracted. Since Cony had taken up residence on the periphery of the colony, the weasel came upon his scent first. Suddenly, beneath his favorite rock overhang, Cony found himself confronted by the fierce predator. He quickly turned and ran, instinctively scrambling as fast as he could go, squeezing into narrow crannies, darting through a maze of tunnels, scurrying along runways and into crevices, with the weasel frighteningly close behind him and gaining.

A scientist once observed pika behavior where, when one was pursued by a weasel, two or more colony members join in taking turns running relays against the predator. It's what saved Cony. As he raced through the colony, oblivious to territorial boundaries, his heart pounding in panic and nearly exhausted, whether on purpose or by accident, another member of the colony darted in behind him. It diverted the weasel from Cony and onto the other pika's trail. It was a dangerous game. But confused by several frightened pikas suddenly darting in and out in front of him, the weasel finally became frustrated and gave up the chase, leaving without its intended meal.

Later, that autumn, a group of scientists hiked up to the talus slide and quietly positioned themselves with binoculars where they could observe the pikas. When the people sat silent and motionless, the little animals appeared undisturbed and went about their customary activities. One person whispered to another: "Pika-boo, first it's here, than it's over there." Another

Earle F. Layser

The hoary marmot found at high elevation in the Rocky Mountains frequently inhabits rocky habitat with the pika (photo by the author).

declared, "I think it has to be one of the cutest animals in America—a little agrarian wonder!"

The scientists were conducting a field trip as part of a wide-reaching seminar topic: "Pika: The Miner's Canary of Alpine Environments." They had learned through their research that these flower-gathering relatives of rabbits were sensitive barometers—bellwethers—of climate change in alpine ecosystems. Monitoring studies were recording the extinction of pika colonies along the low-elevation margins of their range in response to warming climate. Pikas are well-adapted to cold alpine environments, but their thermoregulation is quickly compromised by warming. They reportedly can perish under even moderately warm conditions. One study found pika were unable to survive for six hours when exposed to a temperature of seventy-eight degrees Fahrenheit.

Time passed, and a road was proposed to be constructed into the high-elevation setting through the mountain pass where the colony of little haymakers existed. Proponents for the road development argued, "Opening the area up to motorized recreation was needed, so that everyone could enjoy the scenery. Not everyone can or wants to walk that far."

There were a few critics who took the unpopular position of questioning the need for the road. They attempted to make their point by, among other things, evoking conservationist Aldo Leopold's observation: "Recreational development is not a job of building roads into lovely country, but rather of building receptivity into the human mind." In the end, the developers prevailed. Boosters for the local economy labeled it "progress."

Not long afterward, an engineer and a heavy-equipment operator got off their four-wheelers after switch-backing up the mountain and walked over to examine the talus slope. The engineer remarked, "Looks like it'll make good aggregate." The equipment operator grunted, "Looks like nothin' but another pile of rocks to me."

Pointing to a place near the base of the talus, the engineer said, "We'll set the rock crusher up over there."

When the noise and physical impact of the rock excavation and crushing began the following spring, the golden-mantled squirrels, ground squirrels, chipmunks and marmots were shaken from any lingering winter dormancy. The voles and white-footed mice scurried away at night, as did the woodrats. The pikas, which had made the talus slope their home for centuries, had nowhere to go or hide. Their fine-tuned, habitat-specific adaptations, evolved over tens of thousands of years, were no match for man-caused disturbance in their alpine habitat.

Bighorn sheep rams in Yellowstone National Park (photo by Judy Wantulok).

# 7

## Mountain Monarchs Help Save a Town

*Sheep hunting becomes a passion, pursued to the ragged edge of human endurance.*
– Charles F. Waterman, *The Hunter's World*

Long ago, an ancient mountain people lived within the heart of the Rocky Mountains. They ranged throughout what today is central and southeast Idaho, southwest Montana and northwestern Wyoming, living in small kin-based groups. They referred to the different but related groups by what they ate— Buffalo Eaters, Rabbit Eaters, Pine Nut Eaters, Sheep Eaters. Later, white men gave them the name Snake or Shoshone.

The group known as the Sheep Eaters or Mountain Shoshone, the *Tukudika,* made their home within the mountains of the Greater Yellowstone region. They were masters of mountain survival, and undoubtedly the first people to scale the regions highest peaks. Mountain man, Osborne Russell, in *Journal of a Trapper*, described them as "neatly clothed in dressed deer and sheepskins and perfectly happy."

The Sheep Eaters' lives and sustenance were closely patterned to mountain sheep; an animal born in the age of the Pleistocene, more than ten thousand years ago. The Mountain Shoshone followed the seasonal movements of wild sheep throughout the awesome settings of the Absaroka, Beartooth, Gros Ventre, Teton, and Wind River mountains—the Yellowstone cordillera. In those bygone times, the Indians situated their winter camps within the foothill ranges of the mountain sheep, and in this way they coexisted with, and preyed upon, wild sheep in a sustainable manner for thousands of years.

The Sheep Eaters were skillful artisans who were renowned for the powerful bows they fashioned from the wild ram's massive horns. The bows were capable of driving an arrow clear through a buffalo. Large ram's horns can grow up to fifty-two inches long in a spiral and eighteen inches across. The massive horns weigh up to thirty or forty pounds, equaling the sheep's entire skeleton in weight. To soften the horns and make them workable, the Indians soaked them in the hot springs occurring within the Yellowstone region.

Today, the Sheep Eaters and their way of life are vanished. An 1868 treaty compelled them to move onto reservations. The final chapter was Colonel P. W. Norris's removal of all Indians from Yellowstone National Park to the Wind River and Fort Hall reservations around 1879.

Place names, like Spearhead Peak, however, bear testimony to these aboriginal sheep hunters and their prehistoric presence high amid the Teton Range. Archaeological evidence indicates Native Americans pursued sheep in the Tetons as far back as 6,000 years ago. Other evidence of the Indians' venerable way of life was discovered west of present-day Cody, Wyoming, at a place where wild sheep still winter along the North Fork of the Shoshone River. Not long ago, a rock shelter with a mummy dressed in a sheepskin robe was uncovered there.

At the place the Shoshone called the "Valley of Warm Winds" (the Wind River Valley in the vicinity of Dubois, Wyoming), within the bighorn sheep's winter range, ancient Sheep Eater artifacts exist. There, in boulder-strewn Torrey Valley, rock shelters, sheep "catch pens," and boulders bearing prehistoric rock art abound. The site is listed on the National Register for its remarkable petroglyphs. Torrey Valley is a unique spot; it resonates with a feeling of timelessness, echoing of a sacred place.

While the Sheep Eaters are gone from Torrey Valley today, the majestic bighorn sheep still remain—albeit in greatly reduced numbers—descendants of the same animals among which the Mountain Shoshone once made their winter camps.

Nearly all the lofty mountain ranges in the world were once inhabited by wild sheep. In pre-settlement time, bighorn sheep were among western North America's most successful species. Today, in Wyoming, only eight small and isolated populations of Rocky Mountain bighorns exist, remnants of the once abundant herds. The Wind River Mountains, adjacent to Torrey Valley near Dubois, boasts the largest group occurring anywhere in the conterminous United States. They are called the Whiskey Mountain herd and consist of an estimated seven hundred to eight hundred animals, down from an estimated two-to-five thousand over the last twenty years or so, due to disease inflicted die-off.

The Whiskey Mountain-Torrey Valley area has undoubtedly served as bighorn habitat since the glaciers began receding ten thousand years ago. Most of the year the sheep live in small bands, each is led by a dominant ewe. For much of the year, they inhabit rocky cliffs that are rarely disturbed by humans, deep within the Wind River Mountains' Fitzpatrick Wilderness.

Petroglyphs in Torrey Canyon near Dubois, Wyoming (photo by the author).

Bighorn sheep evolved remarkable adaptations to their mountain habitat. Specially adapted hooves, hard at the outer edges and spongy in the center, allow good traction even on sheer rock. The sheep possess acute eyesight and a unique physiology, which allows them to endure extreme elevation and temperatures. They are actually capable of moderating their heart rate in response to elevation and the need to conserve energy.

A bighorn sheep ram has a muscular body weighing up to three-hundred pounds. In late autumn, head-butting rams can sometimes be observed fiercely contesting one another on Whiskey Mountain, their foreheads and horns crashing together, an unforgettable sound and sight. The cracking sound of the colliding mountain monarchs can be heard a mile away. It is a ritual of endurance that they repeat over and over until the stronger ram prevails; he then gets his choice of ewes.

The extraordinary horns are made up of a fibrous protein called keratin (same as your fingernails). "Full curl" horns are defined by the tips being level with the horn bases. They are coveted by trophy hunters. Generally, it takes a ram seven or eight years to achieve a full curl. This fact has raised questions about bighorn trophy hunting, which selectively takes only the dominant large-horned rams. Some scientists regard this practice as undesirable, because it removes the most genetically fit animals from the gene pool.

Weaker and less fit animals are under normal circumstances least likely to pass along their genes. If not carefully regulated, trophy hunting can lead to the reverse happening. This is not mere speculation. Research biologist Marco Festa-Blanchet of the University of Sherbrooke in Quebec has found a 25 percent decline in the size of horns on bighorn sheep over the past thirty years, and the bodies of both male and female are reportedly getting smaller also, a type of unnatural selection that favors runts.

Conversely, the revenue generated from sale of bighorn sheep hunting licenses benefits management for the species. In so-called "acts of largess on the part of generous benefactors" (read: a wealthy trophy hunter determined to get a tag and tired of waiting on luck of the draw), a sheep tag can fetch large amounts of money at auction. In Wyoming, for example, the governor gets five complimentary sheep permits annually that are then sold to the highest bidders. In 1999, they averaged $24,000 apiece. The "Governors Tags" are in addition to regular licenses, which, in Wyoming in 2009, cost $122 for a resident and $2,266 for a nonresident through the limited draw application and lottery process. In another program, the Foundation for Wild Sheep auctions off a single permit each year at its annual meeting from those states with huntable wild sheep populations. The money raised must be used for mountain sheep conservation projects. In 1994, a single permit from Montana fetched a record $310,000.

From time immemorial, mountain sheep have wintered along snow-line in the foothills of Torrey Valley adjacent to Whiskey Mountain feeding on woody plants such as sage and rabbit brush and cured forbs and grasses. In early spring, they retreat for lambing to the most inaccessible cliffs within the nearby Fitzpatrick and Bridger Wildernesses. A ewe gives birth to a single lamb. After the lambs are a few weeks old, the gathering migrates to alpine ranges high in the Wind River Mountains.

Bighorns are gregarious creatures, often touching noses in greeting. The lambs are playful, engaging in games such as "follow the leader," while making bleating sounds. The ewes can vocalize a guttural baa, which generally serves as a warning. Because of the extreme habitat the sheep occupy, the only predator a young lamb generally need fear is the golden eagle. The males also spend summers in the high country, but separate from the ewes and lambs. Bighorn sheep live up to twenty-four years in captivity, less in the wild.

Despite being well-adapted to their habitat, American wild sheep have notably low reproductive rates, an important point being, they do not and cannot respond to population losses with a rapid rebound in numbers.

In 1988, the town of Dubois's primary industry, a Louisiana-Pacific sawmill, shut down. A small number of activists from Fremont and Teton County, Wyoming, had vigorously objected to the mill because its timber source was primarily obtained from the surrounding national forests. Over the course of a decade, they were successful in closing the mill down by purposefully opposing and appealing any and all timber sales on nearby national forests, thus choking off the mill's timber supply. Without the mill, local demand for timber from the national forests went away.

The local economy was thrown into a tailspin. Residents, forest workers and civic leaders alike asked, "What can we do to keep our town and economy alive?" They took a lesson from the Sheep Eaters and turned to the bighorns. It was an unusual twist, a type of "mutualism" between wild sheep and the townspeople. Generally, humans nowadays think in terms of "saving wildlife," not vice versa.

In July 1993, after much cooperative planning, meetings, and negotiations between the townspeople, agencies and organizations, Dubois, Wyoming, became home to the National Bighorn Sheep Interpretive Center, the only facility in the country dedicated to celebrating and educating people about North America's wild sheep. Federal and state agencies, the National Bighorn Sheep Association, and the Center work together in the management, research, and habitat acquisition for the Whiskey Mountain bighorn sheep herd. Animals from this herd have been transplanted throughout the West to augment ailing sheep populations.

At last count, the Center was receiving over ten-thousand visitors a year. What provides distinction for the facility is the cooperation of the bighorns themselves: from December to May, hundreds of sheep are generally viewable on the lower grassy slopes of Whiskey Mountain and from the road along Torrey Valley. The Sheep Center provides educational and guided eco-tours that provide a rare opportunity to photograph and view bighorn sheep.

The 420-acre Ring Lake Ranch—a retreat center for young people devoted to renewal through the natural world—also lies within Torrey Valley. The ranch donated a conservation easement on the property to the Jackson Hole Land Trust in 2009. The retreat center was conceived in 1965 after the property's owner discovered a spiritual connection to the place, not unlike the Mountain Shoshone felt centuries earlier. Participants at the Ring Lake Ranch retreat center come from all over the world.

Wild sheep were once abundant throughout the foothills of western United States, a majestic animal of the mountainous West. European exploration and settlement took its toll. Wild sheep are very good to eat; they were a logical and relatively easy food source. Fur trappers, miners, meat hunters hired by wagon trains, settlers, market hunters, and big-game hunters all preyed upon them. In the 1890s, while survival of America's bighorns remained in question, New York's finest dined on "roasted wild sheep with puree of chestnuts" at the Waldorf Astoria. The railroads made supplying wild game meat to restaurants on the East Coast possible. Only the wild sheep occupying the most remote and hard to reach places in the mountains managed to survive.

A small population of bighorns that precariously exist at elevations above 10,000-feet in the Teton Range epitomizes survival through having retreated to a hard to reach place. How they manage to persist today in the severest of alpine winter conditions, and within habitat where forage appears virtually non-existent, presents a conundrum to researchers studying them. The isolation and extreme habitat conditions they endure reduce the possibility of contact with disease carrying domestic livestock, most hunters, and other predators.

The ancestors of those sheep were not always isolated in inaccessible terrain at lofty elevations. They appear to be the remnants of herds, which according to the journals of early explorers and trappers, once occurred in great numbers as low as the floor of Teton Valley in Idaho and Wyoming. The bighorns occupying the lower elevations were exploited to extinction by year-round hunting. Even those that managed to hang on in the remotest reaches were not safe.

Hunters pursued the remnant bands of mountain sheep in the Teton Mountain's into the furthest high basins and summits in the early twentieth century. After their annual fall hunts, local lore claims the Idaho hunters would turn their pack horses loose with panniers filled with illegal sheep meat to find their own way back to the barn. In *A Community of Scalawags, Renegades, Discharged Soldiers and Predestined Stinkers,* authors K. and L. Diem quote an early twentieth century Teton Valley guide and outfitter, W.A. Hague, who bragged: "Their aren't any game wardens on this side [of the Tetons] in Idaho." Once back across the mountains and into Idaho, the poachers were safe.

While mountain sheep were among the most plentiful animals found by early explorers, they were also one of the first wild animals to fade from the West in front of an onslaught of over hunting, habitat destruction, and diseases carried by domestic livestock. It is a well-documented scientific fact, that as part of their normal respiratory system, domestic sheep carry bacteria fatal to bighorns. Once a bighorn is infected, their social behavior of nose-touch greeting is one way the pneumonia can be spread catastrophically throughout the herd. For example, in 2010,

Nevada wildlife officials reported 31 percent mortality within the Humbolt Range wild sheep population due to a pneumonia outbreak.

As a result of the severe exploitation and introduced diseases, entire races of wild sheep have gone extinct, such as the rimrock bighorn, Texas bighorn and Audubon's. In 1833, when artist Karl Bodmer painted his *Chapel* landscape along the upper Missouri River in Montana, Audubon's sheep were an integral part of the landscape; he included them as a natural part of his scenes. By the early twentieth century, they had faded away forever.

The total remaining bighorn sheep in the United States today are believed to be as low as only one percent of their pre-European settlement numbers. The total number of wild sheep estimated to exist in the Greater Yellowstone region today is about 7,500. This number represents a significant proportion of all the wild sheep in existence in the world today.

Biologist James Morgan puts it this way: "The beauty and promise of [untold] years have been pitched to the edge of oblivion in an evolutionary instant." The bighorn survivors persist only in remote rugged mountains and canyons, where they eke out a noble existence in spite of all odds against them.

The National Bighorn Sheep Interpretive Center and nearby Torrey Valley resemble a type of wild sheep shrine honoring them and their once larger presence throughout the western United States. Torrey Valley, in addition, is endowed with a sacred quality because of its rich prehistoric connections to a vanished aboriginal mountain people.

Mountain goat near Logan Pass, Glacier National Park, Montana (photo by the author).

# 8
## Rocky the Great Northern Logo

*When locomotives crossed the northern Rocky Mountains, they took on a different image and a different name—the iron horse became instead the iron goat.*
— C.W. Guthrie, 2004

In the northern Rocky Mountains, there is a snow-white, goat-like animal that lives amid stunningly picturesque glacier-carved terrain. It fearlessly inhabits inaccessible high-elevation crags and cliffs and the most inhospitable and brutal of alpine environments.

With its suction-cup hooves, strong muscular forequarters, and keen vision, it nimbly traverses sheer walls and cliffs, leaps across exposed ledges, cavorts along narrow windswept ridges, and sure-footedly negotiates stark and rocky headwalls, all with relative ease and all where one misstep might mean a free fall of a thousand feet. It is a superbly adapted animal possessing daring mountaineering skills—a mountaineer extraordinaire.

The animal has been given the moniker "mountain goat," but it is really not a goat at all. Rather, it is a member of the antelope family related to the European Alps' chamois, a "goat-antelope." It is the only genus and species of its kind in the world, representing what scientist's call a "monotypic genus."

The mountain goat's body is well-insulated by white wool-like under fur and a heavy coat of thick hollow hair. Its coat effectively repels wind and water—picture wind-blasting ice storms—while retaining heat. Male and female mountain goats look similar, with their shaggy white coats, curved black horns and massive fur leggings. Adult males can weigh up to three-hundred pounds.

Much of the year, the adult males or "billies" are solitary loners, while "nannies" and lambs gather in small groups. Adult females rank highest in the pecking order; dominant nannies are the ones in charge. Mountain goats do not mate until they are two to three years old, and then produce only one kid a year. Their low productivity can make recovery from population losses tenuously slow.

The juveniles are taught critical lessons in survival from the nannies. If the daredevil climbers survive their early years, longevity is normally twelve to fifteen years. A mountain goat's beard can be an indicator of age. An adult's beard extends beyond the full length of the face, a goatee reaching a length of a half-foot or more.

Mountain goats have one of the highest natural mortality rates among all big game animals—over 50 percent in the first year—due to the dangerous terrain and hostile climate in which they live, not predation. Even when alarmed, mountain goats generally limit their gait to a deliberately determined pace to match the terrain. They rely on their cliffy habitat for security and escape, so they are not very wary of human hunters with long-range rifles.

Although, mountain goat hides were obtained by Captain Cook as early as the late 1700s, it was presumed they were from "white bears." Later, in 1789, Alexander Mackenzie, in his explorations, characterized them as "white buffalo." Lewis and Clark were also introduced to the animal by skins that Native Americans showed them. The species was scientifically described by George Ord in 1815. Still, little was actually known about the mountain goat until the early twentieth century.

At the beginning of the twentieth century, famed biologist George Bird Grinnell described hunting mountain goats in *Forest and Stream* magazine. He found them amid the rock and ice grandeur on Goat and Otokomi Mountains in what is now Glacier National Park, where, as he described, "sparkling blue lakes were 'walled-in' by towering peaks." Grinnell later became a leading figure in the 1910 establishment of Glacier National Park, which he characterized as the "Swiss Alps of America."

In the late nineteenth century, titans of capitalism—the railroad barons—competed to extend rail systems throughout the country. The Union Pacific, Northern Pacific, Southern Pacific, Atchison, Topeka and Sante Fe railroads all relied on government subsidies and land grants to do the job; that is, all but one: James J. Hill's Great Northern Railway. Hill's proposal to build a railway across the top of the nation, through uninhabited prairies and wilderness, was not supported by Congress. Rather, it was dubbed "Hill's folly."

Hill was a determined, ruggedly-built, barrel-chested man with massive shoulders, short-stout legs, and a goatee-like white beard. Sometimes he wore knickers. He was remarkably nimble in business dealings. One might say there were extraordinary parallels between him and a Rocky Mountain goat. Hill was also a man of unusual vision. In 1883, he elected to build his transcontinental railroad despite the lack of government support.

Two other major obstacles beset his plans: he would have to cross Indian reservations and scale the Rocky Mountains. Lobbying Congress for crossing permission took care of the first hindrance; the second hurdle was not so easily conquered.

Hill had heard of the existence of a northern pass that Indians used in bygone times.   Moreover, in 1840, scholar Robert Greenhorn, drawing upon earlier accounts, had shown the pass on a map he prepared for fur companies. Explorers had unsuccessfully tried to locate the pass, but fierce Blackfoot warriors kept the route secret and guarded from discovery and use.

However, by the time of Hill's quest in the late 1880s, the Blackfoot nation no longer had the will or people to guard their once vast hunting grounds. The white-man wars, the elimination of the bison, small pox, traders' whiskey, corrupt reservation agency officials, and starvation had taken their toll on the once fearsome guardians of the region. Reportedly more than five hundred Blackfoot Indians died from starvation in the severe winter of 1883-1884 alone.

By 1887, the rails had reached Montana and Hill hired engineer John F. Stevens to find the pass for him. Stevens was considered the best mountain-country location man there was, but no Blackfoot Indian would accompany him as a guide. In the winter of 1890, alone on snowshoes in subzero temperatures, after his Flathead Indian guide had given up and deserted him, Stevens discovered the mysterious and legendary Marias Pass. At 5,280-feet elevation, it offered a broad and open crossing of the Rockies.

For that feat, Stevens earned the John Fritz Medal, American Engineer's highest honor. His distinguished career later took him to Russia and China to build railroads. Where U.S. Highway 2 crosses Marias Pass, at the southern-end of today's Glacier Park, there is a monument honoring him.

As tracks were laid across Montana's northern prairies, settlements sprang up along the water tower and siding stops. These became places where the trains picked up grain and livestock. The names the towns acquired were curiously unimaginative and unrelated to the high plains: Harlem, Hinsdale Glasgow, Malta, Zurich. Some say they were named by a railroad executive in the corporative office in Minneapolis by spinning the globe and stopping the motion with his finger, wherever it came to rest became the town's name. Another story, probably the more likely one, is that Hill's daughter spent a year in Europe before traveling west in her own private Pullman. She named the water tower and siding stops after places she had visited in her travels.

By 1891, tracks were laid across the high plains and into the mountains, through Marias Pass, and around the southern border of the Blackfoot Reservation, complete with snow sheds, tunnels, trestles, and steep grades. Whereas the "iron horse," breathing fire and smoke, thundered across the prairies to the south, Hill's locomotives, which scaled the rugged mountain terrain of the northern Rockies, were likened instead to the sure-footed mountain goats they encountered—the "iron goat."

In those years, the Blackfoot Reservation included all of what is now Glacier National Park. In 1895, Blackfoot leaders accepted $1.5 million from the government for the land, which fifteen years later—through the lobbying efforts of Grinnell, Hill and others— became Glacier National Park. The Park adopted the mountain goat as its official symbol.

John Muir hailed the park as "care-killing scenery;" and Grinnell labeled it "The Crown of the Continent." The Blackfoot, in short, would later call it a rip-off.

With the Great Northern Railway's facility development, and promotional and business acumen behind it, Glacier National Park soon became a world-class tourist destination.

In 1921, Louis Hill, James's son who succeeded him, chose the mountain goat for the logo of the Great Northern Railway. "Rocky," the iconographic mountain goat posed on a summit crag, became a widely recognized and symbolic link between Glacier National Park, the Great Northern Railway, and one of the park's most showcased animals.

How the mountain goat logo was adopted is an amusing and Great Northern corporate legend. The layman's story goes that at one time a newspaper boy named Bill Kenny worked outside the Great Northern headquarters in Minneapolis, Minnesota. His load of Sunday morning papers became too heavy for him. However, in the true entrepreneurial spirit of the era, he somehow acquired an old goat, which he would hitch up to a wagon to haul his papers.

Eventually, there were protests about the odors coming from Billy's goat shed. He ended up selling the goat to a Midvale (the east entrance to Glacier), Montana, rancher who had advertised for a distinctive long-whiskered domesticate goat to crossbreed with the Rocky Mountain goat lambs he was keeping in captivity. Billy's goat fit the description: it had a really long goatee. Billy sold the goat, delivering it to Midvale via the Great Northern.

Billy Kenny was ambitious and had been studying telegraphy on his own. And it wasn't long before he was on the payroll of Hill's railway company. Sometime later he was among those on the top rungs of the corporative ladder.

One day Billy's job necessitated a stopover at Midvale. He had the railway officials make an inquiry about the Midvale rancher: "What became of the goats the rancher was raising?" Tom Dawson, a Great Northern official whose portrait now hangs in a Glacier lodge, replied, "The goats all got loose and answered the call of the wild. The country is full of 'em, all the way to Canada." (Tom and Kenny obviously had a lax attitude towards differentiating between domestic goats and mountain goats. Superficially, they can be similar-appearing animals, but they are totally unrelated.)

Several days later on a trip with Louis Hill in the area of Many Glacier, Kenny saw goats everywhere. He trained his field glasses on one standing on a rocky high point, and there he thought was the veritable reembodiment of very goat that used to haul his newspapers: "There's the grandson of my Billy goat, I couldn't mistake that goatee."

That settled a long-standing question for Mr. Hill—who was then Chairman of the Great Northern Railway—one he had pondered for years: "He's our trademark, Bill," Mr. Hill said to Kenny, "no other animal of these mountains deserves more respect or fame."

Today, if you travel the Going-to-the-Sun-Highway to Logan Pass in Glacier National Park, you will likely be rewarded with seeing mountain goats. It's as if the totem of Glacier Park is nearly always on duty at Logan Pass and has planned a personal welcome. Perhaps it's James Hill himself, the tough, old iron-goat reincarnated.

Close-up viewing of the mountain goats is an experience many park visitors fondly recall for the rest of their lives, not unlike those who rode the Great Northern rails to Glacier Park a century ago did, too. The park's scenery is still "care-killing" and the iconic mountain goat provides a living link to the past, reminding us of Hill's ambitious undertaking and taking us back further, too—back in time to when glaciers covered the park's mountains.

The Miller Butte mountain lion with kittens (photo by Thomas Mangelsen).

# 9

# The Miller Butte Mountain Lion: A Wild Emissary

*In the end our society will be defined not only by what we create, but what we refuse to destroy.*
—John C. Sawhill, The Nature Conservancy

On the National Elk Refuge, just north of the town of Jackson, Wyoming, a prominent butte rises from the valley floor. It is vegetated with grasses and scattered dark-green junipers. The south and east sides have cliffs and outcroppings of gray rock that is richly colored with splashes of white and orange lichens.

Long ago, Native Americans, the *Tukudika* or Sheep Eaters, hunted there and also used the butte's south summit as an observation point. Possibly they watched the movements of game in the valley below, and perhaps the awesome setting served to inspire a spiritual connection with the land.

Later, Teton Jackson, Jackson Hole's most notorious nineteenth-century outlaw, and his predatory gang, situated their hideout just south of the prominence. Local lore says the outlaws used the butte as a holding pasture for their stolen horses. Legend also has it that Harry Thompson, one of the gang members, once drove off a posse with rifle fire from a rock outcrop on the butte.

In 1883, John Carnes and John Holland, Jackson Hole's first permanent settlers, took up homesteads on the valley floor just north of the eminence. It became known as Carnes' Butte. Also around that time, settler Robert Miller bought Teton Jackson's squatter's claim and log shacks from him. Miller became a respected and preeminent early-day Jackson Hole personage. The prominence became renamed Miller's Butte or Miller Butte.

In 1912, the National Elk Refuge was established. Over time, the homesteads surrounding the butte were acquired by the government. Only the log home and outbuildings of the Miller Ranch remain today. They are listed on the National Register of Historic Places and are preserved and maintained for public viewing. All the other homestead structures that existed within the shadow of the butte are gone, moldered to dust beneath wind-worried grass. The old-timers who remembered those hardscrabble ranches sardonically referred to the elk refuge as "the government's ranch."

Jackson Hole's settlers subsisted on elk year-round. It is reasonable to assume the pioneers living around Miller Butte and nearby winter ranges in Curtis Canyon, like the Sheep Eaters, also supplemented their diet with mountain sheep. Little, however, was recorded about predators specific to Jackson Hole's earliest settlement period. It stands to reason mountain lions, wolves and bears would have shown up around the butte back then, too.

A mountain lion's pelt had little value for the fur trade of the time. However, in 1884, the Wyoming Territorial Legislature authorized a bounty payment of five dollars for each lion killed. Clearing the land of predators was considered an essential part of settlement. In 1890, the year Wyoming achieved statehood, the bounty was raised to six dollars. In those days, that was more than enough monetary incentive for annihilating lions.

At the beginning of the twentieth century, the U.S. Bureau of Biological Survey, local hunters, stockmen and U.S. Forest Service combined their efforts in Jackson Hole to concertedly wipe out any and all predators. In 1917 alone, the *Jackson's Hole Courier* enthusiastically informed that 311 wolves, 1,812 coyotes, and 132 wildcats (these likely included both Canadian lynx and bobcats), and two mountain lions were expunged. Some ranchers undoubtedly made more cash money hunting and collecting bounties than they did ranching.

Earlier, in 1912, Edward Preple, of the U.S. Biological Survey, had gratifyingly announced: "One of the most destructive natural enemies of the elk, the puma or mountain lion is practically exterminated in the Jackson Hole region." In 1924, E.A. Goldman of the Biological Survey, declared: "Large predatory mammals ... no longer have a place in our advancing civilization."

Predator mania was foremost on Jackson Hole's annual stockmen's meeting agenda in April 1924, where a resolution was passed stating: "The protection of animals of a predatory nature is unfair discrimination against the livestock industry and the public in general." That statement implies that there were at least some people who didn't agree with killing any and all predators even back then.

In 1924, federal and state governments in the West spent more than $1,340,000 for the destruction of predatory animals. The Biological Survey employed 412 government hunters—

Government hunter Cleve Miller won local acclaim by killing five mountain lions in three days hunting in Arizona's Apache National Forest in c1922 (photo courtesy of Western History Collection, Denver Public Library, Stanley Young papers, Z-1573).

experts in poison baits, trapping, trailing hounds, and shooting—
who were in the forefront of the "predatory animal campaign."
Their bloody tally in the western United States for 1924 alone
was: 562 wolves, 193 bears, 3,507 bobcats and lynxes, 34,092
coyotes, and 237 mountain lions. In the years 1915-1924, 1,236
mountain lions were poisoned, trapped, or otherwise hunted
down and killed. For mountain lions, it was discovered to be
effective to cover poison baits with oil of catnip.

The first documented mountain lion sighting on Miller Butte
is from the 1930s, recorded in the U.S. Fish and Wildlife Service
files. Since there was continuing heavy emphasis on predator
control throughout the 1930s, it's probably no accident that this
report coincides from near the time the last wolf was sighted
on the refuge. In those years, the wolf was being persecuted
into extinction throughout the West. Remarkably, though, the
elusive ghost-cat hung on.

Nowadays, wintering elk file up and down Miller Butte, and
when winter drives them down from the Gros Ventre Mountains
and out of Curtis Canyon, a remnant band of fifty or more bighorn
sheep forages along the butte's flank. An improved gravel road
runs along the butte's east base. The road receives a lot of
human traffic—tourists, joggers, dog walkers, cyclists, motorists,
and more—the entire spectrum of Jackson Hole humanity.

Wildlife viewing is a preoccupation of Jackson Holers, so
the road users are always scanning the butte for golden eagles,
coyotes, deer, elk, and bighorn sheep. The refuge rules confine
the human commotion to the road, and somehow the critters
understand this arrangement. Wildlife on the butte has mostly
learned to ignore the coming and going of people, as well as the
town's close proximity.

While concentrations of ungulates tend to attract predators,
normally all the human activity keeps inherently cautious large
predators out of sight or off the butte. Aldo Leopold dubbed large

predators such as grizzly bears, wolves, and mountain lions "wilderness species," they survive best where man's presence is least. Certainly, considering the ruckus of people, the animal one might least expect to observe on the butte's open terrain in daylight hours would be a mountain lion. It is among the most timid of the world's large cats.

Mountain lions are notoriously secretive and reclusive; under most circumstances they avoid people. Moreover, if a mountain lion is either bold or foolish enough to leave a recognizable track anywhere during Wyoming's lion hunting season from September 1 through March 31, it is often not long before houndsmen—hunters specializing in hunting lions with dogs—take up its trail. The big cat is wise to be wary.

Mountain lions hold the *Guinness* record for the animal with the greatest number of names, such as cougar, puma, catamount, panther, painter, ghost-cat and mountain screamer, to name a few. With over forty names in English alone, it's sometimes referred to as "the cat of many names." People's reactions to mountain lions are just as varied, from fear and loathing to admiration and adulation. It is deemed the most contemptible of animals by some, the most magnificent and spectacular by others.

At one time, cougars had one of the most extensive ranges of any North American animal, prowling every state in the nation. Early European settlers confused the eastern cougar with the African lion. For them it was a hideous symbol of evil, dangerous, and a voracious competitor. The big cat's mesmerizing and green-glowing eyes, retractable claws, and stealthy movements, where the rear paws found the exact placement of the proceeding forepaws, invoked fear and superstition. Our forefathers rushed in an organized and paramilitary manner to eradicate the eastern panther.

On the other hand, the Inca and Navajo Indians elevated the cougar to deity status. In the belief that the mountain lion represented a deity, author Zane Grey's Navajo guide refused to participate in hunting it. The Cherokee called it *Klandaghi*, "Lord of the Forest," and the Zuni Indians referred to it as the "Father of Game," in recognition of the lion's place in the natural scheme of things. The Apache believed eating the well-muscled meat of the cougar's neck would covey the cat's strength and agility to the hunter; as did bounty hunter Ben Lilly, who was given the moniker "Dean of twentieth century lion hunters."

Lilly was a tenacious predator hunter; some might say he was obsessed. He boasted of destroying nearly a thousand cougars over the course of his bloody career. He is also credited with killing the "largest grizzly bear ever recorded" in the Southwest (its hide and skull are at the Smithsonian). Lilly's manifesto was: "Anybody can kill a deer, it takes a man to kill a varmint," meaning in his mind a mountain lion, wolf or bear. The fact that in 1920 he was removed from his government hunter job with the Biological Survey for enthusiastically wiping out too many non-stock killing bears is evidence of his over zealousness.

Charles "Buffalo" Jones is best known for his efforts to preserve the American bison and his appointment by conservation President Theodore Roosevelt as Yellowstone National Park's game warden. However, Jones's mindset was similar to Lilly's when it came to predators. He is credited with wiping out forty mountain lions in Yellowstone National Park around 1902, in just one of his predator-control campaigns. Jones himself claimed to have killed a total of seventy-two lions while employed with the park. Following Jones's example, in the years from 1904 to 1925, 121 lions were destroyed in Yellowstone National Park.

Jones was also celebrated for his daring feats in roping cougars in legendary hunts along the north-rim of the Grand

Canyon described by Zane Gray in *The Last of the Plainsmen*. But that was then. We are apt to excuse Jones, Lilly, and other predator hunters of that era by saying they had an "antiquated Victorian attitude" toward wildlife. People today, we like to think, are more enlightened regarding the natural role of predators. As William Stolzenburg points out in *Where the Wild Things Were,* "They serve a crucial regulatory role and their absence leads inexorably to ecosystem simplification."

It is an understatement to say not everyone agrees with those recent findings and ideas regarding the role of predators. But at least mountain lions have been upgraded from varmint to the big-game list in every state except Texas. In Wyoming, the big cat was reclassified from predator to a trophy game animal in 1973.

The truth is, though, the old attitudes toward predators still flourish. In 2000, Jackson Hole newspaper reporters interviewed Wyoming lion hunters, including professional guides. The recorded comments are both revealing and sobering: "I turned to lions to add more depth to my trophy and big-game hunting repertoire ... We have more lions than the area can support ... Lions living close to people could become a threat ... Once a person develops a taste for lion hunting, it becomes an addiction ... There are not going to be any moose or deer left if we don't do something. The lions will take anything ... We are loosing thousands and thousands of deer a year to lions ... We're not frightened or hysterical, [but] oh jeez, if we don't kill these lions, they're going to kill people."

There's a huge difference, however, between Ben Lilly's method of lion hunting and use of hounds as compared to those nowadays. Lilly's methods were low-tech. He relied on his experience, skill, athleticism, and perseverance in hunting lions. He hunted alone on foot or by horseback with his hounds in virtually untracked wilderness. When he was in pursuit of a lion, he would gather his dogs and sleep where night found him. The next day, or however long it took, he and his hounds would run the big cat down and kill it; except on Sunday, he had a personal rule of not hunting on the Sabbath.

Contrast that to a contemporary hunt. After a fresh snow, the guide or his helper drives backcountry roads, or snowmobiles with his hounds towed in cages on sleds, until a fresh track is cut. When the hounds are released, the only challenge may be getting all the dogs to follow the scent in the right direction, rather than back tracking it. Once good hounds pick up a hot trail, the lion has little chance of escape. Despite their speed and agility, lions generally tire quickly and are brought to bay.

Traditionally, hunting cougars has involved chasing them down with dogs, but now technology provides an additional edge. The dogs commonly wear radio collars with trip switches. After the hounds are released on a track, the outfitter might chose the luxury of sitting in his warm 4x4 truck playing country-western music, listening to world news and drinking coffee until the trip switch signal indicates a treed cat. He does not necessarily have to walk or ride horseback over hill and dale trying to keep up with his dogs. An electronic signal directs him to where the dogs are holding the cat at bay, without any wasted effort. The guide is, after all, the organizing brainpower for the hunt. And in all fairness, to properly train lion dogs takes know-how, patience, time, and work. And, also, some houndsmen prefer the physical challenge of following their dogs on foot without benefit of the latest technology.

State law in Wyoming and Montana prohibits a person who was not present at the time the mountain lion was treed from arriving and shooting it, as well as use of two-way communications. But that is not always true elsewhere. Some places, if the guide has a paid client holding a cougar permit, he can notify his prospective hunter by cell phone that a cougar has been treed.

In what is known as a "guaranteed hunt," the client, who might live hundreds of miles away, has been waiting for a call. He has paid handsomely for the opportunity to kill a lion to have as a big-game trophy. But for whatever reason, he doesn't want to take the time to participate while the guide does the grunt work of scouting for track and running the hounds. If necessary, the luckless cougar may be held treed for days until the client arrives.

The client flies or otherwise travels to the prearranged place where the guide's helper picks him up. Using a four-wheel drive vehicle, snowmobile, or a four-wheeler he takes the client as close to the treed cat as he can to minimize the distance they may have to walk or ride. They approach the lion that is calmly sitting in a tree, and the client shoots it from close range. In selling an opportunity to shoot a lion out of a tree, "fair chase" is not an issue.

For those who perceive the cougar as a dangerous, predatory animal, killing it is a macho act. What they fail to realize is there is more to hunting than just killing. Cougar expert Harley Shaw, in *Soul Among Lions*, makes no bones about it: he denounces the shabby tales from such hunts as "lame lies."

Sometimes, too, there can be unintended or undesirable secondary effects from mid-to late-winter cougar hunts. Invariably, the mountain lions are found within or adjacent to big-game winter ranges. Potentially, the disturbance from hunting cats in those areas—snowmobiling, baying hounds, humans on foot, shouting and shooting—can potentially stress and drive off wintering elk, deer, moose or bighorn. In 2000, for instance, two different Wyoming mountain lion guides were ticketed for violating critical wintering big-game range closures.

If the citizens who witnessed the violations had not followed up, insisting on agency enforcement, nothing would have been done about it. Closures were something the agencies had not been enforcing for lion hunters. Perhaps their reluctance to do so says something about the responsible agency's institutional attitude towards predators and predator hunting, too.

In the Greater Yellowstone region and elsewhere in the northern Rockies, lion hunters have recently discovered an additional complication: wolves are triggered to defend their territory from the invasion of hunting hounds. In November 2009, the Buffalo Pack killed three out of nine hounds that had been released on a cougar trail in the upper Gros Ventre drainage in Wyoming. Needless to say, having their hunting hounds killed by wolves does not further endear wolves to sport hunters.

One Montana houndsman, in "Mountain Lion Basics," January 2010, *Big Sky Outdoor News and Adventure*, says, "The days of starting old tracks and letting the dogs run them up new are over with. The population growth of wolves has hindered our ability to effectively free-cast the hounds like we used to. Nowadays, you need to stay close to the hounds for obvious reasons ... wolves can, and will, run the dogs down and kill them."

There can be non-lethal approaches to the sport of mountain lion hunting, too. In one of those, the guide is familiar with a particular animal's home range. From experience he generally has a good idea where to look with his hounds. A lion's use of territory is flexible and may vary with the season, but generally the cat remains faithful to its home range, even if frequently pursued. The client is required and actually wants to participate in the chase. He or she has physically prepared for the challenge of riding horseback, snowshoeing, or walking in rugged terrain— from dawn until dark, if necessary. When the lion is brought to bay, it is not killed. The client photographs it. The photograph seeker is still required to purchase a special license or permit, but the ghost-cat is allowed to live and have its image recaptured in other photography hunts.

Also, favoring the lions, in a move applauded by some wildlife enthusiasts, Oregon and Washington have banned the use of hounds to hunt cougars.

A cougar's home range can encompass a hundred or more square miles—one of the most extensive ranges of any terrestrial predator. Telemetry studies have revealed that the secret lives of cougars consist of much random roaming within their territory and a lot of plain-old lazing around and sleeping. They sometimes sleep sixteen hours a day, which is hardly in keeping with the image of a relentless, non-stop aggressive killer.

In the late 1990s, just across the mountains from Jackson Hole in Teton Canyon, a cougar killed a wintering yearling moose less than a hundred yards from where cross-country skiers frequently passed. Earlier that fall, a mountain biker had seen a cougar on a trail he was riding. The cyclist belonged to a nonprofit organization involved with developing and maintaining trails in the valley. E-mail messages began circulating back and forth alerting the membership to the dangers involved in cougar encounters, citing rumored lion attacks in California. Around the same time, deer hunters blamed cougars for the low mule deer population in southeast Idaho, not severe winters or over-hunting. Ranchers eagerly chimed in, claiming they had experienced livestock losses from cougars, too.

Complaints and alarmist phone calls poured in and the politically harassed Idaho Department of Fish and Game instituted unlimited winter hunting for lions in southeastern Idaho. In 1997-98, forty-four cougars were recorded killed; the next year, ninety-four were destroyed. Another unlimited hunting season was set again in 1999-2000. To their credit, the lion hunters themselves finally protested that it was being overdone, mountain lions were being wiped out.

Likewise, in Montana, after a child was mauled by a cougar in Glacier National Park in 1989, the state's Fish, Wildlife and Parks Department received seventy-seven calls from people who felt threatened by the existence of lions. Montana's cougar harvest went from 159 in 1988 to 604 in 1994-95 and 776 in 1998. The latter was a record number harvested from any one state as a "game animal." Again, it was the houndsmen who stepped in and protested. Montana has since instigated an extensive research program and is in the process of drafting a mountain lion management plan.

On a clear day in early February 1999, a runner made her way out Jackson Hole's National Elk Refuge road. While jogging, she studied the craggy south-end of Miller Butte. An unusual movement and form on the butte caught her attention. She stopped and carefully studied the spot, which was surrounded by rock outcrops and cliff band. Whatever it was, its camouflaged coloration matched the rocks. But the lighting was just right; her eyes had not deceived her. Even from that distance, she could make out the long tail on the large, tawny animal. It was a mountain lion!

The keen-eyed jogger excitedly pointed out the cougar to others along the road, who in turn brought it to the attention of more people. From 125 yards, a small gathering watched in amazement. Someone noticed there were several more below the first cat; they were smaller and cryptic-gray in color. "Cubs!" they all exclaimed at once: "Three of 'em!"

Word spread in the town of Jackson. Someone excitedly called the Wyoming Game and Fish Department office. The Game and Fish regional wildlife coordinator was unimpressed. He played the sightings down: "There are cougar almost every year on Miller Butte... This year they're just in a more visible place." The state wildlife coordinator did not get it. The non-hunting public was thrilled to be able to view the cougars, and they did not want them killed.

What the Game and Fish Department employee said was true, however. A refuge biologist had documented that a female with two kittens had lived on the butte for an extended period in 1994-95, occupying some of the same terrain as the more recent arrivals. Some liked to speculate it was the same cougar, this time with three kittens. There was a big difference, though: the 1994-95 cougars had managed to mostly stay out of public sight. That winter seventy-seven lions were reported harvested statewide.

A refuge biologist dutifully documented the arrival of the more recent lions. On February 12, 1999, he had been attracted to an elk carcass on the butte, a kill the mother cougar had made. In the course of examining the carcass, the biologist noticed the big cat watching him from a hundred yards away. The biologist leaked the fact the cat was living on the butte to a renowned Jackson Hole wildlife photographer and others. The word spread.

The biologist and general public had discovered the Miller Butte cougars around the same time. Here was the infamously stealthy, secretive, and wary ghost-cat with three cubs actually residing in a small cave or rock recess on the butte and hunting almost within full public view, not all that far from town.

Wildlife experts, photographers, and outdoors people jumped at this unique once-in-a-lifetime opportunity to view a mother lion and three cubs, exclaiming, "Before this, in their entire careers, they had never been lucky enough to see a lion in the wild." Someone named the lioness "Spirit." Collectively, the four lions were hailed as the "Spirit of the Rockies."

All the history, myth, natural history, attitudes, and human contentiousness surrounding mountain lions converged for public examination, reflection, critique, and perhaps reinterpretation, at Miller Butte. One observer documented it as the "most magical wildlife event that has ever touched the valley" of Jackson Hole.

Does viewing wildlife have value? Well, within days, the number of wannabe cougar watchers burgeoned into a crowd of mountain lion paparazzi. Up to five hundred people gathered at a time along the Elk Refuge road to watch the mother lion and her three kittens. Some worried the cougars would become habituated, and therefore more vulnerable. Large carnivores with no fear of humans have short lives.

Friends chatted, cell phones rang, dogs barked, while a phalanx of long lenses on tripods commanded the front ranks. Several famous wildlife photographers, as well as writers, were among the crowd. Wildlife watchers from other states, anxious for the opportunity to see a mountain lion in the wild, traveled to Jackson. A parking area was plowed out and a sign posted: "Parking for Mountain Lions." No mountain lions parked there, but hundreds of people did.

The local newspapers carried weekly editorials and tabloids about the lions, reporting on their habits, behaviors, and the juvenile lions' playing. The mother's hunting skills and kills were also closely tallied.

For decades the U.S. Fish and Wildlife Service and Wyoming Game and Fish Department have stressed a need to reduce the number of elk wintering on the refuge. Human hunters have generally fallen short of the harvest goals. Both biologists and hunters could take some lessons from the mother lion's effectiveness. She stalked wintering elk that unwarily wandered onto the butte, killing one about every four days. Then she would return to the den and lead her cubs to the kill. In this setting, few appeared to begrudge her preying on elk. A decade later, in December 23, 2009, *JH Weekly* reporter Brigid Manderm, in writing about the National Elk Refuge said, "if natural predators regain their traditional hunting grounds and help control the elk [in Jackson Hole on the Elk Refuge] ... wildlife officials will be more than happy to have their help."

How many people viewed the Miller Butte cougars over the course of the forty-two days they lived on the butte? Well over a thousand. The mother lion had inadvertently acted as an emissary—an ambassador—to moderate some of the bad rap mountain lions have traditionally gotten. Cougars are difficult animals to portray in human terms, their inherent stealth and secretiveness often spooks people. However, in this case, having a lioness and her nearly grown kittens viewable to so many people helped to humanize them and it allowed people to relate to them in a more compassionate way. It generated some empathy for the lions and helped increase tolerance for cougars everywhere.

On the other hand, not everyone saw it that way. Few things more rapidly disclose basic philosophical differences between people than their attitudes towards large predators. There were those who felt loathing and were edgy, and even openly angry, about the cougar celebration. The Wyoming Game and Fish Department received complaints and thirteen phone calls from worried people.

The sympathetic portrayal of mountain lions by the media, the surrounding hullabaloo, and the fact that the lions were blatantly living nearby on the National Elk Refuge outraged some native sons. These were, after all, the very predators their forefathers had despised and worked hard to destroy less than a century ago. Predator phobia appears to be deeply ingrained and passed along through generations in some segments of our society.

It should not come as a surprise, then, to learn the following year, in 1999-2000, the Wyoming Game and Fish Department raised the quota for the Jackson Hole lion-hunting unit from five to twelve lions. For the first time ever in the state, licenses to kill more lions invoked public ire. The Miller Butte lions had worked a unique emissary magic and had gained some human allies.

The Game and Fish Department was pressed by the public to justify the "fuzzy science" behind the unprecedented rise in harvest numbers. Letters to the local newspapers protested the increase. Public meetings were held, and the department's decisions questioned. In Jackson, where sixty people packed into a small meeting room, tempers flared. A police officer was called in and asked to stand by, just in case.

The state's biologists confessed that for the purpose of setting harvest quotas, "It's virtually impossible to get an accurate count on the actual lion population." A biologist in Jackson's regional office privately disclosed, "The quota was raised because of the recent increase in lion sightings and a concern over the cats showing up around urban areas [subdivisions]."

Critics argued that the increased lion sightings, in northwestern Wyoming and elsewhere, were attributable to rapid ongoing residential development and growing numbers of people encroaching upon lion habitat, rather than to any increases in the number of mountain lions. It was also pointed out there had never been an attack on a human in Wyoming history (since then there has been one, near Laramie in 2006).

Some called for an outright statewide ban on lion hunting. In the end, it did not stop an increase in the quotas. Behind the scene, local officials, ranchers, state politicians and game commissioners still pulled the Game and Fish Department's bio-political strings. Regardless, a new era had dawned. It was the first time the killing of mountain lions had ever been questioned in Wyoming.

Another issue was highlighted, as well. While Wyoming had outlawed killing female lions with cubs at their sides, research showed it was pretty much an empty regulation. Mother lions generally leave their kittens at the den site. Hounds rarely tree the entire family. In fact, hunters often didn't know or couldn't tell if a female had kittens. If the cubs are young—under ten months of age—when the mother is killed, they more than likely starve to death. Further, recent research had shown that females with cubs were the ones most frequently encountered and taken by hunters.

The regional supervisor for the Game and Fish Department conceded, "If there's going to be lion hunting, there will likely be some orphaned kittens." Proponents for killing lions played the anti-hunting card: "I think this issue is driven by people who do not want hunting at all." Critics responded by calling for a separate sub-quota for female lions.

The Miller Butte cougars were agents for other progressive events. In response to the above issues, the Jackson Hole Cougar Fund was established in 2001 by professional photographer Thomas Mangelsen and conservationist and author Cara Blessley. Its stated mission: "to protect the cougar throughout the Americas." The Fund educates the public on the value of cougars in nature and promotes the gathering and application of sound science. By advocating sustainable populations of mountain lions, it helps ensure that these creatures may exist in ways that enjoy public support.

Shortly after the Cougar Fund was established, it helped to transfer four orphaned kittens to the Denver Zoo, when their mother was killed by hunters. Moreover, the Fund began successfully lobbying for agencies to provide hunters with training courses across the West, so that they no longer mistakenly killed females with kittens. The lion hunting controversy and the Fund's enlightened insistence on the application of better science in lion management statewide also spurred critically needed cougar research and management planning.

In September 2006, the Wyoming Game and Fish Department completed a *Mountain Lion Management Plan.* Prepared through a collaborative effort of Game and Fish personnel, the Cougar Fund, sport hunters, and wildlife enthusiasts, it has been held up as "one of the best plans in the country" in that it provides science-based management guidelines. A mortality unit hotline has been set up with a requirement that hunters must call to learn the quota status in their unit before hunting. When the pre-established quota for a unit is met, hunting is supposed to end.

However, when the 2008-09 statewide mortality objectives were set at 315 lions, it raised eyebrows. For comparison, before the plan in 2003, total statewide mortality was 216; and in 2005, it was 189, plus an inadvertent additional twenty-one orphaned kittens. The state used the new plan to increase quotas.

Quota numbers obviously remain a point of contention. Transparency of the rationale behind the setting of particular harvest quotas is a key issue. Some claim too much discretion has been given to regional managers. There is concern that some are inclined to accommodate local political agendas and anti-predator attitudes through biased implementation of the plan and policies. In short, the equivalent of unlimited hunting can be achieved simply by regional and local managers establishing high quotas.

Despite unresolved issues, stomach-churning contentiousness, and the initial begrudged responsiveness from a Game and Fish Department unused to being harried about mountain lion harvest numbers, in the end, what continues to emerge from the 1998-99 Miller Butte lion's visit is a positive step forward for the lions, sport hunters, conservationists, biologists, and the public alike. But still, in truth, regardless of management plans, only the lions themselves know how well or poorly they're doing, and the big cats are not prone to tell us.

In a replay of the earlier Miller Butte mountain lions' visit, in February 2007, a twenty-month-old female cougar showed up on the butte. It wowed spectators for a week or more; an encore to the 1998-99's cougars. Some liked to speculate it was a granddaughter of Spirit. Earlier, Beringia South, a locally based wildlife research group, had collared the young lioness and dubbed her "F30." The "F" stood for female; "30" her ear tag number.

Shortly thereafter, a Cache Creek homeowner near the National Elk Refuge complained to the Game and Fish office in Jackson, alleging that a mountain lion had peered through a window into her home. F30 was accused of being a Peeping Tom.

In retrospect, there is question that the mountain lion had done anything of the sort. An eight-foot-high woven wire fence separates the south end of the National Elk Refuge from the town's residential area. The fence extends from the Refuge's Broadway Street south-entrance north for one-half mile. It is possible the mountain lion could have gone around the fence and into the residential area. But others feel, following an upbeat newspaper story about F30, that a false complaint was disingenuously called into the Game and Fish office by the homeowner, who coincidentally, it turns out, was an anti-predator activist.

If that's true, the mean-spirited action demonstrates the irrational hatred of predators still present in our society—a type of theriophobia, "fear of the beast." The activist may have resented the possibility of another mountain lion garnering favorable public attention similar to those on Miller Butte in 1997-98, and may have rationalized his or her action on the belief that killing lions improves sportsmen's deer or elk hunting success. Whatever motivates such thoughts and behaviors seems to originate from a dark and spooky region of the human psyche.

What happened next is an all-too-common tragedy in today's urban-wildland interface. Because of liability issues, government entities take no chances. Recently, Idaho wildlife biologist Rob Cavallero confirmed this in response to a mountain lion incident in Teton Valley: "When there are carnivore conflicts, we have to be able to respond quickly in order to manage the public trust."

The young, radio-collared cougar was readily tracked and treed, tranquilized, and then moved to the western side of the Teton Mountain range. A few weeks later, she was discovered dead from stress and starvation resulting from her relocation. In the end, control over nature, regardless of the employment of modern day methods and technology, still remains a war with nature.

Three years have passed since a cougar was last reported sighted on Miller Butte. Will another ghost-cat ever allow itself to be vulnerable enough to be viewed over an extended period by the public on the butte again?

Barren-ground caribou bulls migrating along the Kongakut River in the Arctic National Wildlife Refuge (photo by the author).

# 10

## The Last Great Migration

*They travel without any knowledge of what may have happened to their breeding grounds, their wintering grounds, or any of the places in between since the last time they made the journey ... an act of faith and courage.*
—David S. Wilcove, *No Way Home*

At one time, within the borders of what is now the United States, two of the most extraordinary annual migrations on Earth took place: bison on the Great Plains and passenger pigeons in the eastern deciduous forests. They were incredible natural phenomena both from the sheer enormity of numbers and the remarkable distances traveled.

Both of those migratory marvels were destroyed. The passenger pigeon was hunted to extinction. The bison only narrowly escaped a similar fate. Today, the relatively meager numbers of bison survivors are prevented from following any instinct to journey beyond established reserve or park boundaries. The purposeful destruction of those that do wander is a type of dysgenic selection against any residual migratory tendencies.

True, there are still many animals in the conterminous United States that display seasonal and attitudinal migrations between winter and summer ranges, but such movements are relatively localized. The freedom for significant terrestrial animal migrations in the conterminous United States has mostly been eliminated by highways, fences, farms, and housing and industrial developments. We are a developed nation, and as author David Wilcove states, there is "no way home" for animals that would otherwise roam.

One exception stands out for the conterminous United States—a residual reminder of a grander natural past. Approximately two hundred antelope annually make a 340-mile round trip from Grand Teton National Park to the upper Green River Basin in Wyoming. In small groups the pronghorn, not unlike the antelope in the upper Hoback Basin, too, sneak their way across and around man-made obstacles—under fences, around dogs and ranches, across forest roads and highways, and through housing developments and industrial oil drilling operations.

Much of their migration route from Teton National Park up the Gros Ventre, and over the Kinky Creek Divide into the Green River Basin is now protected by conservation easements purchased through monies provided by a wide-range of organizations and grants. The easements are being held by the Conservation Fund.

These antelope, we may presume, represent a remnant of the herds that were genetically programmed to navigate this ancient path in a once regal outpouring of antelope, bison, elk and deer from Jackson Hole and the surrounding mountains of western Wyoming onto the prairies and winter ranges in the Green River and Bighorn Basins. In bygone years, such migrations were represented by astounding numbers of animals. Today, we are talking about a remaining pitiful few hundred, but disproportionably important, antelope.

Sheer numbers were once the imposing hallmark of terrestrial animal migrations. It is still possible to witness this on Africa's Serengeti plains or in the vastness of arctic North America. The last great terrestrial migration spectacle that exists on U.S. soil is the Porcupine Herd in Alaska's 19-million-acre Arctic National Wildlife Refuge, or the Arctic Refuge, as it is frequently called. Arctic Refuge is the only classified Wilderness on U.S. soil representative of an Arctic ecosystem.

There are approximately 120,000 caribou comprising the Porcupine herd—named for the Porcupine River, a tributary of the Yukon, which flows through a major part of their range. The distance they migrate is around fifteen hundred miles a year. Along the way they endure fierce arctic storms, navigate across mountain ranges, and cross forty swift-flowing rivers.

The distance they migrate is about three times that of the Serengeti's famed wildebeest migration. The caribou range over parts of the Yukon and Northwest Territories, in Canada's Ivvavik and Vuntut National Parks, and Alaska's Arctic Refuge, a migration crossing national jurisdictional boundaries and encompassing a range area twice the size of New England.

The drama of the caribou migrating across the arctic vastness is a rhythm that has been repeated since the Ice Age. They circulate north onto the tundra from tree-line until autumn storms force them south, then they move to winter ranges spread out across the taiga (boreal forest) of northeastern Alaska and the Yukon; then as soon as possible, they migrate back north again, the cows heading towards the calving grounds on the coastal plain, and the males, driven by a search for food, not habitat for offspring rearing, move into the foothills and mountain valleys of the Brooks Range.

The importance of the coastal-plain calving grounds to the caribou can not be overemphasized. At first glance the flat, austere coastal-plain is unremarkable. But it's there that the best forage for nursing cows is found, predators like wolves and grizzly bear are scarce, and because of the cool wind coming off the Beaufort Sea, there is relief from biting insects. Faithfulness to this calving area is what defines the Porcupine herd. The coastal-plain calving area is the cornerstone for its survival.

Evidence supporting the caribou herd's fidelity for calving on the coastal plain is not merely anecdotal or hypothetical; empirical data are available. The U.S. Fish and Wildlife Service have generated computerized maps from aerial survey data for the years 1983 to 1999, unquestionably defining the areas of the coastal plain used for calving.

Inupiat Eskimos and Athabascan Indians have sustainably subsisted on the caribou for thousands of years. Sixteen native villages, eight of which are in Alaska, are strategically located in relation to the pattern of caribou movements. Indeed, the caribou have been called "the buffalo of the North," a mainstay for the people who reside within their range.

In 2001, my wife, Pattie, and I joined a small group outfitted by a Fairbanks, Alaska, company called "Arctic Wild." We planned to paddle the Kongakut River from deep inside the Brooks Range to Siku (meaning "icy" in Inupiat) Lagoon on the Beaufort Sea coast, and then along the coastal plain in Siku Lagoon to Demarcation Bay. A goal of our trip, besides experiencing wilderness in its truest form, was to witness part of the caribou migration—the return of the deer from the coastal-plain calving area into the Brooks Range foothills—what scientists term the "post-calving aggregation."

Just traveling to our put-in on the Kongakut River was an ambitious journey in itself. After the commercial air flights from Wyoming to Fairbanks, our planned drop-off on the Kongakut River still lay 450 air miles to the northeast across unroaded wilderness. No roads or tourist services exist inside the Arctic Refuge. Yellowstone National Park's 2.2 million acres receives over three million visitors annually; the 19-million-acre Arctic Refuge, maybe twelve hundred.

In a four-seater aircraft with one seat removed in order to facilitate stashing gear, we flew from Fairbanks across the White Mountains and then the Yukon Flats, where water and wetlands spill endlessly across the landscape. Next, we crossed the Arctic Circle, then never-ending taiga, and finally we reached the southern slopes of the Brooks Range. There we located and flew up the Chandalar River, seemingly forever. Eventually, the Chandalar led us to Arctic Village. And still, we had not yet entered the Arctic Refuge.

Arctic Village—a scattering of log cabins and a 1918 log church listed on the National Register of Historic Places—is home to about 152 Athabascan souls, who call themselves the Gwich'in. They represent the northernmost Indian nation in North America. Their cultural and traditional values are tightly linked to *tutta*, the caribou. It is no coincidence their village is located within a portion of the Porcupine herd's winter range; their livelihood depends on *tutta*.

After refueling, we boarded yet another bush plane flight from Arctic Village across the Brooks Range. Between Pattie and me, the pilot, and all our crammed in cargo, I was nervously reminded of the sputtering overloaded and rickety aircraft in *Never Cry Wolf,* a Hollywood movie based on Farley Mowat's novel.

The Brooks Range represents the northernmost extension of the Rocky Mountains and the northernmost mountain range in the world. Its vastness defies imagination. The Brooks Range gives perspective to words like "expansive", "remote", and "awesome." We flew across a jumble of nameless snow-patched, ragged and jutting peaks, which opened up into one astounding uninhabited valley after another. We passed the spectacular 9,000-foot glacier-covered Romanzof Mountains in the eastern Brooks Range and crossed nameless rivers that seemed to flow randomly in all directions. It brought to mind Robert Service's colorful lines: "Have you ever gazed on naked grandeur where there's nothing else to gaze on... big mountains heaved to heaven ... which the blinding sun blazons... the mountains are nameless and the rivers run God knows where."

We crossed renowned conservationists' Olaus and Margaret Murie's beloved, widely-meandering Sheenjek River and climbed over the Continental Divide onto the north slope of the Brooks Range, beyond the northern limit of tree growth. And, some time later, began a descent into a massive canyon, where the gin-clear waters of the Kongakut River flowed. Mountaineer John Kauffman summed it up in his book, *Alaska's Brooks Range: The Ultimate Mountains*: "There is no more frontier to experience, but the vast expanse of the Brooks Range may come the closest."

On our landing approach, we flew low within the narrow confines of the Kongakut's canyon walls while being violently tossed about by thermal air currents. Glimpses of Dall's sheep on rocky slopes flashed past. No resemblance of a landing field greeted us. Instead, our attention focused on a sliver of gravel bar rapidly rising to meet us. With a sudden jolt, amid dust and flying gravel, and reverse engine roaring, we came to an abrupt landing on the gravelly riverbank. The pilot loudly cursed the gravel which had been kicked-up and dinged the plane's propeller. Now we knew from experience why the Inupiat called it the Kongukut, meaning in their language "the farthest away river." It was about as far away as one could get, almost off the map.

Stepping out of the plane, we were welcomed by tundra that from mountain slopes to summits was adorned with Lilliputian wildflowers—Arctic forget-me-nots, Arctic poppies, Dryas, glacier avens, dwarf rhododendron, pasque flower, and others. Stunning 360-degree mountain vistas sparkled with sunlit snow patches. Small bands of bull caribou with intensely-black velvet antlers surged past and through our camp site with pulse-like regularity. On a far slope, a solitary white wolf, seemingly indifferent to our presence, trotted purposefully toward its canine destination.

We were amazed and exhilarated by the natural splendor that surrounded us, and it showed in everyone's uncontained smiles and enthusiasm. Contrary to what some would have us believe, it was not a "barren land of perpetual snow and ice." Conservationist Margaret Murie, in *Two in the Far North*, accurately described it as "a steady serene beauty that sings ... and soaks into one's being."

The sun was relentless. Its round-the-clock energy and intense lighting effects pervaded the huge landscape and one's entire being. In *Vanishing Arctic*, author T.H. Watkins aptly called it "the sun as Earth knew it in the beginning." At first we basked in the boundless radiant joy, but soon we were forced to surrender to our frailties, seeking relief behind long sleeves, glacier goggles, brimmed hats, sunscreen and Chap Stick. Our tents heated up like ovens; temperatures inside them became unbearable. The Arctic is truly a land of extremes and contrasts.

On the third morning, we broke camp and began an eighty-five mile paddle, following the river's course toward the Beaufort Sea. The Kongakut is mostly fast-flowing Class II water, but like most northern rivers, its channel is braided. We proceeded down river in fits and starts, hanging up in shallow braided channels

Earle F. Layser

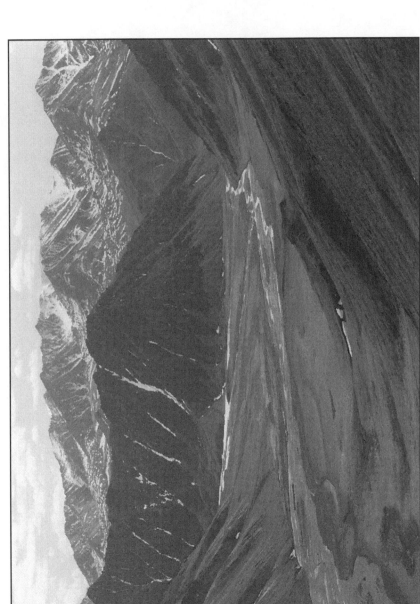

The awesome Brooks Mountain Range and Kungakut River valley in the Arctic National Wildlife Refuge (photo by the author).

and dashing through narrow gorges on fast-flowing rapids. We floated through miles of eerie mists while walled into narrow passageways created by the fifteen-to twenty-foot high remains of winter ice buildup caused by overflow and ice dam blockage. The ice buildup is termed "aufeis." In the surreal quiet of the dense fog, the soft tinkling sound of sloughing "candle ice" could be heard, contrasting with startling thunder booms of large blocks of aufeis calving into the river. In *A Naturalist's Guide to the Arctic*, E.C. Pielou noted, "the aufeis is a reminder that in the Arctic, warm weather never lasts for long."

A serene mountainous landscape, unembellished with trees, drifted past with the days. Dall's sheep and caribou speckled the mountain sides. Occasionally, a grizzly bear or wolf made an appearance. At places, thickets of tall willows, decorated with large, erect catkins that looked like candles, lined the river. The species had an appropriate common name, "Alaskan willow." We only dared to venture into the willows while apprehensively and loudly singing out "Bear, bear... are you in there?" We practiced "no trace" camping, while grizzly bears, on the other hand, made huge backhoe-like excavations into the tundra in pursuit of doomed arctic ground squirrels.

As we approached the coastal plain the mountains gradually became more gentle and subdued and the foothill valleys broadened. From the rounded summits one could view the coastal plain and behind it the blue-gray haze that hung over the Beaufort Sea icepack. Where the foothills transitioned into the plains, we came upon shaggy musk oxen, an Ice Age relict the Eskimo call *imummak* —"the bearded one."

One could not look in any direction in the foothills without seeing pockets of caribou scattered across the landscape. Bands of 'bou, mostly bulls, dramatically and frequently crossed the swift-flowing river close in front of us. If there was a common direction to their movements, it was hard for us humans to discern it. They were, in the way only the caribou themselves knew, enroute to join up with the cows and calves returning from the coastal plain.

When we planned the trip, we had envisioned seeing a large aggregate of cows and calves returning from the coastal plain, an amassed and iconic migration gathering, similar to those pictured in the books we had studied, such as pictured in John P. Kelsall's book, *The Caribou*. We were not to be disappointed.

For a day hike on that particular morning, Pattie and I selected a low broad valley that gradually extended for miles from the river. It appeared to form a pass through to the coastal plain. As we hiked up and across tundra beset with flowers, we disturbed nesting ptarmigan that were cloaked in an impressive disarray of molting colors. Lapland longspurs and golden plover scurried before us, calling "chu-leet, chu-leet." Our guidebook recorded the Arctic Refuge supported 160 migratory and resident bird species. Caribou trails laced the landscape, but no 'bou were visible.

At lunch time, we rested on a ridge at the head of the valley. The ridge was composed of smooth, very thinly-bedded gray shale. The chartaceous shale was scattered in heaps, bits and pieces along the ridge, as if the Earth was exfoliating. It was not plastered with the brilliantly-orange crustaceous lichens we had commonly observed on other rock outcrops, rather, its weathered appearance conveyed a sense of agelessness.

The coastal plain is approximately thirty miles wide and flatter than Kansas. Like the prairies, it is dominated by "big sky." Distant objects shimmer across space in rising air currents; and mirages appear, similar to what you might experience in deserts. The tundra vegetation—Arctic willows, sedges, and cottongrass—on the coastal plain is low-growing. To avoid being wind sheared, the prostrate plants hide between the mounds formed by cottongrass, creating what is innocuously known as "tussock tundra." While caribou seem to negotiate it easily enough, it's renowned for the challenge it presents for people to negotiate it on foot. One can try to hop from tussock to tussock or resignedly slog in the greasy muck between tussock pedestals.

In *Arctic Refuge: A Circle of Testimony*, writers Hank Letfer and Carolyn Servid summarize an ancient Gwich'in tradition: "In a distant time the caribou and the Gwich'in were one ... the tundra sustained the caribou and the caribou sustained the people." The Gwich'in have long chosen not to hunt caribou along the coastal plain, calling it "the sacred place where life begins."

Biologist George Schaller described the Arctic Refuge and its coastal plain as "a place of living grandeur, one throbbing with life." Conversely, it's the same place the George Bush administration's Secretary of Interior, Gale Norton, flew over in the early 2000s and described as "vast, white and barren." A cynic might suggest it was this myopic observation that contributed to her securing a job with Dutch-Shell Oil in 2006.

Perched on the ridge, my wife and I mused on the fact that after eighty years of individuals and organizations from all over the world fighting to preserve this unique and ecologically intact landscape, it still remained in political limbo. At the time when it was being proposed for protection under the Wilderness Act, 1.5 million acres—constituting 75 percent of the coastal plain within the refuge—were omitted in a last-minute compromise action. It essentially left the refuge's coastal plain open for oil and gas leasing. The omitted acres comprise the very habitat the Porcupine herd is dependent on for calving. It is also the place that some claim harbors large oil reserves. How large no one knows. The U.S. Geological Survey estimates, the reserves might supply five to twelve months of the total U.S. demand for oil.

The contested 1.5 million acres have been named the "1002 lands," after clause number 1002 that was inserted into

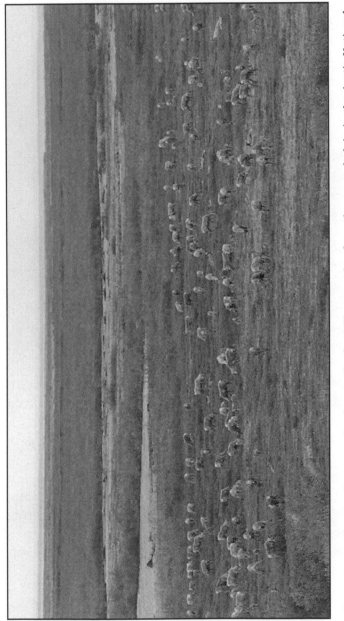

Porcupine caribou herd cows and calves in the foothills returning from the coastal plain in the Arctic National Wildlife Refuge (photo by the author).

the Alaska National Interest Lands Conservation Act. Over an eight-year period, beginning in 2001, powerful pro-development forces in the U.S. Congress and Senate, supported by an ex-oil-man president and vice president, gave opening up the "1002 lands" for oil and gas development their highest priority. What drove them were not necessarily the potential oil reserves, rather for them, it was an ideological battle.

Had they succeeded, not only would have one of the world's last great terrestrial mammal migrations been at risk of being destroyed—much like other animal migrations in North America that have vanished overtime in the face of development—but with it, too, North America's last true aboriginal subsistence cultures. An entire Arctic ecosystem complete with its people stood to be lost forever.

From our ridge top, we continued to glass the broad valley below us with binoculars. As if by magic, a lone caribou materialized in the distance coming from the direction of the coastal plain. She proved to be a vanguard. In minutes, as we watched, others streamed into view, fanning out behind the lead cow in a wedge-shaped pattern. More followed. Soon there were thousands spread out before us, the ancient primal spectacle of cows and calves returning from the coastal plain. Individuals progressed in a stop-start manner characteristic of their kind on the march. Stopping to briefly forage, then trotting ahead, and pausing again to snatch another mouthful, then moving ahead again. Thousands!

We were too far away to hear their characteristic snorts, grunts and clicking of tendons or dew claws, but as we watched the moving mass of animals, those primitive sounds played in our minds. Observing large numbers of migrating animals can be as much about their sounds as the sight itself.

Margaret Murie called the caribou "the land's rightful owners... the living, moving, warm-blooded life of the Arctic." In

*Caribou and the Barren-Lands,* author George Calef wrote: "The bison have vanished from the plains, the flocks of passenger pigeons are gone... but the majestic herds of caribou cross the tundra as they always have." History tells us we can not take this grand natural phenomenon for granted. It is one of the last of its kind remaining on Earth.

Let us hope that in the future our grandchildren and great-grandchildren will still be able journey to the Arctic, and in its vast and awesome wilderness setting, see grizzly bears digging up tundra in pursuit of ground squirrels, observe gray wolves trotting across radiant sun-illuminated snow patches, marvel at musk oxen packed together head down in their defensive stance, and witness one of Earth's last great land animal migrations—the spectacle of tens of thousands of caribou spread out and moving across unbounded arctic plains and foothills.

The Arctic Refuge still gives meaning to Robert Service's century-old tale, not only for us, but for generations to come: "Can't you hear the wild, it's calling you. Let us journey to a lonely land ... let us go." We can only pray "the wild" will always be there to call and for future generations to be able to journey to and experience.

Portrait of a cow bison from the Grand Teton National Park bison herd (photo by the author).

# 11

## The Great Escape: Free-Ranging Bison Return to the Hole

I rise, I rise
I, whose tread makes the earth rumble.
I rise, I rise,
I, in whose thighs there is strength.
I rise, I rise,
I, who whips his back with his tail when in rage.
I rise, I rise,
I, in whose humped shoulder there is power.
I, rise, I rise,
I, who shakes his mane when angered.
I rise, I rise,
I whose horns are sharp and curved.
—Osage Indian song

Twenty-five thousand years ago, giant bison, *Bison latifrons*, with imposing seven-foot horn spans, thundered across the North American grasslands. The remains of these enormous bovines were discovered in sediments around American Falls Reservoir in Idaho. They were the progenitors of today's American bison, *Bison bison*, the largest land animal on the continent. Bison inhabited North America long before man. Then, for thousands of years, the lives of bison and indigenous people were closely interrelated. Native people revered them. They relied on the bison for their life necessities. Less than two hundred years ago, the shaggy beasts blackened the American landscape; it was the most numerous large wild mammal on Earth. Bison dominated the ecology of woodlands, plains and prairies. They were the archetype keystone species. Today, it is the human race that blankets the continent. Despite the bison's shameful and wanton slaughter by European man, the iconic beast of the American plains and prairies still survives. It rightfully remains among our most treasured animals. Millions of tourists travel to our western National Parks from all over the world to glimpse them in their natural habitat—an animal that once ruled the land, and whose history on this continent looms as colossal as the creature itself.

In August 1978, I led my two sons, ages 11 and 14, on a backpacking trip. We began at the Darwin Ranch, a private inholding within the Gros Ventre Wilderness near Pinedale, Wyoming, and followed the Gros Ventre River to its source—the place where it emanates from persistent cornices and snow fields north of Corner Peak.

From there we crossed over the lofty watershed divide and made a steep mountainside descent without benefit of a trail to Shoal Creek. Shoal Falls, along our route, I knew, was a favorite spot of the late Donald "Doc" McLeod, the second medical doctor ever to practice in Jackson Hole and a strong supporter for congressionally designating the Gros Ventre Wilderness. From there, we crossed another drainage divide and proceeded down the mountains to the forest road on Granite Creek.

At the time of our trip, the Gros Ventre Wilderness had yet to be officially declared. In the entire trip, from the Darwin Ranch to Granite Creek, we encountered no other people. Try that nowadays.

The first night we camped on a terrace downriver from Ouzel Falls. The tangible odors of mountain meadow, sagebrush, and lodgepole pine forest pervaded the air. From our campsite we could hear the river gliding past boulders. Our presence disturbed a family of coyotes, which put on a howling good performance, serenading us throughout the night. It was a memorable Wyoming wilderness outing.

In the morning, my youngest son followed a game path to the river. It was not long before he returned, excitedly wanting to show me a large bone protruding from the river bank. After some careful excavating, it turned out to be a truly rousing find: a buffalo skull!

For me, the skull was a nostalgic link to more than a century earlier, when the land was still truly wild. In those bygone times, the rattling of dewclaws and snorting of great shaggy bison could be heard in the resplendent summer meadows of the Gros Ventre Mountains—amid the "beaver meadows" below Ouzel Falls and the river's Upper Falls, and in the shrub-grasslands along the part of the river valley that later became the Horn Ranch. Back then, the bison owned the land.

In late August, when the first dusting of snow arrived on the mountain summits, the bulls would make their presence known through a commotion of roaring, pawing up clouds of dust, and urinating in the exposed dirt and then rolling their hulking one-ton bodies in it. The sound of bellowing bulls filled the mountain valleys; it could be heard from miles away. The bison shaped the ecology of the Western meadows, plains and prairies.

My son insisted on carrying his find, so we tied it on top of his backpack, and he proudly lugged the extra weight up and down the mountains for the rest of the trip. The skull hung in our Jackson, Wyoming, home for a number of years. Recently, I gave it to my grandson. I have since learned others have similarly found buffalo skulls below the Gros Ventre River's Upper Falls and on the river terraces and prairie about the old Horn Ranch homestead.

Later, that autumn, when I was doing fieldwork in the spruce forests at the head of the Green River on Pinyon Ridge, an area freckled with kettle lakes at the north end of the Wind River Mountains, I happened to look under a tangled pile of wind-thrown trees. Lying on top of the ground beneath the windfall was a large skull that was obviously not a cow's cranium. Crawling under the pile of limbs and woody debris, I retrieved the bleached-white skull of a cow buffalo. What was it doing lying out on top of the ground under a windfall in a heavily forested area? Where had it come from, how old was it, and how long had it lain there? It remains a mystery.

Obviously, a large animal had dragged it under the down fall, or so I imagined. Hard to believe it had managed to remain reasonably intact, tossed around on top of the ground and chewed upon by animals for what would seem at least eighty or more years. Could a few bison have survived here well into the twentieth century, hidden in this remote timbered area at the head of the Green River? The Pinyon Ridge bison skull joined my son's find above our fireplace mantle. Sometime later, I collected several well-weathered bison-horn sheaths in the sagebrush prairie in the Green River Basin near Big Piney. They fit nicely onto the skulls we had on display.

Years later, in the mid-1990s, I was doing wetland consulting work on the mountainside subdivision that had once been the Crescent H Ranch south of Wilson, Wyoming. An exposed moss-covered bone in the middle of a seepage area caught my eye. After some careful unearthing using my shovel, it became apparent it was a very large buffalo skull lying face down, sunken in the black mire. It boggles the mind to think it must have laid there intact in the muck for over a century.

Afterward, in talking with the developer on an adjoining lot, I found he had taken it upon himself to excavate a nearby similar, but larger, spring with a backhoe. "I had that bog hole dug out before someone fell in it. There was a lot of old horse bones buried in there." When I told him, "Those weren't horse bones, they were bison," his expression went from disbelief to defiance. He thought I was being absurd. So I showed him the huge buffalo skull I had just found.

Historically, bison may have been plentiful at times along the valley floor in Jackson Hole and in the surrounding high-mountain meadows. One source makes reference to a "large herd of buffalo in the valley" of Jackson Hole in June of 1833. But by late autumn, undoubtedly many migrated or drifted out of the mountains to lower-elevation prairies; although, it is possible some small bands may have also toughed it out in the high-mountain valleys, too. In the *History of Teton Valley,* Mountain Man Dick Leigh was quoted describing a herd of buffalo that perished in 1857, when it attempted to winter along Fox Creek on the western side of the Tetons. Whether they were shot or winter-killed isn't clear.

With their shaggy coats of long hair, which are thickened with wool, and other physiological adaptations, bison are well suited to withstand extreme weather conditions. Those that weren't able to survive the brutal winters left their skeletal remains behind; the ones we discovered more than a century later, perhaps.

Technically, the American bison is not a buffalo. True buffalo are indigenous only to Africa and Asia. It is more evidence that our English ancestors were not very connected to the natural world and were also lousy taxonomists. It is believed the colonists adopted the name buffalo from a corruption of the Canadian voyageurs *boeuf*, meaning ox or cattle, or the French explorers' *bufflo* or *buffelo,* referring to "good hide." Similarly, the colonists confused the African lion with the eastern cougar—they finally figured out the latter didn't have a mane—and *wapiti* with the European *elch, elg or elk,* which is the animal we call moose. I will use the names buffalo and bison interchangeably, recognizing the name buffalo is powerfully emblematic of the American West. The Lakota called the buffalo *Tatanka,* the bulls were *Tatanka Wan.*

Of all North America's wild animals, perhaps none has had more of a historical impact on more levels for the peoples of this land than the bison. Bears, wolves, mountain lions, moose, elk and others contribute much to what we consider to be wild country, but as author Harold Danz points out in *Of Bison and Man,* other animals are apt to "skulk in the darkness or flee, whereas bison courageously occupy the land."

Mountain men and early explorers recognized different races of buffalo. Those that inhabited the mountains in small bands, such as in the high-mountain valleys around Jackson Hole and the Yellowstone region, were called mountain buffalo. Colonel Richard Irving Dodge described the mountain buffalo as "inhabiting the deepest, darkest defiles, or the craggy, almost precipitous, sides of mountains." Those that made up the large herds on the Great Plains were called plains buffalo.

The skulls that my son and I found within forested areas in the mountains would definitely have been the mountain variety if, in fact, there really was any biological basis for considering them a separate subspecies. Modern genetics research suggests there was essentially no difference between the two. It probably boils down to wild bison adapting and behaving differently depending on where they lived.

It is the work of zoologists to argue about such things, but for most of us today the question is moot. If the beasts occupying the mountain and plains were indeed different subspecies, the genetic, morphological or behavior differences between them were lost forever when they were hunted to near extinction and interbred as a result of early twentieth-century restoration and restocking programs.

Another race of bison also once occurred in the deciduous forests of eastern North America ranging from northern Georgia to Hudson Bay. These were called wood or forest bison. Today, we mostly think of bison as an animal of the western United States, but our European ancestors found plenty of wild bovines in the forests east of the Mississippi River, too. It was another wild creature that was resolutely cleared from the land wherever it was in the path of settlement. For whatever reasons, less attention has been paid to the forest bison's past occurrence and demise. They were hunted to extinction before scientists could learn much about them—a *fait accompli*.

Henry Shoemaker's *A Pennsylvania Bison Hunt*, published in 1915, describes one late eighteenth-century hunt. Settlers had taken over the bison's winter range and driven them into the mountains, and they were starving. The famished beasts returned and rampaged through a homestead, allegedly "killing three children and their mother" and laying waste to the farmstead. Fifty hunters and a large number of dogs were assembled. They marched in a military manner into the mountains, where they pursued "the brutes" for two days before catching up with three hundred of them. The bison were impeded by deep snow and "the work of the slaughter quickly began." After the last animal was killed, the hunters lit a huge fire, "a signal to the women and children in the valleys below that the last herd of Pennsylvania bison was no more."

As late as 1773, when pioneer Philip Quigley settled on the West Branch of the Susquehanna in Pennsylvania, he described a northern herd comprised of twelve thousand buffalo. When settlers moved west across the mountains through the Cumberland Gap, they did so following worn "buffalo paths." Daniel Boone wasn't just shooting bears and deer on the western slopes of the Appalachian Mountains. There were thousands of buffalo around the salt licks in Kentucky, with buffalo paths as wide as country lanes. When traveling, the bison chose the easiest grades and their trails later formed the routes of railroads and modern highways. In the Big Boone Lick vicinity, settlers complained the abundance of bison prevented the progress of agriculture. The forest bison were totally annihilated, not unlike the fate buffalo suffered a century later on the western plains and prairies.

By the early nineteenth century, hundreds of thousands of bison had been destroyed east of the Mississippi. When settlers carrying firearms encountered wild animals, such as bison, they invariably killed them. The last bison recorded killed in Pennsylvania was at a place aptly named Buffalo Crossroads near Lewisburg on January 19, 1801. A large bull stood its ground in the road before Colonel John Kelly, a veteran Indian fighter and Revolutionary War soldier. Like a gavel rap, the shot that rang out conveyed finality to the word extinction.

Bison were among the first animals to disappear from the eastern forests. The elk, cougar, wolf, fisher, beaver, passenger pigeon, and the seemingly boundless virgin forest habitat itself soon followed, compliments of our ancestor's biophobia, commercial hunting, and an attitude that natural resources were god-given, unlimited, and inexhaustible.

When the white man began exploring the plains and prairies west of the Mississippi in the early nineteenth century, he was surprised to find that the prairies were an ocean of wildflowers, and astonishingly, amid the sea of blossoms were millions upon millions of buffalo— "a wondrous blanket of dark brown stretching to the horizon."

Lewis and Clark's 1806 observations on the abundance of bison—"We discovered a moving multitude, which darkened the whole plains"—were not unique. Haunting superlatives and testimonials of the bison's abundance are given by explorers, travelers and hunters in early nineteenth century historical accounts. The number of bison existing at that time has been estimated at 60 million.

In a vision, Plenty Coups, an Absaroke (Crow) Chief, described the origins of the once great bison herds: *From a peak in the Crazy Mountains [in Montana], I suddenly saw a buffalo bull... Look! I said pointing. Out of the hole in the ground poured buffalo bulls and cows without number. They spread wide and blackened the plains. Everywhere I looked, great herds of buffalo were going in every direction, and still others without number were pouring out of the hole in the ground to travel on the wide plains.*

The buffalo were not alone: incredible numbers of antelope, elk, and deer were amply mixed into the scene, and behind them trailed large numbers of wolves. Meriwether Lewis wrote, "immence hers of Buffaloe, deer, Elk ... in every direction." It was the greatest aggregation of large mammals the Earth has ever witnessed; a wildlife display unrivaled even by the Serengeti's fabled plains. The stunning spectacle staggered the imagination and defied description. Some excerpts from various sources:

*Vast herds... immense quantities... we were surrounded by buffalo, elk and deer... innumerable herds... they covered the plain as far as the eye could see... the herds extended many miles in length... a great mass of moving creatures... hundreds of thousands... remarkable and massive herds... almost unbroken herds for 120 miles... The plains were blackened with them... ten thousand buffaloe within a circle of two miles... The distant pounding of their hooves sounded like ocean's roaring ... It did not seem possible to pack another buffalo into the space.*

At places it appeared Eden-like, Meriwether Lewis wrote: "The buffaloe, Elk and Antelope are so gentle that we pass near them... they frequently approach us more nearly to discover what we are."

But what happened next also staggers the imagination. In breathtaking swiftness, roughly from the 1830s to 1880s, the bison that had once numbered in the tens of millions were slaughtered in an unrivaled bloodbath and driven to the edge of extinction. So abrupt was the total destruction of the vast herds that by 1884 only three-hundred buffalo hides were shipped east, compared to hundreds of thousands each year in the previous years. Hides from the bison were used to manufacture the tough leather belts and other implements that served to drive the machinery of the Industrial Revolution worldwide.

Meat hunters, hide hunters, sport hunters, wealthy hunters from abroad, Native American hunters, the improved Sharp's rifle, settlers, the railroads, industrial demand, political policies, foreign commercial markets, natural disasters, eliminating competition for cattle, public apathy, and a driving compulsion to simply to kill bison all converged in deadly efficient unison. The United States government encouraged the killing mania: frontier Army posts shamelessly provided free ammunition to hunters.

The Sante Fe newspaper, the *New Mexican*, spoke out against it, calling the carnage "wantonly wicked." In a matter of decades, the incredible biological abundance and diversity that had evolved over eons on America's western plains and prairies was suddenly gone.

Old hunters swore the buffalo were "hiding up north" somewhere and would return. They never did. Eminent naturalists George Catlin and John Audubon, and plainsman Francis Parkman, had earlier foreseen and prophetically forecasted the buffalo's demise, even while their numbers still appeared inexhaustible to many. Audubon predicted, "The buffalo's doom is sealed;" as did Catlin, who said, "Before many years, the buffalo will vanish." Catlin was ahead of his time, proposing that a "Nation's Park" should be established for the Indian and buffalo. His idea for a park went nowhere.

General Phil Sheridan, on the other hand, believed each hide hunter ought to be decorated with a medal: "Let them kill, skin and sell until the buffalo is exterminated, as it is the only way to... allow civilization to advance."

In the aftermath of the carnage, the skeletal remains virtually littered the plains. Bones lay so thickly that they were a nuisance to the farmers who followed. "Bone picking" became an industry in itself. Author Michael Punke, in *Last Stand*, sums it up: "Killed once, but harvested twice: once by hide hunters; once by bone pickers."

Homesteaders harvested the onetime cash crop; it paid better than farming. The bones were shipped east by the railroad carload to manufacture glue, fertilizer, and char for refining sugar.

The bones of Indians set out of respect on burial scaffolds eventually spilled their contents onto the plains, too, mingling with those of the bison. Where that occurred, both were gathered up and sold. Bones were bones. A ton fetched seven to ten dollars. Bones disappeared from the plains and prairies even more rapidly than the bison themselves.

When bones ran low, Native Americans dug them out from beneath buffalo jumps, the places where their ancestors had once slaughtered bison by driving them off cliffs. At one time, the Indians believed the bones were capable of rising back up into new buffalo—the skull represented a form of rebirth to many tribes—but times had changed.

The amount of bones and sums of money paid out for them is hard to comprehend. The Michigan Carbon Works reportedly produced 650 tons of buffalo bone ash per year. On the average, it took one hundred buffalo to make a ton of bones. In Kansas *alone,* between the years 1868 and 1881, $2.5 million was paid out for the bones supplied to Carbon Works. That sum of money, at eight dollars a ton, represents over 31 million buffalo.

Bones of the great herds, laced with that of the plains Indians, were eventually widely spread across American farmlands in the form of fertilizer, returning the ashes of the wild herds and those of the people who had relied upon them back to the soil from whence they had originated.

Danz, in *Of Bison and Men,* suggested that perhaps we should view the hunters, hide men, and other opportunists who ushered the great herds out of existence as Tolstoy describes in his epilogue to Chapter 7 in *War and Peace*: "They remove moral responsibility from those men who produce the events. At the time, they do the work of brooms that go in front to clear the rails for the train: they clear the path of men's moral responsibility."

When the fury of the hunt subsided, the shabby myth of inexhaustible resources was laid bare. The rapidity at which settlement followed was astonishing. Earlier, nineteenth-century pundits predicted it would take five hundred years—that is, centuries—to populate the West. Instead, it was only a matter of decades.

Remote high-mountain valleys with hard winters were the last to be settled. Permanent settlement in Teton Valley, Idaho, did not occur until 1882. Pioneers did not make permanent settlement in Jackson Hole until 1883-84; fifteen years after Wyoming had convened its first territorial legislation session. The bison were mostly gone from there by then, too. One of the last reports of wild buffalo in that vicinity was when commercial hunters wiped out a herd of 165 somewhere near Jackson Hole in the winter of 1884-85. That was also about the time the last of the northern herd in Montana was finished off, too.

The fear that the bison were about to become extinct motivated the Smithsonian to take action, simply for the reason none had been preserved in their museum collection. In 1886, hunter and naturalist Dr. William Hornaday, who was the chief taxidermist for United States National Museum at the time, arranged to track down survivors of a small wild herd somewhere between the Yellowstone and Missouri Rivers. Hornaday, who later founded the American Bison Society and became a tireless campaigner for bison restoration, contributed to their near extinction by killing a total of twenty-nine over the course of two hunting trips. Six of those bison were mounted and put on exhibition at the Smithsonian in 1887.

The six mounted bison are known as the Hornaday Group. Over the years, the large bull in the collection was the model for a number of national symbols: the Wyoming state flag, the Great Seal of the Department of Interior, the National Park Service badge, postage stamps, and coins. When it was wounded and finally run down, the bull had courageously stood its ground. Hornaday, who later described the hunt in *The Extermination of the American Bison,* wrote: "Nearly every adult bull we took carried old bullets in his body." In the large old bull that ended up in the mounted display, Hornaday had found "four [bullets] of various sizes that had been fired into him on various occasions."

Hornaday's mounted bison display was dismantled in 1955. In 1996, after years of neglect, the bison were dusted off and returned to Montana, where today the mounts are on exhibit at the Museum of the Northern Great Plains at Fort Benton.

By 1887, the harried, shy, and wary survivors of the once-great herds are generally reported to have existed in the wild in only two locations: Canada and Yellowstone National Park. Six hundred bison were estimated to remain alive in the United States; two hundred of those were in Yellowstone Park, the rest in private herds and zoos. But there is some evidence a few also survived elsewhere in remote locations at that time yet, too.

Yellowstone National Park was established in 1872. Coincidentally, it was the same year more than two million bison were massacred across the West. The legislation establishing the park protected against "wanton destruction of the fish and game [or]... the destruction for purposes of merchandise or profit," but there were no provisions for enforcement. Congress appropriated no funding to run the park for the first five years. The act reserved two million acres "as a public park or pleasuring ground for the benefit and enjoyment of the people." Instead, it became a killing ground, a shooting gallery. Within a few years after its establishment, Superintendent Norris reported four thousand elk had been poached inside the park.

Today, while park visitors excitedly "shoot" wildlife with cameras, back then they shot it for "the pleasure of killing." Anarchy reigned in Yellowstone. In 1886, the U.S. Calvary was finally brought in to administer the nation's first national park. Captain Moses Harris was the first to conduct patrols in winter, the season when the poachers were apt to be most active. Before Harris, winter afforded poachers *carte blanche*.

Still, even with the Army operating winter patrols, flagrant pilfering continued. Buffalo heads and robes were in big demand. Prime heads fetched five hundred dollars and more from taxidermists. Settlements close to the park border— Ashton, St Anthony, Marysville, and Henry's Lake, Idaho, and

Gardiner and Cooke City, Montana—harbored calloused and notorious poachers. Elsewhere, the plunderers set up semi-permanent camps just outside the park borders, waiting for any game to wander out so they could kill it. Superintendent George Anderson called them "border pirates." Taxidermists in Livingston, Montana, illicitly sold mounted buffalo heads to places as far away as London. The park's wildlife was literally put in a state of siege from illegal hunting.

The outlaws were not the plain-vanilla variety who might occasionally shoot a deer for subsistence. They were dangerous, hardened and disreputable frontier riffraff and, in some cases, fugitives from justice. To avoid arrest, some of their ilk would have felt no compunction at all in shooting an apprehending officer. They fully believed that wildlife was put there solely for their taking, their God-given right.

A few snowshoe cabins existed in the southwestern part of Yellowstone by 1897, but the Bechler Solider Station was not built until 1910. The Army lacked sufficient scouts and resources to effectively patrol the entire park. Describing the situation in the park's southwestern corner, Superintendent Anderson wrote: "There is a section of country beginning at Henry's Lake and extending south [that is]... inhabited by a merciless and persistent lot of head and skin hunters."

In his journals, *Beaver Dick: The Honor and the Heartbreak*, trapper Dick Leigh recorded a bison being killed in 1875, outside the southwest corner of Yellowstone Park. By 1895, some of the last remaining Yellowstone bison were known to occur in the Fall and Bechler River basin area. In *A Community of Scalawags, Renegades, Discharged Soldiers and Predestined Stinkers*, authors Kenneth and Lenore Diem cite an 1897 letter from St. Anthony's Sheriff Pincock warning Yellowstone's superintendent that "parties are waiting for snow to crust up [in late March] to go after eleven bison wintering in the [southwestern part of the] park." Those words were an epitaph for the last bison inhabiting that region of the park. The immense Bechler Meadows, where bison historically roamed, remain relatively empty still.

In the early years, if the soldiers were actually able to catch poachers in the act, the only punishment the Army could render was to seize the perpetrators' property and escort them from the park. The frustrated officers in charge got creative. They force marched the captured pilferers to the most distant boundaries to expel them. The biggest and meanest sergeant was given the job of conducting the escort and literally kicking the poachers out of the park. In one particularly active week alone, sixteen were booted out.

In the northeastern part of Yellowstone, a rat's nest of outlaws operated out of Cooke City. There, one of the most ruthless buffalo poachers was a hard case known as Edgar Howell. He performed his grisly business in winter on skis. It is believed that during the time Howell was active, he single-handedly killed eighty Yellowstone buffalo—40 percent of the wild bison then alive.

While Native Americans were holding onto the dream of the return of the buffalo through the mystical and religious Ghost Dance, the U.S. Calvary were faced with the hard reality of protecting Yellowstone's last wild buffalo from poachers. In a twist of irony the U.S. Army, which had earlier promoted the destruction of the buffalo, had afterward been given the assignment to protect them. To their credit, the Army contributed much to making the object of the Ghost Dancer's dream—the return of the bison—an eventual reality.

The capture of Howell in the act of slaughtering bison in Yellowstone's Pelican Valley in the winter of 1894, as told by Punke in *Last Stand*, was a saga pitting a few dedicated, seasoned Army scouts on homemade ten-foot cross-country skis against tough and experienced frontiersmen who were

The confiscated bloody plunder of poacher Edgar Howell in Yellowstone National Park, c 1890s (photo courtesy of National Park Service, Yellowstone National Park).

used to hardship and experienced in winter survival and travel. The incredible winter routes, distances traveled, and extreme conditions under which the poachers operated, and the army scouts sought them, would present challenges even today with modern mountaineering equipment.

If it had not been for the combined efforts of a relatively few dedicated individuals in the Army's administration of the park, reporters, and conservationists—particularly naturalist and publisher George Bird Grinnell and his use of his magazine, *Forest and Stream,* as a pulpit—along with a precious few congressmen, and finally, importantly, at long last, public outrage, the last wild bison in the United States would have, without a doubt, been extirpated by illegal hunting.

Instead Howell's capture and the publicized wanton and illegal killing of the park's bison set off a firestorm of public outrage, and, as a result, Howell inadvertently contributed to the May 1894 passage of the Lacey Yellowstone Protection Act.

Iowa congressman, John Lacey was a conservationist and advocate for wildlife protection. His new law made bison hunting in the park illegal. It also provided funding to reestablish a healthy bison herd within Yellowstone National Park. Regardless, though, by 1902 the damage was done; only about twenty-five wild bison remained alive in Yellowstone. Wild mountain buffalo were on the slippery brink of extinction in the United States.

Not surprisingly, not everyone agreed with idea of saving the bison. An *Indianapolis Star* editorial asked "… why [should] any intelligent person care for the preservation of these moth eaten, ungainly beasts, when their place might much better be taken up by modern blooded cattle, beautiful to look at, is a conundrum no one has answered."

Yellowstone Park records note that a single bull bison showed up out of nowhere in Jackson Hole in 1901. It was undoubtedly promptly dispatched. But buffalo are quite capable of "getting smart." While it's generally thought wild bison survived only in Yellowstone, small bands had actually managed to stay alive elsewhere, too. They hid out in far-flung places like the rugged and inaccessible Missouri River breaks in Montana, Wyoming's Red Desert and the upper Green River, and Colorado's Lost Creek wilderness, up until the twentieth century. Wyoming geologist David Love claimed a small group of eight to twelve wild, free-ranging bison persisted in the Red Desert into the 1950s. But when these fugitives were discovered and word got out, they were invariably ruthlessly hunted down and killed. Western states never afforded the buffalo game animal status.

In earlier years, in the aftermath of buffalo hunts, orphaned calves were often left wandering the prairie and would sometimes follow a rider home; others were sometimes captured by lassoing them. Buffalo Jones' record was capturing eight wild buffalo calves in one day of riding and roping. Back at the ranch, they were nursed by domestic cows. Beginning as early as in the 1870s, in this manner, some men—or you could say prescient entrepreneurs—like Samuel Walking Coyote, Charles Allard and Michael Pablo, Fred Dupree, Charles Goodnight, Charles J. "Buffalo" Jones, Gordon "Pawnee Bill" Lillie, James "Scotty" Phillip, and others, started private herds. Their motives were not simply altruistic or sentimental; they foresaw practical opportunities beyond buffalo barbecue for friends. They recognized the buffalo's existence was justifiable from a practical and utilitarian standpoint. While the last wild bison in Yellowstone and elsewhere were struggling for survival, private bison reserves were growing. The progenitors for many of the herds that exist today originated from those private sources.

Charles "Buffalo" Jones was a former buffalo hunter who atoned for his participation in the bison's slaughter by capturing and preserving a large number of them in captivity, reportedly 150 head. His method of lassoing wild bison from horseback captured not only some of the last buffalo, but also the public's attention. His exploits made him famous as detailed by authors Robert Easton and MacKenzie Brown in *Lord of Beasts* and Zane Grey's *Last of the Plainsmen*. Jones' legacy is that his captured bison eventually contributed to the reestablishment, and original establishment in some cases, of a number of herds within the United States, including Alaska, and also in Canada and northern Mexico.

But through Jones' energetic efforts to develop and promote what he envisioned would be a superior breed of range animals by cross-breeding bison and cattle (the cattalo), another, but less fortunate, legacy proved to be the inadvertent pollution of the bison genome with domestic cattle genes. However, Jones was not the only one who engaged in crossbreeding. Buffalo hunter "Yellowstone Vic" Smith was also involved in capturing buffalo calves for ranchers who wanted to crossbreed them with cattle. And Charles Goodnight and Canada's Dominion Range Experiment Station actively participated in this type of experimental hybridization, too. No one then knew or could even imagine what that might potentially portend for wild bison in the future.

By 1906, the Allard-Pablo herd in the Flathead Valley of Montana, numbered six hundred pure wild bison; James Phillip's herd was estimated at one thousand to twelve hundred head at the time of his death in 1911; and, the Goodnight herd numbered 125 in 1910.

Because of his experience and knowledge, Buffalo Jones was employed by President Theodore Roosevelt in 1902 to restore the bison in Yellowstone. Jones built a fenced enclosure at Fort Yellowstone (Mammoth) and acquired fourteen animals from the Allard-Pablo herd, three from Goodnight's herd in Texas, and several from his own herd. Additionally, he captured three wild bison in Yellowstone to give what he called "primitive strength" to the captive herd. The bison were semi-domesticated and maintained like livestock.

The plains bison introduced from Goodnight's herd, and the bison from the other sources, eventually hybridized with Yellowstone's indigenous mountain bison. In 1907, the operation with twenty-eight bison was moved to the Lamar Buffalo Ranch, where until 1930, bison were ranched and raised like cattle and then released to supplement the park's depleted natural herds. The program was a success. The number of bison in Yellowstone grew: in 1909, there were 95; by 1954, 1,500; in 1997, 3,500!

In 1925, after a near mishap, Yellowstone's chief ranger, Sam Woodring, decided a large bull bison in the Buffalo Ranch herd known as "Old Tex" had become too dangerous for the semi-ranching operation. The cranky, old bull was the offspring of a Goodnight plains bison from Texas that was pregnant when she was brought to Yellowstone in 1902. Ranger Woodring, who is credited with shooting Old Tex—the massive skull displays three bullet holes—earned the unique distinction of becoming the only national park ranger to inadvertently make the Boone and Crockett record book for killing a park animal. Old Tex tops the list of record bison yet today.

Over the years, visitors to Yellowstone National Park have been awed by Old Tex's huge skull hanging in the chief ranger's office at Mammoth. It is a replica of the real skull which is stored in the Yellowstone Museum as catalogue item "No. 5297." The museum also houses Old Tex's hide; albeit somewhat worn, Superintendent Horace Albright used it for a rug in his office. Unfortunately, the bull bison's weight was not recorded, but his record-size skull lends some credence to the claim that the plains bison were larger than the mountain variety.

Old Tex was a bison born from another time and place. His aggressive temperament and size were positive attributes for a wild bison having to survive and compete on the open plains.

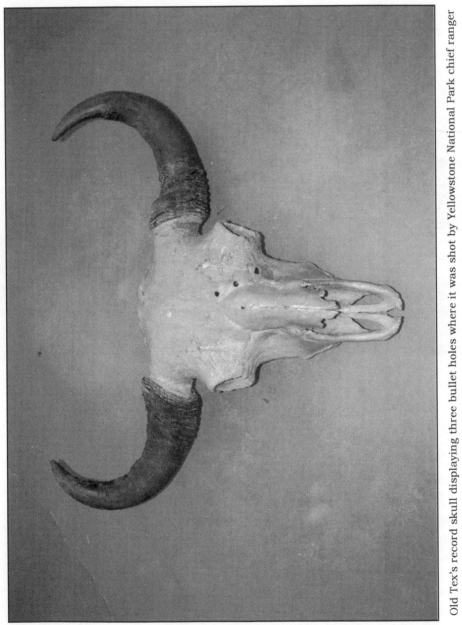

Old Tex's record skull displaying three bullet holes where it was shot by Yellowstone National Park chief ranger Sam Woodring in 1925 (photo by the author).

In a ranching situation, though, where the preferred trait is docility, he was a liability.

The treatment of Native Americans and wild bison in the late nineteenth century mirrored one another—aggressive and independent individuals suffered the fate of being removed from the population, while the survivors were consigned to reserves. The loss of a way of life for both bison and an indigenous people went hand in hand. But both survived, physically. In rebirth there was adaptation, but the old way of life, not only for Native Americans, but for bison as well, was gone forever. Old Tex's skull is more than just a tourist curio or a Boone and Crockett record; it is a token reminder of the last wild plains bison and a vanished past.

Bison are America's most emblematic animal. They are popularly pictured on official seals, flags, and logos, named as a state mammal, and used as sports team mascots and for official coats of arms. Few apparently see this widespread display of admiration for the bison as paradoxical or ironically conflicted with a shameful history of exploitation and persecution of the animal.

In wicked irony, from 1911 to 1938, the U.S. government commemorated the bison by stamping out 1.1 billion "buffalo nickels." The designer intended the coin to represent what was "most symbolically American." He chose a bison. Except for Yellowstone, buffalo were extinct on publicly owned land when the coin was first issued, but politicians in Washington put bison in the pockets of every American. The sculptor who was commissioned by the mint modeled the coin's buffalo after "Black Diamond," a lone bull bison living at the Bronx Zoo. While the government was stamping out buffalo nickels, Black Diamond was auctioned off for three hundred dollars and processed in New York's meat-packing district.

In March 1943, a 221,000-acre Jackson Hole Monument

was set aside by President Theodore Roosevelt amid a furor of outraged local protests. Still, the monument was minimal; it included only the mountainous terrain above the valley floor. From 1945 through 1947, following on the heels of its establishment, ranchers and legislators in Jackson Hole angrily introduced several bills and vigorously lobbied to abolish it. None of those bills passed. But Grand Teton National Park, the special place as we know it today, was not actually legislatively created until 1950.

The long and contentious battle for Grand Teton Teton Park is chronicled by Robert Righter in *Crucible for Conservation.* At a small gathering of conservationists and supporters for the park in the 1940s, Jackson Hole author and dude rancher Struthers Burt described his concept for the national park as a "museum on the hoof." It turned out to be a prophetic vision.

When the monument was first declared, several animals were conspicuously absent from the original cast of native wildlife: the wolf, grizzly bear and bison. With the establishment of the monument, and particularly later the park, the stage was set for the bison's encore with the sky-piercing Teton Mountains forming the stage's backdrop. By the time the monument was declared, bison had been gone from the Hole for over sixty years.

As if to celebrate the monument, two years after its declaration three bison resembling apparitions from out of the past materialized on the prairie north of Jackson. The advance scouting party of wild bovine made their way south through the valley. Where they came from, and where and how they subsequently vanished, no one today really knows. No doubt, after the bison took out some fences along the way, ranchers sent them to join the vast herds in the great beyond. Settlement of the frontier was too recent a memory among Jackson Hole's leading citizenry in those years to allow a return of free-roaming wild bison. The same mindset that so rigorously opposed the Jackson Hole Monument would likewise have been opposed to bison reoccupying their ancestral ranges in the Hole.

In 1946, after much cooperative planning, a lease agreement was executed by the National Park Service that permitted the construction and operation of a fifteen-hundred-acre Jackson Hole Wildlife Park—a fenced wildlife preserve within the monument. The Park Service was not too keen on the idea, and while Jackson's eminent biologist and wilderness proponent, Olaus Murie, did not openly oppose the wildlife park, his contempt was barely contained. He referred to it as "a zoo."

The wildlife park was conceived and operated by a nonprofit corporation sponsored by the New York Zoological Society, Jackson Hole Preserve, Inc., and the Wyoming Game and Fish Commission. Its purpose, as Laurence S. Rockefeller described in the 1948 dedication ceremony, was "so people could identify, observe and better appreciate the wildlife they are being asked to conserve." It showcased the monument's wildlife for the public to see and for scientists to study and was a part of Rockefeller's larger ongoing conservation agenda in Jackson Hole at the time.

The wildlife park served as a public exhibit for large mammals for five years. The Jackson Hole Biological Station, a part of the facility, however, continued to operate in conjunction with the University of Wyoming and the New York Zoological Society at the site up until 1978.

Today, few people who stop at the popular and scenic Oxbow Bend parking area realize that the natural-appearing setting they gaze across—east and west of Oxbow Bend, south of route U.S. 287 to the Snake River—was once the site of a Wildlife Park and Biological Station.

The wildlife park was approved in 1946, but it was not dedicated and opened to the public until two years later. There

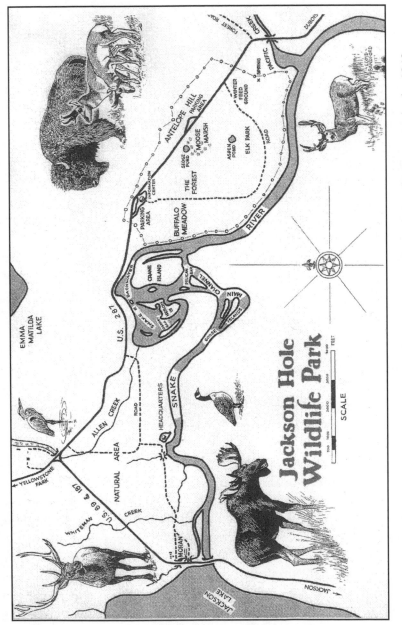

The Jackson Hole Wildlife Park was located within Jackson Hole National Monument in the 1940s (courtesy National Park Service, Grand Teton National Park archives Fabian collection).

was a construction difficulty. Building the wildlife park's biological field station, public exhibit buildings, barn, corrals, loading chutes, and roads was not the problem; the setback came in erecting fence around four hundred of the installation's fifteen hundred acres. The fencing was required to be stout enough to contain big game animals, including bison.

It is axiomatic that bison require strong, high fences to contain them. They have the agility to leap fences in a single bound that will contain cattle. Five-foot-high buck and rail fences pose no problem to jump. It is said that, if a wild buffalo can get its head over a fence, it will jump it. Male bison, which can weigh a ton and stand over six-feet tall at the shoulders, are capable of knocking down woven-wire fencing and leaping six-foot-high corrals. It can depend on how determined the animals are to get out, too. Generally, nowadays, electric fences are used to effectively contain bison.

The total amount of high-strength, woven-steel-wire fence constructed at the wildlife park to enclose large animals was 26,854 linear feet (5.01 miles); 18,837 feet were built to be eight feet in height, and the remaining 8,017 feet of fence was made six feet in height. A wire net was also strung across the Snake River to prevent the animals from escaping by swimming. It all required no small amount of labor and investment. The maintenance and upkeep of the wildlife park's fence system, combined with the bison's indomitable spirit, figures large into the story of the origin of Jackson Hole's modern day bison herd.

The history of bison survival and restoration in Yellowstone National Park also becomes recognizably relevant for today's Jackson Hole herd when we learn that twenty wild buffalo—three bulls, twelve cows, and five calves—from Yellowstone were reintroduced into the Hole at the wildlife park in 1948. They were intended to be a part of the wildlife exhibit. After a sixty-four year hiatus, bison had returned to Jackson Hole.

Reintroducing bison back into the Hole and penning them up at the wildlife park was apparently a non-issue at the time. It was ignored by the monument's detractors. But to have simply proposed a direct transplant of bison into the monument itself, or later into Grand Teton National Park, would have undoubtedly ignited a firestorm of local outrage. It would have been impossibly controversial. However, no one at the time foresaw that the wildlife park would inadvertently become the venue by which free-roaming wild bison would return to the Hole.

At the wildlife park dedication ceremony July 19, 1948, a horseman was employed to haze the bison and elk back and forth in the background meadows behind the speaker's platform. Once again, bison were used to provide a wildlife spectacle to symbolize man's conservation efforts.

In September 1948, *Animal Kingdom* magazine contained an article entitled, "The Inauguration of Jackson Hole Wildlife Park." In the summer of 1948, over 120,000 people had visited the wildlife park. Two full-time employees had been hired to prevent tourists from getting themselves into dangerous predicaments with the bison. A *Salt Lake Tribune* article in September 4, 1949, called it "the wildest park in the nation," with everything "from grizzlies to chipmunks." To get them through the winter, the wildlife park's seventy or more big game animals were required to be fed.

The wildlife park's bison herd was maintained at fifteen to thirty animals. Those considered excess were turned over to the state. After the establishment of Grand Teton National Park in 1950, the National Park Service took over the facility in coordination with the Wyoming Game and Fish Department. In 1963, tragedy struck: brucellosis disease was discovered in the little herd.

Bison are believed to have originally been infected with brucellosis from domestic livestock. Some of the bison in

An unidentified worker feeding the bison at the Jackson Hole Wildlife Park, n.d. (photo courtesy National Park Service, Grand Teton National Park).

Yellowstone National Park were found to be infected with brucellosis-causing bacteria as early as 1917. The general health of Yellowstone's bison does not appear to be affected by the disease. They seem to build a natural résistance to it, but the rub is cattle do not. Brucellosis can cause cows to abort their calves, and it is the source of undulant fever in humans. The livestock industry considers it a scourge.

As a result of the discovery of brucellosis-infected individuals, all the adult bison in the wildlife park herd were destroyed. Four yearlings that had been vaccinated earlier and five vaccinated calves of the year were retained. The following year, twelve certified brucellosis-free bison—six adult males and six adult females—were brought in from Theodore Roosevelt National Park in North Dakota, lifting the little herd's number back up to twenty-one.

Today's Jackson Hole bison herd is of mixed genetic provenance. Their lineage potentially includes: original Yellowstone bison, Buffalo Jones' herd, Goodnight's Texas bison, the Montana Allard-Pablo herd, and those brought in from Theodore Roosevelt National Park. The Roosevelt Park animals were originally obtained from Fort Niobrara National Wildlife Refuge in Nebraska in 1956. The Nebraska refuge had received their bison as a gift from the New York Zoological Park and the American Bison Society, their original source is not known.

In recent years, a small sampling of Grand Teton National Park's bison were tested and found *not* to have been "watered down" by cattle gene introgression. Regardless of their potentially diverse ancestry, those tested appeared to be pure wild bison.

They behaved like wild bison, too. The disconsolate penned-up beasts became habitual and practiced escape artists. In their bovine way, they must have recognized a better world lay beyond the fenced enclosure. Beginning in the1960s, invariably and routinely, several times a year, Wyoming Game and Fish personnel were called in to recapture the Houdini-like bison.

Rounding up escaped bison became a routine event. Keep in mind the original fence had been installed twenty years earlier, and presumably its maintenance was not a first priority for the park's limited funds.

Coincidentally, around this time, in 1963, a group of scientists from outside the National Park Service headed by A. Starker Leopold—son of the legendary forester and conservationist, Aldo Leopold—were commissioned by the Secretary of Interior to prepare what would become known as "The Leopold Report." It set forth a visionary goal for management of the national parks that "each Park be maintained, or where necessary recreated, as nearly possible in the condition that prevailed when the area was first visited by the white-man... a National Park should represent a vignette of primitive America... and create the mood of wild America." It scolded the National Park Service for its failure to apply sound stewardship principles in the management of its biotic resources. Its recommendations were heralded as revolutionary by the scientific community.

For Grand Teton National Park, the report recalled Struthers Burt's earlier vision for "a museum on the hoof." And it echoed of National Park Service biologist George M. Wright's ambitious leadership in the 1930s to restore original wildlife conditions within the national parks.

The wildlife park had served its purpose in an earlier time. The new era in national park management, ushered in by the Leopold Report, challenged the wildlife park's concept and existence. At the time, no doubt because of the administrative headache the unruly bison presented, the herd had been reduced in number to eleven adults and four calves.

In 1969, the wayward, pen-crazed bison crashed down the fence. And away they galloped—their large brown eyes rolling, slobbering, tongues lolling, and with tails held erect—the literal embodiment of the expression "high-tailing it out of there." Bison are capable of galloping more than 32 mph. It was the buffalo equivalent of the *The Great Escape*, a Hollywood movie about a mass flight from a fenced prisoner of war camp.

Robert Wood, the park's biologist at the time, is said to have exclaimed (expletives deleted), "Now we have a problem." Park Superintendent Howard Chapman, on the other hand, wasn't rattled. He viewed it as a unique opportunity to put the recommendations of the Leopold Report to a test. The Park Service benignly neglected to round up the escaped bison. Chapman went on to become Director of the Western Region of the National Park Service. Wild, free-ranging bison had returned to their ancestral haunts in the Hole.

The manner in which bison returned to the Hole recalls an ancient Apache-Comanche origin myth that says: "It was coyote, the trickster, who released all the bison from the buffalo corral, so that they would scatter across the Earth." Perhaps the trickster coyote conspired to arrange an encore through the bison's escape in Grand Teton National Park.

The woolly fugitives stayed out of sight. Hiding like the last survivors of their kind did at the turn of the century. They spent the easy summer months in the little-visited pothole area of the park and along the inaccessible east side of Signal Mountain. In winter they resided within the shelter of the old-growth cottonwood and spruce forests along the Snake River north of Moose. It was remarkable they hung on at all. Remember, these were animals that had been raised and held in captivity all their lives. While they were acclimated to Jackson Hole's severe climate, they were nonetheless used to being fed in winter.

To graze in deep snow, bison use their powerful shoulders and necks, sweeping their massive heads back and forth to plow snow out of the way to expose forage. But in the three to four feet of snow that generally settles into the Snake River bottom north of Jackson each winter, they literally had to crater their way down to dried and frozen vegetation. As a final survival strategy, they resorted to browsing shrubs, gnawing bark from aspen trees or off the limbs of cottonwood trees felled by beaver, and grazing riparian vegetation growing in open spring creeks. It was tough for the bison to make a living in winter in the northern part of Teton Park. The only other ungulate capable of doing it was the moose; but they are browsers that generally feed on woody plants sticking out above the snow, whereas, bison are usually grazers foraging on grasses and forbs.

That they managed to survive winter after winter in the deep snow and cold speaks loudly for the bison's superbly evolved adaptations. In the 1970s, an Alberta veterinarian conducted studies on animals for cold tolerance. He found Hereford cattle hit their critical temperature at fourteen-degrees Fahrenheit, whereas the bison's metabolic rate was still decreasing at minus twenty-two degrees. Bison's hair thickness is twice that of cattle; their dark color absorbs heat; their large long trachea allows pre-warming of cold air; and short hair above the eyes prevents freezing around the eyes.

When snow and hoar dramatically clings to them during winter storms, it profoundly reminds us that these are indeed creatures descendent from the Pleistocene epoch.

Still, the extreme conditions the bison struggled against held their population growth in check. By 1975, six years after their escape, the herd had only grown to twenty-one.

Winters during the late 1970s in Jackson Hole were notable for record snow and cold. One storm alone during that time dumped over fifty inches of snow on the town of Jackson; that was on top of an already existing foot or more. Around 1978-79, the town of Jackson recorded January temperatures of minus sixty degrees.  North of Moose along the foot of the Teton Mountains, the snow was generally deeper and the arctic air settling into the river bottom even more frigid.

Sometime during those extremely cold and snowy years, around ten years after their escape from the enclosure, the bison instinctively drifted south, down the valley, toward the north end of the National Elk Refuge. There, strong winds periodically swept portions of the foothills and buttes free of snow, exposing cured grass and forbs. Conditions were still demanding, but it was easier to make a living in winter on the foothill buttes than in the river bottom. Over the next four years, the little herd grew to thirty seven.

For the first ten years after their escape, the bison had been reclusive and mostly stayed out of sight. Unlike the bison in Grand Teton Teton Park today, they were rarely seen by the public. Most people were unaware free-ranging, wild bison actually existed in Teton Park in those years—at least as "free-ranging" as any bison are allowed to be nowadays.

Bison can live to be forty years of age. Perhaps some of the original animals from North Dakota were approaching that age by the 1980s. Maybe the newer generations were less wary or less bound by established behavior patterns. In any case, sometime around the winter of 1980-81, the shaggy bovine wandered far enough south on the National Elk Refuge to discover the supplemental winter feeding being provided to more than seven thousand elk. Not to be outdone, the bison bullied their way into the feed lines.

In the words of senior park biologist, Steven Cain, that was a "pivotal event." Another way of putting it is that even for bison there's no such thing as a free lunch. It was like eating the fruit of Eden, it came with a price. The U.S. Fish and Wildlife Service and the Wyoming Game and Fish Department and sportsmen were not pleased with "the park's bison" taking over the elk feed lines and consuming the alfalfa pellets and hay meant for elk. They took issue with it.

By 1984, because elk were being driven off the feed lines and pushed around by bison, separate feeding stations were laid out to accommodate them. In Wyoming, elk are prized game animals. The bison were viewed more as a nuisance that interfered with the Game and Fish Department's single-minded elk management program. By 1989, the Wyoming legislature authorized a "wild bison reduction season." Bison have never been given "game animal" status by the State of Wyoming. But, ironically, in 1985, the bison had been adopted as Wyoming's state animal.

Inside the park, the bison were protected from hunting. But when they left the park and ventured onto the adjacent national forest, and later the National Elk Refuge, too, they unknowingly entered into another agency's jurisdiction, where a different set of rules applied.

Around this time period, a photograph of a group of bison splashing across the Snake River with the snowcapped Teton Mountains in the background appeared widely in Jackson's art galleries. The spectacular image was not solely responsible for alerting the public to the majesty of Grand Teton National Park's bison herd, but it no doubt contributed. Jackson Hole's bison were finally becoming more visible to the general public.

With life made less rigorous by supplemental feeding, coupled with the impressive protectiveness of mother bison, the bison flourished. Bison cows can and do repel grizzly bears and wolves from vulnerable calves. A mother bison missing her calf will reportedly walk around for days calling—a rumbling exhaling that sounds like drumming—and looking for it. By the millennium year of 2000, the park boasted five hundred bison on the hoof. As a rule, 95 percent of those were showing up for winter handouts on the National Elk Refuge. Only a small number of recalcitrant bulls stubbornly refused the easy life, preferring to tough it out on their own up north.

Hunting for bison had been allowed on the national forest adjoining the park since 1990. During the period from 1990 to 2005, no fewer than six of the bison hunters had taken had made the Boone and Crockett Club's record book. Besides their skull and horn measurements, to qualify for listing, they are also required to be "wild and free-ranging game animals taken in a fair chase." Despite the State of Wyoming's reluctance to classify bison as game animals, permits to hunt them are avidly sought by sportsmen.

It was little publicized, but the bison began dispersing from Jackson Hole, similar to those that today attempt to migrate from Yellowstone National Park north along the Yellowstone River Valley at Gardiner, Montana, or west down the Madison River near West Yellowstone, and also down the Shoshone River near Cody, Wyoming. The Jackson Hole bison instinctively found and followed the age-old migratory paths to the Green River Basin. In 1988, a bison made a surprise appearance near Marbleton, Wyoming; in 1990, three showed up at Cora, Wyoming; and two more at Cora in 1992. Without man's interference, the plains would eventually be repopulated with bison again. But wandering bison are not tolerated.

Like in Yellowstone National Park, the ecological habitat for bison in Grand Teton National Park is also only marginally self-contained. Under original natural conditions bison could freely migrate to more favorable ranges if conditions demanded. The unfortunate aspect of the persistent destruction of wild bison that disperse or migrate beyond the national park's borders is that it selects against animals with migratory instincts, potentially erasing the genetic memory of migration. Migratory instinct under natural conditions can aid a species' survival, but for bison nowadays it is a death sentence. Yellowstone and Teton

National Parks' wild bison are considered to be "free ranging," but with a caveat—free ranging within the park's legislatively designated boundaries only.

In 1994, a wildfire swept through the sagebrush-grassland at the south end of Antelope Flats around Mormon Row in Teton Park. In the years afterward, the burned prairie celebrated its renewal, bursting forth with an incredible display of wildflowers and native grassland vegetation. The bison grazed amid the belly-deep blaze of wildflowers with the Teton Mountains providing a snowcapped backdrop. Those people fortunate to have witnessed the spectacle will remember it for the rest of their lives. It was a sublime vignette of past primeval America.

Meanwhile, some biologists had begun wringing their hands, claiming "habitat degradation" from the growing bison population. Moreover, they opined that "the bison herd had grown to levels above what had historically existed in Jackson Hole." Nobody really knows what existed historically; there are no accounts. Those advocating herd reduction were blocked from killing the bison by lawsuits from concerned conservation organizations and the public. So the herd happily continued to grow. By the winter of 2007, it was 1,100 strong!

In April 2007, the hugely controversial "Jackson Hole Bison and Elk Management Plan/EIS" was finally approved. The plan and environmental statement generated 11,900 written comments from the public. Balancing wildlife management and conservation issues with social and political issues obviously presents a challenge in the twenty-first century. Obviously, too, the Jackson Hole bison have a large following of concerned and sympathetic supporters.

Among other things, the approved plan allows controlled bison hunting on the National Elk Refuge and adjoining National Forest. An objective for the bison herd size was set at five hundred animals. The 2008 hunting season reduced the herd by two

Earle F. Layser

A gathering of Jackson Hole bison in Grand Teton National Park in June 2010 (photo by the author).

hundred and fifty. After the initial fusillade, the bison that had remained standing wisely moved back inside the park. Those individuals whose desire for alfalfa pellets overcame any innate wariness ended up being removed from the herd. An aerial survey after the hunting season counted 875 bison still on the hoof.

In an interview after the 2009 hunting season a refuge biologist remarked, "We've had very low bison numbers on the south end of the refuge this year. There's the possibility that the bison after three years of hunting them have learned that the refuge is not a safe place for them this time of the year." As was discovered a century or more ago, wild bison are quite capable of "getting smart."

On September 26, during the 2009-10 Jackson Hole bison hunting season, a Riverton, Wyoming, hunter, accompanied by experienced guide Johnnie "Horse Caller" Filbeck and his assistant, Cole Campbell, were attempting to kill a bison with a .50 caliber handgun that would qualify for the record book. The client shot a large bull bison three times at close range before it dropped. Filbeck's assistant and the client walked up to the downed bull. It lunged onto its feet and fought back.

Unlike a domestic bull, a charging bison keeps its eye on its enemy, and despite its size is agile enough to swerve and turn in pursuit. It caught Campbell and tossed him high into the air twice. The enraged bull then threateningly stood over the stunned assistant guide. The client emptied his handgun with no effect, then got his rifle and finally put the bull down.

The seriously injured guide assistant was flight lifted to the hospital suffering from seven broken ribs, major bruises, and a massive goring in the buttocks. In an interview, Filbeck laconically commented: "It could have been worse, it could have happened to the client." The park's bison entertain tourists all summer, but make no mistake, the green fire still burns in them; they are wild animals with a long history of surviving adversity.

Modern day bison management issues in Greater Yellowstone region and elsewhere are not simply an aside to this story, lingering frontier attitudes are revealed in the treatment buffalo are frequently accorded. In recent years, bison from Yellowstone National Park's northern range have been killed by the thousands when they annually migrated out of the park onto private land and the adjoining national forest—victims of Montana's brucellosis slaughter. Since the 2000 millennium, about 3,700 have been killed; *déjà vu* the nineteenth century. In 2007-08 alone, figures vary, but between 1,616 and 1,725 were destroyed for venturing outside the park's boundaries. Yellowstone had about four thousand bison in 2007, only about half of that number remained in 2008-09 after so-called "brucellosis control measures" were undertaken by the Montana Department of Livestock.

The management of Yellowstone National Park's bison poses modern day wildlife ethics issues. Wild bison leaving the park are being rounded up or captured, penned up in holding corrals, and trucked to slaughter like cattle. The Montana Department of Livestock has been ruthlessly uncompromising: it makes neither exception nor little effort to find alternatives. The agency at the insistence of the ranching community even rounds up bison on national forest lands where no cattle grazing allotments exist.

Putting the Department of Livestock and ranching community in charge of wild bison guarantees short-sighted prejudicial treatment. It's not all that long ago that their granddaddies worked to clear the range of competing wild herbivores. What underlies the fear of bison reoccupying historic habitat is not unlike that for the wolf: it lets the wild back into Western lands.

In a *Bozeman Chronicle* article entitled "Bison after brucellosis" by Daniel Person, Errol Rice, executive vice president of the Montana Stock Grower's Association confirmed the issue goes deeper than disease control. Rice is quoted saying: "I think the rancher's No. 1 fear is brucellosis. But yeah, I can honestly say there is fear for competition for grass. But it is more than competition for grass, it is fear of being pushed off the land entirely."

Meanwhile, as bison were being rounded up and trucked to slaughter, sportsmen applications to legally hunt bison in Montana were at record levels. In 2009-2010, more than 10,000 people applied for a license; 44 were granted. One might ask why sportsmen have not loudly protested the Department of Livestock's killing of a potentially valuable game animal and why they have not asked for more opportunity for regulated hunting of bison?

After the slaughter of 2008, and a change in the presidential administration, the federal Government Accountability Office released a scathing criticism of the bison's treatment. But controversy over letting bison access winter range outside the park continues, even on adjoining national forest. The policy is inconsistently administered by the different western states. Bison are allowed to range onto parts of adjacent Bridger-Teton National Forest from Teton National Park in Wyoming; likewise, elk also may carry brucellosis. But stockmen zero in on bison and oppose letting *any* leave Yellowstone Park. Simply put, the management of bison on the National Forests adjacent to Yellowstone National Park needs to be carried out in a more reasonable, scientific, and less short-sighted, political, and draconian manner (see the Discussion section for more on this issue).

The western Great Plains, prairies and mountain valleys, that once comprised one of the largest grasslands on Earth, have today been reduced to vestigial remnants surrounded by towns and cities, corporative agricultural enterprise, private farms and ranches, and sown with introduced grasses. The bison were cleared from the land to make way for this progress. In the twenty-first century, is there no room left for bison to roam within the 20-million acre Greater Yellowstone ecosystem and elsewhere on public lands outside of the two National Parks? Must wild bison be confined to within the borders of the national parks only?

Bison are in little danger of extinction today. Over 450,000 are estimated to exist nation-wide, but still 95 percent of those are on private ranches or farms and many have genomes polluted with cattle genes. What originally "saved" the American bison was their utilitarian value. Media magnate Ted Turner is the largest single private owner with an estimated fifty thousand. If you want a glimpse of what old Montana may have looked like, visit Turner's ranch on Spanish Creek near Bozeman in spring. The herd spreads out across verdant native-grassland foothills and the calves gambol amid the golden-yellow flowers of balsamroot.

The importance of Grand Teton and Yellowstone National Parks' wild bison goes deeper than just their numbers and potential utility alone. While overall, many buffalo may exist on private ranches and farms, few of those are free from cattle-gene introgression. As was pointed out, not all bison are entirely real bison. The Nature Conservancy estimates only ten thousand of the half-million bison in North America are free of cattle genes. In five hundred random samples collected from Yellowstone bison from 1997 through 2002, *none* were found to harbor genetic material from cattle.

Genetically pure bison herds, such as those in Grand Teton and Yellowstone National Parks, have disproportionate ecological and conservation value. They are the closest thing remaining today to the true wild bison genotype, *Bison bison bison*. They are the "heirloom variety." Their conservation is not just about nostalgia, sentimentalism, or wildlife viewing by tourists, it's about preserving biodiversity and the species' singular ecological adaptations and fitness. Yellowstone National Park's wild bison, along with a few other tested small herds, have been designated "genetic rescue populations." They represent important genetic reservoirs or "source herds" for the preservation and restoration of North America's true indigenous wild bison.

In recent years, white buffalo have been born in Wisconsin, South Dakota and North Dakota; a relative spate of rare births, since the chance of a true white buffalo occurrence is thought to be one in every ten million. There are several different ways a buffalo may be born white: they may be leucistic (have blue eyes), albino (no pigment), and in the case of cattle gene introgression, the white comes from their cattle ancestry. In any case, it caused a furor among Native Americans. They recalled the Lakota prophesy wherein the sacred white buffalo signifies a rebirth for humanity; a heralding of hope and peace. At the National Buffalo Museum herd in Jamestown, North Dakota, which bills itself as "The Buffalo Capital of the World," two white bison were born. The one in 2006 was named *mahpiya ska,* Dakota for "White Cloud," and the other in 2007 "Dakota Miracle." At a special ceremony honoring the event, Lakota Joseph Chasing Horse spoke: "We are praying that mankind does wake up and think about the future, for we haven't just inherited this Earth from our ancestors, but we are borrowing it from our unborn children."

Grand Teton National Park's bison population may have peaked in 2007, but the future of the herd appears secure. The park's bison are beloved by many. Whenever my son and grandchildren visit us, it's tradition to do a game viewing drive around Teton Park's Kelly Loop to view the bison. I feel as if I've traveled a great circle from years ago, when my sons and I unearthed the bison skull in the riverbank along the upper Gros Ventre.

The earth may never give up another mountain bison skull

to my family and me as it did back then, but my grandchildren today have something more valuable than just skulls and bones. They have the opportunity to actually view wild bison restored to their native habitat in Jackson Hole—a vignette of the once great herds. Teton Park provides this opportunity for millions of visitors to enjoy annually, including people from all over the world.

The bald eagle may be our national symbol, but the bison, more than any other animal, is tangibly and emblematically interwoven into the fabric of the history and development of our country. If we were ever to select a national animal—for instance, in India the national animal is the Lord of the Jungles, the tiger—it would have to be the creature that once owned the land, the American bison.

A male wolverine photographed on the west-slope of the Teton Mountains
during the Alta 4-H study which was dubbed "Wolver-Dan"
(photo by the Alta 4-H club's motion sensory camera).

# 12

## Wolveranne: The Alta 4-H Skunk Bear Project

*People may think that they know about animals, but it isn't true; a human's powers are insignificant. We are people; we know only a little about animals and their ways. Animals have special abilities which they depend upon to live, giving us only the powers which they no longer need.*

—"The Wolf and Wolverine's Revenge," Dene story in *Wolverine Myths and Visions.*

In the northern part of Wyoming's Grand Teton National Park and the west slope of the Teton Range within the Jedediah Smith Wilderness on the Targhee National Forest, there are high-elevation basins forested with ancient Engelmann spruce. The dense understory in these stands consists of tall shrubs, such as mountain ash, *Sorbus scopulina*, wild currants, *Ribes spp.*, thimbleberry, *Rubus parviflora*, and fool's huckleberry, *Menziesia ferruginia.* The forest has an aspect similar to what you might expect to find in northwest Montana, hardly Wyoming.

The forested basins are interconnected by remote high-mountain plateaus, ridges and alpine crags, where snow persists, and which lead north to Yellowstone National Park and beyond. The land resonates as prime habitat for bears, wolves, moose, pine martens, maybe lynx.

In the past, there had been infrequent sightings, but it was never confirmed, that the rarest of the rare occurred here, too: wolverine. But no one knew for certain. That is, until one made an unprecedented appearance at a residence near Moran, Wyoming, in the mid-1990s, and was photographed eating suet at a bird feeder!

The wolverine is another animal with many names—carajou, bear skunk, nasty cat, mountain cat, Indian devil, woods devil, beaver eater, and devil bear. To the Blackfeet Indians, it is known as the skunk bear, to the Ojibway Indian, big skunk. The Alaskan Inuit named it *kee-wa-har-kess,* "the evil one," while the Cree call it *Ommeethatsees,* "the one who likes to rob." Scientifically, it is known as *Gulo*—"the glutton."

To Alaska's Koyukon people, the wolverine has the most powerful spirit of all animals, even more than the grizzly bear. The wolverine features prominently in the mythology of indigenous people of northern Canada: for the Innu people, it is the creator of the world, and to the Dene (*Den Dhaa'*—the "ordinary people"), it is the original trickster and a link to the spirit world, the archetype of supernatural cleverness. It is a creature that science, up until only recently, knew little about. It still remains mysterious in many ways.

The wolverine is a wilderness animal traditionally associated with the romance of the north country. It is an amazing and feisty animal known for its fearlessness, ferociousness, cunning, and remarkable strength, all out of proportion to mere size—it can be a powerful whirling mass of long canine teeth and claws. One Alaskan researcher attests to the wolverine's astonishing strength and ferocity by the fact they sometimes chew through and escape from live traps made of steel and 11-gauge chain-link fencing.

In *Lives of Game Animals,* naturalist Ernest Thompson Seton described the wolverine this way: "Picture a weasel ... that little demon of destruction, that small atom of insensate courage ... sleepless and tireless, incredibly active ... multiply that some fifty times, and you have the likeness of a wolverine."

Skunk bears are only as large as a small to medium-size dog: fifteen to thirty pounds for females, up to forty pounds for males. Still, wolverines are the largest terrestrial member of the weasel family—the Mustelidae. But they're not built long and lean like weasels, rather, they are short and stout like a small bear. Genetic studies indicate the American marten is the wolverine's closest relative.

Wolverines have broad heads, small eyes and short rounded ears. They are powerfully muscled, especially their shoulders, head and neck. Their amazingly strong teeth and jaw muscles allow them to crush bones as thick as the femur of a moose to get at the bone marrow, an astonishing feat of strength for an animal their size.

They have short but incredibly sturdy legs, oversize broad feet, and impressively sharp and long curving claws, all of which facilitate their tireless travel across snow and ice, up rock walls, and across alpine ridges, and in tree climbing, digging, and even swimming. In the animal world, wolverines are the ultimate all-terrain machines.

Their endurance is legendary. The skunk bear is capable of crossing astonishingly large distances of rugged terrain, at any season and under any conditions, to scavenge on carrion or some pitiful leftover scraps. They have the strength to burrow like a backhoe on steroids through six to eight feet of snowpack, tunneling down to food caches or den sites. In the northern Rocky Mountains, the dens are generally secreted in uninhabited and isolated boulder-strewn, high-elevation terrain. Even with aid of modern telemetry and technology, up until very recently, the number of wolverine den sites that had ever been located could be counted on one hand.

While the wolverine is thought to dine mostly on winter-killed animals and leavings from other predators, including those left by man, they are also omnivorous, consuming almost anything that's edible—ground squirrels, mushrooms, berries, insects, and bird eggs.

Like their skunk family cousins, wolverines have anal glands that can emit a potent musky odor; hence the moniker "skunk bear." Wolverines' scent-mark food caches with their disagreeable urine and musk to discourage other scavengers; they also emit a powerful musk when they are being aggressive or threatened. The smell has been described as "foul" or "ugly"— the *eau de cologne* of wolverine.

Wolverines have a circumpolar distribution, traditionally generalized as "isolated northern areas." Recent research correlates their occurrence in the conterminous United States to high-elevation areas with persistent or late-spring snow cover.

Little is known about their pre-European settlement occurrence and population density. Records indicate a northward (and to ever-higher altitudes) contraction from the animal's original pre-settlement distribution as a result of the fur trade, hunting, and habitat encroachment by man. By the 1920s-30s, wolverines were reported extirpated from the lower forty-eight states.

The late-nineteenth and early-twentieth century hide and bounty hunters', as well as the later massive-predator control programs' practice of lacing carcasses and baits with strychnine to kill wolves and coyotes, were deadly efficient in wiping out wolverines, too. The "1080" and the sodium-cyanide "coyote getter" poisons were potentially similarly effective. Author Michael J. Robinson, in *Predatory Bureaucracy*, reports three wolverines were killed in Colorado between 1918 and 1919 in predator control actions by the Bureau of Biological Survey. They were the last wolverines seen in Colorado's mountains for ninety years afterwards.

Beginning as early as 1877, the park superintendent reported ungulate carcasses in Yellowstone were being poisoned for "wolf and wolverine bait." with strychnine by freelance "wolfers." Another very effective method of getting rid of species like the wolverine has proven to be the European settlers' and modern-day developers' fragmentation of wilderness habitat.

Fifty years after they had been reported extinct, wolverines were occasionally showing up in Yellowstone National Park. From 1970 to 1978, in "YNP Research Note No. 5," park biologist D.B. Houston recorded twenty-seven reliable sightings within or adjacent to the park, indicating a few skunk bears had managed to survive.

While wolverine are rarely associated with depredation of livestock in the United States (there is a single report by a rancher in 1998 of a wolverine killing sheep east of Buffalo, Wyoming), mammalogist David MacDonald, in *The Encyclopedia of Mammals*, attributes the reason for wolverine control and their consequent historical decline in northern Europe to their alleged killing of livestock (sheep and reindeer).

The wolverine suffers from other liabilities in its relationship with man. Foremost, it has one of the most striking and prized pelts of all fur-bearing animals—a rich, glossy, dark- brown pelt with two pale yellow strips that sweep along each flank to the base of a long bushy tail, and with white patches marking the chest, forepaws or legs. Its fur is in high demand for trim and lining of clothing. Frost mysteriously and readily brushes off of the thick, oily, dark and exceptionally hydrophobic fur. A single wolverine pelt can fetch up to four hundred dollars in today's market. In 2009, the author saw a wolverine pelt in the general store at Ninilchik, Alaska, priced at $299.

The states of Alaska and Montana still allow trapping of wolverines. Until recently, up to twelve were being taken annually by trappers in the Treasure State, where it is classified as "a furbearer of restricted harvest." Montana has since initiated a quota system with four designated "wolverine management units" and a current annual statewide harvest limit of five.

Prior to Montana implementing their limited quota system, one research biologist in Montana had remarked, "For the price a trapper can get for a wolverine pelt in Montana, a consequence can be the complete elimination of wolverines from an entire mountain range." Montana Fish, Wildlife and Parks has since closed wolverine trapping in some of the state's "island mountain chains," which are believed to be important ecological connectors.

Trappers have generally despised and demonized wolverines for their destructiveness. They eat the trappers' catches, carrying off traps and all; and they've been known to wreak havoc with cabins and supply caches. What they don't eat or destroy, they spray with their disagreeable musk and urine. The trappers' tales of the skunk bear's cunning and rapacious destructiveness are celebrated north-country lore.

Recently, it has been recognized that wolverines are ecologically linked to wolves through carrion availability. In Canada, it has been documented that wolverines scavenge carrion remains from wolf kills. We might presume the reintroduction of wolves is a positive for wolverines in the conterminous United States. It follows that impacts to wolves and their prey have potential to impact wolverine, too.

Most of us will never observe a live wolverine. Maybe seeing the relentless pacing of one at the zoo is possible, but glimpsing a skunk bear in the wild, interacting with its natural habitat, is something only an infinitesimally small percentage of people will ever experience. Wolverines occur in such low densities, over such vast geographic areas, and generally in such rugged terrain, that chance encounters by people are very rare. The increased numbers of backcountry skiers in recent years could possibly result in more sightings.

In 1994, the Biodiversity Legal Foundation filed a petition with the U.S. Fish and Wildlife Service to list the wolverine under the federal Endangered Species Act, initiating what has become an epic conservation saga. The Fish and Wildlife Service used the animal's rarity and mysterious nature to deny the petition. The agency claimed there was not enough information available on the animal to warrant listing. Catch-22, the animal's rarity was used to prevent it from being listed.

Subsequently, six more conservation organizations petitioned for listing the wolverine. In the years of legal wrangling that followed, a federal judge ruled in 2006 that the U.S. Fish and Wildlife Service were required to review the threats against the wolverine. But two years later, the Bush-Cheney administration decided that since the wolverine was not endangered in Canada, it needn't be listed.

Conservationists countered that the United States should protect its own wildlife, not rely on Canada to do so. A lawsuit to overthrow the Bush-Cheney administration's decision has been filed; a dozen conservation organizations are party to the appeal.

A *Casper Star Tribune* newspaper Web site, which allows reader comment, had the following sampling of responses to a 2008 article entitled, "Groups Plan Wolverine Lawsuit": "Wolverine advocates?! NO. Just another left-wing liberal attempt to shut down energy production in Wyoming ... They will sue until all signs of mankind are removed from the earth and only the lawyers and ecos are left. I thought the meek would inherit the earth not the scum."

As a rule, wolverines are renowned for their secretiveness. It is not surprising when even old-timers say they have never seen a wolverine. One such person, who has trapped marten along the west slope of the Teton Range for over fifty years, claims he has never encountered one. Although, we now know wolverine occur there.

On the other hand, the animal is frustratingly enigmatic. In 2004, a wolverine, gorging, not too "cunningly" or "secretively," on road-killed deer along highway I-30, near Fossil Butte National Monument west of Kemmerer—outside what is typically thought of as the animal's habitat—became a hit-and-run victim itself. It was perhaps Wyoming's most curious road kill ever; it caused quite a stir.

The road-killed wolverine was reconstructed by a local taxidermist and is on public display at the Wyoming Game and Fish regional office in Green River.

The 2004 Fossil Butte road kill, the 1998 sheep-killing wolverine reported east of Buffalo, Wyoming, one caught in a trappers snare twenty miles north of Cheyenne in 1996, and another recent accidental trapping in a foot snare near Menan, Idaho, all have one odd thing in common: they were in sagebrush desert, far from the high-elevation, snow-covered, mountainous terrain that typically defines the devil bear's habitat.

Experiencing and learning firsthand about rare wildlife in its natural habitat is something many in our urbanized society today are unfortunately unable to do. Chance sightings or interactions with uncommon wildlife can be treasured experiences. Encounters with rare or talismanic animals, such as wolverines, grizzly bears, mountain lions or wolves, are often described as "unforgettable" and "powerful experiences," sometimes even life altering or as having the power to influence the course of one's life.

Alta, Wyoming, is a small community of scattered residences and farms located along the foothills of the west slope of the Teton Mountains. It enjoys a world-class view of four Teton peaks—the timeless grandeur of Mount Owen, Teewinot, the Grand Teton, and the Middle Teton. The community supports an active 4-H club, the organization's motto being: "Head, Heart, Hands and Health for my club, community, country and my world."

The 4-H'ers "world," in Alta, includes the Teton Mountains just out their back door.

Around 1996, Dick Staiger, the leader of Alta's 4-H Exploring Natural Resources Club at that time, was looking for a project that would get members involved in wildlife management in a meaningful way. Staiger is a quiet, serious outdoor person who, had he been given a choice, would no doubt have rather lived in the nineteenth century in the fur trade era among mountain men. He is not someone you would be apt to call a "greenie." But to say Staiger dared to think big is a gross understatement. The usual Natural Resources Club projects having to do with monitoring deer or elk habitat did not spark his imagination. Instead he ruminated on whether there was someway his club could conduct a study to verify if wolverines actually existed in the Tetons.

The potential players for such a study were informally invited to a gathering at Dick's house. The alchemy of friends included Idaho Department of Fish and Game biologist Jeff Copeland, who, coincidentally, had done his graduate work on wolverines in central Idaho; Driggs, Idaho, resident Gary Lust, of Mountain Air Research, who did contract flying for wildlife telemetry studies; Don Betts, licensed veterinarian; Larry Williamson, the manager of Grand Targhee Ski Resort; and Rex Hibbert and Andy Heffron, outdoorsmen and parents of members of the Resource Club.

As the evening progressed some wine flowed and the wolverine study idea surfaced. Copeland advised on the need for a written plan clearly defining study methods and objectives, including a protocol outlining who would do what, when and how, to ensure consistency, and also the need for workable live traps. Betts agreed to do the surgical implants of the VHF transmitters and Mountain Air Research the telemetry flights. Grand Targhee Resort would provide use of its over the snow machines; Idaho Fish and Game and Wyoming Game and Fish would provide technical support and donate road-killed animals for trap bait; the 4-H parents and kids would build, set and monitor the traps ... and, importantly, also do fundraising for the project. The 4-H members went door-to-door generating local interest and raising money. It all came together informally as a multi-agency, community-member project.

At the time, only a few research studies had ever been conducted on wolverines in North America. The naysayers scoffed: how would untrained 4-H'ers do this project when professional biologists and scientists would be challenged to accomplish it? Hibbert's son, Kyle, later admitted, "My dad's coffee buddies bet him twenty dollars we wouldn't find any wolverines."

It was more than just a project; it was an adventure in the natural sciences that offered the potential to make an original contribution. The participants went to work building the required live traps, no easy feat in itself. Their design followed Copeland's, et al., "A Live Trap for Wolverine and other Forest Carnivores," *Wildlife Society Bulletin*, No. 23 (1995).

The traps were huge and heavy: seven-to-eight-feet long, three-to-four-feet wide, over three feet deep, made from six-to eight-inch-diameter lodgepole pine logs. The log box trap's lid was weighted with a concrete slab; it required a pole lever attachment for one person to raise all three-hundred pounds of it. It took weeks to construct the three curious contraptions.

One was built on-site, while the other two were assembled in the parking lot at Grand Targhee Resort.

In early winter, the box traps were hauled from the parking lot by over-the snow-machines to their separate pre-selected sites on the remote periphery of Grand Targhee Resort's permit area adjoining the Jedediah Smith Wilderness. The traps were initially baited and left open and unset in December; then in January 1998, they were re-baited and set to function. Access to the traps by that time had become no easy matter even with snow machines, because of bottomless, deep-powder snow.

The 4-H kids and their parents took on the responsibility of operating the traps and recording data. Each trap was fitted with a remote radio transmitter that could be monitored from the homes of the 4-H'ers. A motion-sensory camera was also installed at each trap. If an animal entered the trap and pulled on the chunk of bait meat, the lid would drop, trapping the culprit inside and activating the transmitter. The signal would be a call to mobilize and make a snowmobile trip to check the trap. Regardless if a signal was triggered or not, the traps and remote cameras were visited every three days to monitor conditions and any wildlife visits. Everything was carefully recorded in a log book.

The motion-sensory cameras showed the baited traps were visited by gray jays, magpies, ravens, long-tailed weasels, American martens, red foxes and coyotes. Marten and foxes were commonly caught. The captured non-target animals were released without handling. Later, in the second year of the study, an investigating grizzly bear tore one of the log traps apart, ate the bait and left. It was the first documentation of a grizzly bear in that part of the Tetons in nearly a century.

In the first winter, one of the trips to re-bait the traps in late January proved to be particularly exciting—what appeared to be wolverine tracks were discovered! The wolverine had investigated the trap, walked around it and left. The winter wore on somewhat routinely, however, without any more sign of the devil bear. Maybe it was true: *Gulo* was too clever to be live trapped.

In mid-March, when twelve-year-old 4-H member Ben Heffron came home from school, he tuned the receiver to check if any of the trap transmitters had been activated; there was a signal ... "beep, beep, beep." Following their study protocol, Ben and his father, Andy, prepared to check the trap. When they arrived at the ski resort and started out on the snowmobile toward the trap site, a virtual blizzard was raging—the kind of storm only the west slope of the Tetons' adiabatic forces can generate—and it was getting dark.

They parked the snowmobile near the trap. Any animal tracks that had been made were covered over by the snow. What animal would have been out in this kind of weather anyway? With the aid of a handheld light, they could see the trap lid was down. Putting on snowshoes, the Heffrons wallowed through the deep powder to the trap. From experience, they knew "when the animal in the trap was quiet, generally they had captured a fox; if there was a purring sound like an engine running, it was a marten." This time, however, they were met with "a deep, low-throated, grizzly-like growl." Ben later recalled, "It was a growl that could make you wet your pants; it was send-you-running-down-the-hill scary."

The trap was buried to the top in the deep snow. Ben was given the task of lifting the three-hundred-pound lid slightly by pulling down on the pole lever, while his father lay down in front of the trap to look inside with the flashlight in order to determine what kind of creature they had captured. When the lid was cracked opened, Andy Heffron found himself nose to nose with an infuriated skunk bear. It rushed toward him, huffing and snarling, he shouted to Ben, "Down, Down!" meaning for him to drop the trap lid. But in the excitement, Ben thought he meant to push down on the lever, further opening the lid. For an adrenaline-filled moment, Andy thought he was going to have the angry wolverine out of the trap and on top of him. The description—"whirling mass of teeth and claws"—flashed through his mind. It was the first wolverine *ever* to be live-trapped in Wyoming!

With aid of a cell phone, the Heffron's notified Staiger, who then called other members of the study: "We have a wolverine!" A joint decision was made by the study participants, they would wait until morning to process the wolverine.

Word quickly spread about the capture. Early the next morning, thirty community members, parents, 4-H'ers and biologists gathered at the site. Fifth and sixth graders were excused from school in Alta to see the rare animal and witness the procedure of removing the wolverine from the trap and surgically implanting it with a transmitter.

Copeland sedated the skunk bear with Telazol administered by a syringe on a "jab-stick." The wolverine turned out to be a three-year-old female weighing twenty-two pounds. She was measured, photographed, and ear tagged, and blood and tissue samples were collected. There was no indication that she had any kits. The biologists tagged her F468; the 4-H'ers dubbed her "Wolveranne."

Veterinarian Betts surgically implanted a VHF radio transmitter the size of a D-cell battery in Wolveranne. It was a forty-five minute operation. The sedated devil bear was then gently put back into the trap, heating pads were placed around her, and she was left to sleep off the sedation. Betts later remarked, "Pitbull dogs are mild-mannered creatures compared to an irate wolverine."

The 4-H'ers returned to the trap the next morning, Wolveranne was pacing inside, very much alive. When the lid was raised she sprang out of the trap and, with five-foot-long bounds that left a trail of billowing snow dust, she quickly vanished. The crew re-baited the trap and returned to the winter-long routine of monitoring the radios and checking the traps once every three days.

The capture of a single wolverine however, didn't prove the existence of a resident, reproducing population of skunk bears. It could have been a mere transient individual from a northern population just passing through. A new chapter in the study began: aerial tracking Wolveranne.

Strong radio signals several days later indicated she was alive and well, and on the move. That summer she roamed over an area twenty-five miles long by ten miles wide within the Teton Mountain Range. Her transmitter was capable of sending out signals for two years. It was hoped Wolveranne would eventually lead them to the holy grail of wolverine research: a den site.

At the time, only five birthing dens of wolverines had ever been found in North America. Studies involving those den sites and others in Scandinavia indicated that female wolverines can be very sensitive to disturbance during denning, birthing and until the kits are weaned at around ten weeks of age. The studies indicated they are apt to abandon the den sites if disturbed during this critical period.

The Alta 4-H'ers continued their trapping project in 1998-99, adding a fourth trap, which was made from a metal barrel. By then, the study participants had become well practiced. Amazingly, over the course of the second trapping season, two new wolverines were caught: a female, tagged F379, and a male, numbered M399, which the 4-H'ers named "Wolver-Dan." Both of these wolverines were also surgically implanted with VHF transmitters.

Not to be outdone, Wolveranne managed to get herself caught two more times over course of the season, too. It raised

The expansive realm of the wolverine on the west-slope of the Teton Mountains (photo by the author).

questions about the reputed cleverness of wolverines. Someone facetiously remarked, "Maybe she enjoyed the anesthetizing drugs." Her recapture allowed her original transmitter to be replaced with a new one.

Before the study, it was generally believed wolverines were solitary animals. But one of the times in April, when Wolveranne was recaptured and still in the trap, the remote cameras showed Dan was accompanying her. He remained at or near the trap with her after she was inside. He was even photographed standing on top of the trap, while Wolveranne was caught inside. Later, telemetry flights in May showed the two traveling together. It was believed their association was social, for purposes other than mating, on those occasions. This was the first report of wolverines traveling together outside of mating season.

While Wolveranne never did lead the researchers to discover a den site,it was now reasonably certain the Tetons provided habitat for a stable breeding population of skunk bears—a significant finding. The 4-H'ers had accomplished what they set out to do and more.

All during this time, too, the Exploring Natural Resources Club had been active in informing a local and nationwide public of their project. The 4-H'ers made national news. They conducted weekly presentations on wolverine ecology and their project for Grand Targhee Resort guests and other groups. The presentations were still continuing ten years later, taken over by new 4-H'ers. It's estimated over a thousand visitors to Grand Targhee Resort have learned about wolverines at these presentations.

Do folks in Wyoming have an appreciation for wildlife? The answer is an emphatic yes! The 4-H'ers exhibited their wolverine study display at the Teton County Fair, where normally you'd expect scrubbed hogs and currycombed heifers to prevail. Their project received the Grand Champion Award. At the Wyoming State Fair, it received Best of Show Award. It was selected as one of the six best 4-H natural resources projects in the country and was later awarded the best overall project at the sixty-fourth North American Wildlife and Natural Resources Conference in San Francisco. The University of Wyoming also selected the study as one of the top ten accomplishments in the State of Wyoming in 1998.

In 2000, the Alta 4-H group handed off the primary responsibility for the study to the Hornocker Wildlife Institute and The Wildlife Conservation Society. In 2001, their biologists captured an eleven-month-old male wolverine in the Teton Range. They labeled him M304. Wolverine M304 gained national notoriety for his amazing dispersal movements, traveling five hundred miles in seven weeks. In one nineteen-day junket, M304 journeyed south from Grand Teton National Park to a ridge east of Pocatello, Idaho, and back again to the Teton Range, a distance of 256 miles. A few days later, he headed north to Mount Washburn in Yellowstone National Park and then back again to the Tetons, a distance of 140 miles in seven days.

Wolverine M304 didn't settle down after its walk about. Over the next nineteen months, he was located by his VHF transmitter in other far-flung places encompassing eight different mountain ranges: Snake River, Portneuf, Washburn, Gros Ventre, Wind River, Salt River, and Centennial ranges located within Yellowstone National Park, Idaho, Montana and Wyoming. Major highways, rivers, agricultural areas, and lowland valleys, apparently were not impossible barriers for the devil bear.

M304's odyssey was cut short in January 2004, when he was "legally killed" by a trapper in the Montana portion of the Centennial Range. The Centennials can be a vital wildlife connector or corridor for the Greater Yellowstone ecosystem with wildlands in central Idaho.

The information gleaned from tracking M304 demonstrated wolverines function in low densities over incredibly large geographic areas. Indeed, in 2009 this was further confirmed when another rambling young male wolverine made national news. Tagged M56, he traveled over five hundred miles from Yellowstone and Grand Teton National Parks to Colorado, where he is now ensconced in Rocky Mountain National Park. It is known he successfully negotiated crossing I-80, a heavily trafficked highway, sometime between midnight and 4 a.m. early Saturday morning of Memorial Day weekend. Colorado has since proudly announced the first occurrence of a wolverine in the state since they were wiped out in 1919.

Similarly, in 2008, a motion-sensory camera captured an image of a wolverine on the Tahoe National Forest in the Sierra Nevada Mountains of California. The last Sierra wolverine was thought to have been killed in 1922 for use as a scientific specimen. Interestingly, DNA analyses of the new arrival's hair and scat show it to be most closely related to the Rocky Mountain wolverine populations. From the Rocky Mountains to the Sierras is a long and hazardous trek by any route for any wild animal, especially considering the man-made obstacles it would have to successfully navigate.

Studies have been initiated on wolverines in Glacier National Park in recent years, where it has been discovered six to ten skunk bears occupy a five hundred square-mile area. The findings have been rather astounding. They reveal wolverine parents may share responsibility for raising the young, and they confirm the amount of ground wolverines can cover is nothing short of phenomenal. Studies found they are capable of crossing the steep to vertical mountainous terrain comprising Glacier Park in several hours; something it would take very fit person days to do. Besides being an all-terrain machine, the wolverine is the ultimate ultra-marathoner, too.

In 2009, Wildlife Conservation Society wolverine expert Robert Inman estimated 250 skunk bears exist in the conterminous forty-eight states. Ten of those are believed to be in Grand Teton National Park. In the entire Greater Yellowstone region, fourteen are currently wearing radio collars; more are collared in Glacier National Park. Considering wolverines' ability to traverse large distances, they may hold the key to identifying the connecting corridors within and between mountain ranges and major ecosystems in the western United States.

Although the species must still be considered rare, the data suggests Gulo is making a gutsy return to some of its historical ranges within the conterminous western United States. A behind the scene story in the conservation of this far-ranging and uncommon beast is the little known fact that the Alta 4-H project was at the forefront of the current ongoing wolverine research. The 4-H'ers succeeded in making a major contribution to wildlife conservation because they refused to be intimidated by politics, science's "gatekeepers," and other naysayers.

The wolverine is frequently adopted as a symbol; it is a strongly totemic animal. In our contemporary culture, it is Michigan's state animal, although no wolverines have been recorded from there for over two hundred years. That is, until 2004, when one was confirmed near Ubly. Why the name "wolverine" was applied to Michigan residents is not certain, but some believe that when settlers moved into the state and began taking up the Native Americans' land, the Indians called them "wolverines," because in their minds it was the worst thing they could think to call anyone. George Armstrong Custer also called his Michigan Brigade the "Wolverines." It's also the University of Michigan's logo, the mascot of various cities and teams, and is used for business logos. Recently, in pop culture, it is the name for Hollywood's X-Man, appropriately, a character with superpowers.

But most of all, the wolverine remains an enduring symbol of deep wilderness. Knowing the wolverine is still out there in the twenty-first century, crossing remote snow-covered mountainous terrain in its relentless loping gait, inspires an untold confidence in the resilience of our natural world. The Den Dhaa' say, "His tracks go on and on, back to the time before people were living here."

Gray wolf portrait, a member of the Druid Pack from the Lamar Valley in Yellowstone National Park (photo by Judy Wantulok).

# 13

## The Pack's Memoirs

This is a two-part story, the first of which is told through the wolf, or wolves in general—the pack. The wolf recounts his origins, evolution, and the history leading up to the "wolf wars," and the unrelenting persecution and extirpation of wild wolves up until the beginning of postmodern society's changing perspective on wild canines.

In the second part, the Afterward, the author chronicles the story of the wolf's return and restoration in the Northern Rockies since the passage of the Endangered Species Act—the restoration's success, evolving management, conflicting politics, and ongoing controversy. The reader can assess where beliefs have changed in our postmodern society towards large carnivores; but also discover, there are parallels, events, opinions, and rhetoric that are being repeated today that are amazingly little changed from those of centuries ago.

# Part I

*How does a civilization exterminate a species, extinguishing a unique evolutionary lineage that trails back like paw prints in the sand for tens of thousands of years?*
—Michael J. Robinson, *Predatory Bureaucracy,* 2005

The pack's memoirs are a saga of evolutionary fitness, adaptation, and survival stretching far back into the murk of time. It's a tale of bold exploits, struggle, intrigues, travesties, and triumph spanning continents and wildernesses. In recent centuries, it is a story inseparable from the history of man's attitudes towards the pack.

My narrative reveals a great deal of irony, misunderstanding, and antipathy for us. Any errors and omissions in this chronicling, which relies upon history, biology, folklore, and reports recorded by human beings, are not the fault of us wolves but, rather, that of human memoirists. Where people have left written records, we wolves were able to write nothing at all. We have always communicated in very direct ways—scent marking, facial expressions, posturing, barking, yipping, snarling, and howling. It is a vernacular humans rarely understand.

When I speak of "the pack," it denotes my species or wolf packs everywhere in general; otherwise, if I mean a specific group of wolves, I will call them by their name, such as the Druid Pack or Hayden Valley Pack. Additionally, I have chosen to tell my story mostly in "the first person," as compared to merely being spoken of. Some may try to fault the telling of my story as wolfishly one-sided, brash, gruesome, or simplistic; and even question its veracity. Maybe that is to be expected; it is, after all, *my* story.

I can trace my ancestry back more than fifty million years in the fossil record. You would have recognized me in Eurasia nearly a million years ago: *Canus lupus*, the gray wolf. My progenitors migrated across the Bering Land Bridge to North American, long before the self-absorbed biped animal that calls itself "human" did. In fact, the genus *Homo,* only first appeared on Earth about two million years ago.

Calling us *gray* wolves seems somewhat of a misnomer. Gray is a common coloration, but my kin's pelage ranges in color from all shades of gray, tan, and brown to pure white or black. In relatively recent time, humans trained as zoologists, eager to demonstrate their scholarly attentiveness to morphological detail, described twenty-four subspecies of my kind; generally, five are commonly recognized today. Regardless, throughout thousands of years, I have remained recognizable simply as *the wolf.*

My kind roamed North America a very long time before our cousin, *Canus dirus*, the dire wolf, showed up and began pulling down camels. Our dire relative was larger, short-legged, slower and not as smart, if brain size is any gauge. Maybe the latter is why he was an inadvertent victim of the tar pits at La Brae.

Long ago, my clan coexisted with an extraordinary array of predators, as savage an assemblage of meat eaters the Earth has ever witnessed—American lion (much larger than today's mountain lion), saber-toothed cat, short-faced bear, dire wolf. We scavenged their kills—the Pleistocene mega-fauna: huge bison, mastodons, mammoths, camels, and wild horses.

Back then, we were not the top or "apex predator," an animal that preys on others but that no other animal preys upon. Our genetic memory is programmed from when we were potential prey also. It contributes to the protective cohesiveness of the pack and our wariness and cunning. Even today, if we are not vigilant, bears are still apt to dig our young out of the den and eat them. Moreover, in recent time, we were and frequently are still ruthlessly preyed upon by man.

When the Pleistocene mega-fauna began dying off beginning around sixteen-thousand years ago, our cousin the dire wolf could not adapt; he became extinct. What made us unique was our innate intelligence, remarkable physical ability and stamina, and the pack's social structure. We displayed flexibility and adaptability. The ever-changing dynamics of predator-prey relationships were a driving force in our evolution. My kind successfully ranged across nearly all habitats. We evolved different subspecies and ecotypes, but our ancestral type, *Canus lupus,* still remains recognizable, a biological template of great ecological success.

Across time, the territories of Neolithic and Paleolithic people and wolves overlapped. Our species had much in common. Both of us were social species, developing social hierarchies and affectionate relationships among our own kind. We shared the same habitats; both of us practiced communal hunting; we hunted the same prey; and both of us were highly territorial. Science later invented a term to describe the phenomenon: "convergent evolution." As predators, we resembled each other. Ours was a successful way for meat eaters to live.

At first, we did not purposefully hunt together, but we often discovered ourselves in close proximity during the chase for the same prey. All people were hunter-gathers back then. Commonly, we scavenged each other's kills. Fossil records show my bones in association with humans going back 100,000 years; and in North America, ten thousand years or more.

Eons ago, my whelps were taken from their dens and reared by humans. My pups were nursed alongside human babies; my kind were tamed and domesticated. People later named them *Canus lupus familiaris* or, more commonly, dogs. Humans conveniently forgot the biological origins of their pets, animals for which they display much fondness. Recently, it was indisputably established that the dog's original ancestor was none other than me, *Canus lupus,* the wolf. People only reluctantly accepted the truth after findings from DNA analysis left no doubt.

Humans and my tamed kin hunted side by side. They still do, as it is mutually beneficial. Man used our hunting and sensory abilities, and our agreeable and loyal nature—my instinct to bond with the pack—to their advantage. Those of us who submitted to them were employed as guard animals, beasts of burden, attack animals in war, and we were even used as a source of food and fur.

Ironically, humans have a deep distrust and dread that we might use them for food, too. My kind attacking or biting humans in North America is *extremely* rare, and then it is attributable to some anomaly, generally habituation or a wolf-dog hybrid. Only when my kind is crazed by a disease caused by the rabies virus are we likely to attack and maul people. But then, so do hydrophobic coyotes, foxes, skunks, and raccoons; and even humans themselves, if infected, also attack their own kind.

But inherently, humans are rarely satisfied or to be trusted; they are not of one mind, and they often react aggressively for reasons we wolves do not fully understand.

Since the Middle Ages, we wild canines have been categorized as vicious and ferocious by European man, but from our perspective, the menacing, droop-eared, hang-lipped, drooling mastiffs and wolfhounds that humans created for purposes of war and guard dogs are truly frightening and savage monstrosities—they are definitely "emissaries of terror." Many of my kind have been brutishly torn apart by such dogs simply for what some humans consider "sport."

It's ironic that humans strive to confirm and document incidents of aggression towards them by my kind but overlook the number of attacks, injuries, and deaths of people caused by their dogs, such as by Dobermans or pit bulls in urban settings. The odds that a human being will be attacked by a domestic canine in an urban or rural setting are infinitely greater than that of being attacked by any wild canines in the backcountry. Likewise, feral dogs kill nearly as much livestock as wild canines. I find it odd that postmodern humanity ignores those facts, persisting instead in fear mongering and embellishing worn folklore about the dangers of attack and destructiveness from wild wolves.

Native Americans were anthropomorphic and animistic in the way they viewed us and the natural world. Many tribes admired and revered us and sought to emulate us. The pack's behavior provided the perfect symbols for human social groups. They respected our stoicism and stamina. Warrior societies honored their clans by naming them after us; we symbolized courage and bravery. The Pawnee tribe especially identified with our kind, calling themselves the Wolf People. Both the Pawnee and Blackfoot Indians referred to the Milky Way in the night sky as the Wolf Trail, which they perceived to be the route to heaven.

I sense people today often have little appreciation or understanding for the basis of those characterizations by indigenous people. To many people nowadays we appear larger than life, but let me clarify. The pack was among the original hunters of bison on the North American plains. Members of my clan often weigh less than one hundred pounds, although the so-called "buffalo wolf," may have been on the average somewhat larger. Generally, we test for vulnerability before selecting our prey, since animals such as elk, moose and bison are formidably large and powerful. But can you imagine attacking a nine-hundred-pound moose or a two-thousand-pound bison if you weighed only ninety pounds? Little wonder Native Americans respected the pack's team work and bravery.

Those large herbivores are not defenseless. Members of the pack are frequently seriously injured—skulls fractured, ribs broken and legs shattered. In one recent study by humans, 51 percent of my kin had experienced and survived one or more of those kinds of traumatic injuries. The life and death contests we engage in with large, powerful prey require courage and teamwork, something indigenous people identified with and admired about us.

Even when we hunted among the abundant herds of antelope, elk, bighorn sheep and bison that formerly flourished on the Great Plains of North America, there was risk. An American artist named George Catlin once observed my kin attacking a lone male bison and he recorded two pack members were crushed to death by the hooves and horns of the enraged bull.

The pack's tolerable relationship with humans endured for tens of thousands of years, until two things appear in human history: agriculture and religion. The same two things often attributed to large-scale wars between humans. Our relationship with humans who took up farming and the shepherding of domesticated flocks deteriorated. The agriculturists no longer relied on the hunt. Instead they grazed domestic livestock within what was historically our habitat.

Humans extended their concept of territory to include property. They considered their livestock to be property. They began defending property like the pack defends territory. The pack has never adapted to man's concept of equating property to territory. Furthermore, humans adopted a belief that they hold dominion not only over livestock, but over *all* living creatures. Therefore, man considers the prey, which both of us might normally pursue, as uncompromisingly his alone. These strongly held homocentric beliefs of man have resulted in unreconciled conflict not only with us wolves, but with all wild creatures and the natural world in general.

For additional historical perspective, my story requires some asides from the continent of Europe, where at one time we enjoyed heroic stature, too. Legend says Romulus and

Remus, the founding heroes of ancient Rome, one of mankind's greatest civilizations, were raised by wolves. And, in the barbaric wilderness north of Rome, the vast Hercynian forest where pantheistic Germanic tribes practiced tree worship, people kept large wolf-like dogs. The pagans took them into battle with them against the Roman legions. To this day, the dog that bears the name German Shepard still has the greatest resemblance to me, the wolf, of any of my domesticated brethren. The practice continues into modern times. American's have employed this same breed of dog in guerilla warfare in the jungles of Vietnam and the mountains of Afghanistan. In Afghanistan in 2010, 315 military working dogs were employed in finding explosives and other missions.

At one time, Europe's pagans idolized us as companions of the gods. We were objects of worship for devotional cults of pantheists. Christianity's elders' waged war not only against the heathen worship of ancient oaks and groves, but against us wolves, too. The Church ordered the oaks felled, and my kind were demonized and labeled the Devil incarnate, "hell hounds." Our annihilation was demanded by the Church, which allowed no other gods. Our existence was proclaimed as proof that Satan walked the Earth.

The Church used the populace's fear, superstition and ignorance to advance its religion. Wolf-like creatures, such as The Beast of Gevauden, were alleged to have terrorized the common people; it was said to be punishment from God. In medieval Europe, night became known as the time of the Devil. People believed hominids took the form of wolves—werewolves, sinners transformed by God. Nowadays, those times are called the Dark Ages in human history. But those times still influence people's beliefs and attitudes towards the pack yet today.

Humans have recorded that the first organized "control" of my kind was, in fact, sponsored by the Church during the

Inquisition. The Church's influence was incredibly powerful. There are still many people today who fear werewolves—a study in 1992 showed 80 percent of Russian farmers surveyed believed in werewolves. The Church's negative influence towards the pack still echoes loudly in postmodern time.

It is doubtful the English colonists who settled in America were directly knowledgeable of such history. But the perceptions, superstitions and folklore they brought with them to the New World were strongly religious based and disavowing towards nature.

At first the colonists mistook the pack's "haunting and devilish" vocalizations for that of lions; they cowered fearfully at our howling. The colonists thought of themselves in terms of Biblical scripture: "innocent lambs" and "spiritual flocks," identifying themselves with animals we wolves were apt to prey upon. Their strongly held belief was that they had been sent forth "as sheep into the midst of wolves," symbolized as a struggle between civilization and wilderness. They further warned against "wolves in sheep's clothing." In their doctrine, my kind also served as a metaphor for corruption and everything evil; we were branded as "skulking criminals" and "voracious killers," not to be trusted. The green fire in our eyes symbolized the untamed New World, we frightened the colonists; and as you might imagine, the colonists frightened us, too.

Still, it has been discovered in the colonists' journals that they were not above scavenging our kills. It's a commonly accepted belief that the starving colonists relied on Native Americans to obtain food, but it's less well known that they also chased and clubbed the pack off of our kills and took the meat for themselves. The pilgrims' descendents have selectively failed to mention this in their Thanksgiving tradition. It seems ungrateful not to give thanks to the pack, too.

The wilderness that we came to symbolize was hated and feared by the English settlers. Incongruously, though, they built their settlements right up to the margins of deep forest and then turned livestock loose to graze unsupervised. They ignored the fact that it was our ancient habitat, territory long held by us and occupied by other wild creatures, too. They set the stage for our unhappy coexistence. In 1630, they took up the Old World practice of offering rewards for our scalps. The practice of paying bounties for killing wild canines spread up and down the East Coast among the colonies. The reward for killing one of my kind was forty shillings, the equivalent, I am told, of an entire week's wages for a farm laborer.

Interestingly, there are parallels in the settlers' treatment of us and that of Native Americans. The Indians often modeled their war cries after the pack's howling. The colonists declared them "more like wolves than men." The Euro-Americans eventually offered rewards for Indian scalps, too. The pack and aboriginal people became equivalents, both metaphorically and in reality.

The pack struggled as the Euro-American settlers devoured our ecological habitat and usurped our long-standing role as top predators. Puritan minister Cotton Mather set the moral tone and mission, exhorting his followers to make the "howling wilderness into a fruitful field" and to "clear the woods of those pernicious creatures." Pernicious was a fancy word for labeling us destructive, wicked and evil. North America's "wolf wars," a campaign that has continued for centuries, had begun.

Seventeenth-century Euro-Americans organized community "circle hunts," participated in competitions to gather the most wolf scalps, dug "pit-traps," laid snares and deadfalls, turned loose mastiffs trained to tear us apart, and put out baits in which barbed metal hooks, termed "wolf hooks," were fiendishly concealed. Death was not enough. When my brethren were destroyed, they nailed our severed and bloody heads to the town hall. Ironically and oddly, none of this sullied the Puritan reputation for pious somberness.

The circle hunts were macabre affairs. The participants carried burning torches and created a horrific din. While the hunts were ostensibly to rid the forest of the pack, not only was my kind slaughtered, but *all* the wild animals that had the misfortune to be encircled. Invariably, literally hundreds of deer were destroyed. The hunts were said to "tame the woods." Not that the settlers had the ecological acumen to plan it, but they wiped out our food source, the prey base. Yes, we killed and devoured colonists' livestock; to eat, we had little choice. It further intensified the European settlers' hatred and loathing for us.

Early Euro-American settlers were not apt to question their strongly held beliefs, but a century or two later, naturalist-philosopher Henry David Thoreau contemplated the ecological wreckage of the eastern woodlands and wrote: "When I consider that the nobler animals have been exterminated here—the panther, lynx, wolverine, wolf, bear, moose, deer, the beaver, the turkey, etc., etc.—I cannot but feel as I lived in a tamed, and as it were, emasculated country." Thoreau's sentiments no doubt puzzled most pioneers, who viewed the world much improved by the removal of wild animals.

Nowadays, there's a phrase biologists apply to describe predator behavior that entails killing more than can possibly be eaten: "surplus killing." Humans sometimes fault other predators, particularly wolves, for this behavior, but historically it is humans who have foremost engaged in the bloody practice, wiping out entire populations, driving species into extinction. We wolves cannot help but wonder why humans do not judge and describe their own actions and behaviors with the characterizations and rules they apply to other predators.

The colonists and early settlers fabricated outrageous tales about the pack, folklore that generated fear and revulsion for my kind. One frequently told story is about a settler and his family who, while traveling through the forest in an ox cart, were surrounded and attacked by wolves. The family knew the oxen were necessary for their survival, so the parents threw their children out of the cart one by one, until the blood- thirsty wolves were satiated. The remainder of the family was then able to proceed on through the forest. The name *sapiens* in *Homo sapiens* means "to know," but humans don't know; they actually believe such canards and passed them along from generation to generation. People formed their ideas about my kind from these fables, folklore and falsehoods, and unfortunately, frequently do so yet today.

While my kind was suffering the colonists' displeasure and cruelty, in the distant and surrounding unsettled wildernesses the pack continued to follow the natural rhythms of our prey's population cycles, evolved to overcome our prey's defenses and adaptations, and patterned their behavior and existence to that of our prey's migrations and seasonal changes, as we had done from time immemorial. For centuries, after the colonists' arrival, literally millions of my kind lived beyond settlements in a landscape suited to canine predators, coexisting with Native Americans on the western plains, prairies and mountains. Contrary to Euro-American myths, the herds of wild ungulates were not decimated by our presence and predation; instead, they thrived.

When the Euro-American hunters arrived, they trapped the beaver to near extinction and laid waste to the great herds of wild ungulates. After hide and market hunters had nearly eliminated the bison, they discovered a demand for our pelts. A pack member's hide fetched from seventy-five cents to a dollar.

The hunters' single-mindedly chose strychnine for its efficiency and ease in killing the greatest number of pack members possible. They began the insidious practice of lacing the carcasses of animals they killed with strychnine crystals. An enterprising factory in Pennsylvania, and later New Mexico, took advantage of the demand for the poison and mass produced it.

Strychnine is tasteless, colorless and odorless. It is a very potent poison, only a small amount is needed. Its victims experience severe muscle spasms and contractions, along with convulsions and seizures leading to internal organ damage and brain death. It works quickly; it can kill a pack member in minutes. Rarely, a very cautious wolf may survive by quickly disgorging it.

The pack had learned to follow the boom of the hunter's Sharps rifle to scavenge carrion, which at times littered the plains. It is no exaggeration that my kin were poisoned by the hundreds of thousands. Not only were our dead scattered across the prairies, but also bears, bobcats, badgers, coyotes, ravens, magpies, foxes, wolverine, and eagles; the bodies of any and all wild creatures that fed on meat. People sometimes refer to the plains and prairies as "empty," but before the Euro-Americans emptied them, the land was filled with wildlife. Those of us who survived learned to eat only what we killed, or else we were fortunate to have inhabited remote regions overlooked by the traffickers of death.

Historians have lauded the hunters for clearing the way for westward European expansion. Settlers swarmed across the country in the nineteenth century. They brought along their Puritan ancestors' antipathy towards nature, and the folklore, meanings, and methods for dealing with predators—Old World baggage. Nothing wild or native that they encountered was considered sacred in the westward march of progress. It was deemed Manifest Destiny. Native Americans and wild animals, especially the pack and other predators, were viewed as impediments to be overcome. The coexistence of predators and civilization was deemed to be antithetical.

The pack observed that an effective means humans use to assassinate the character and reputation of their own kind is to characterize them as wolves. When a religious group identifying themselves as The Church of Jesus Christ of Latter Day Saints was driven out of Illinois in the late 1840s, they were called "wolves" by their detractors. A mob gathered for what it claimed was to be "a great wolf hunt," although everyone knew what they were really planning to hunt was the Saints.

The Saints learned first hand what it was like to be persecuted similar to wolves. Their prophet Joseph Smith preached that the Saints "were not to kill any animals ... or anything created by Almighty God that had life, simply for the sake of destroying it." Given those experiences and teachings, the pack was expecting the Saints might be inclined to practice tolerance for wild creatures.

However, when the Saints reached the promised land of Utah, or what they first called Deseret, they disregarded Smith's admonition against killing animals simply for the sake destroying them. Instead, they adopted the old Biblical symbolism of identifying themselves as the Lord's flock and as innocent lambs, while wolves were once again cast in the role of the Devil. In 1886, they organized a "wolf-killing competition" between two teams of hunters in the Utah Territory. Together, the two teams reportedly exterminated 1,114 wild canines.

The pack recalls that as early as 1877, ungulate carcasses in Yellowstone National Park were being poisoned with strychnine by "freelance wolfers." Humans who preyed upon us called themselves "wolfers." The park was declared to be a "pleasuring ground" for people, but it was a "killing ground" to wild animals. Already in 1880, Park Superintendent Colonel Philetus Norris noted with satisfaction that "the easy slaughter of wolves with strychnine-poisoned carcasses has nearly led to their extermination." From 1860 through 1900, it has been estimated that as many as two million of my kind were destroyed across the West

Some of us managed to avoid the wolfers' baits and traps and others managed to disgorge the poison and learned from the experience. You might have thought it was enough that only relatively small numbers of us remained. Many wild animals, not only predators, had been hunted to near extinction, ironically not by the pack or other predators, but by humans.

By the late nineteenth and early twentieth century, when the once-great numbers of prey—deer, elk, bison, wild sheep—had been brought to the brink of extinction by sport and commercial hunting, humans blamed us for it. We were made scapegoats for their "surplus killing."

People demanded our complete eradication. In 1915, the Yellowstone Park superintendent labeled us wolves "a decided menace," and in 1919, the park reported, "concentrated efforts to *exterminate* wolves had been mounted" (my emphasis). In 1922, a park report stated, "It is evident that the work of controlling wolves must be vigorously prosecuted by the most effective means available." In the years from 1914 to 1926, over 136 of my kind were hunted down and killed within the park. They said people came to the park to see "nice animals, like deer," not dreadful fanged creatures.

If we were not even allowed to exist within the park, where could we live?

In 1916, the pack recalls, zoologist Joseph Grinnell (George Bird Grinnell and Joseph were distant cousins, both

were biologists; Joseph developed the theory of ecological niche)
was the first person to propose preserving carnivores within the
National Parks.

He was alone with that idea, it went nowhere at the time.
Still, Yellowstone Park was only a reflection, a small microcosm,
of the anti-predator sentiment, compared to what existed in that
era. The last remnant bands of wild ungulates were driven to
retreat into the remotest reaches. Ranchers and farmers moved
livestock onto the plains and into the mountain valleys to take
advantage of the cheap and abundant grazing. In a matter of
decades, not even a blink in evolutionary time, the natural prey
that the pack had interacted and evolved with for eons was
nearly completely gone.

Settlers, farmers, ranchers and livestock spread across
the land. Droves of horses, lowing cattle and bleating sheep
suddenly appeared where only a short time before there had
been wild herds. In the history of the evolution of my kind one
thing stands out, our ability to adapt. With our natural prey base
mostly gone, not unlike what occurred in the eastern forests two
centuries earlier, we turned to open-range livestock in order to
eat. It was an unforgivable transgression in the minds of the
agriculturists, who had taken over proprietorship of the land.
The war against us geared up.

Back in New England, the deeply rooted aversion to what
the pack represented was still recalled, passed down through
generations. In 1913, the community of Lancaster, New
Hampshire, sited a monument of a wolf sitting atop a boulder
on the green between their church and library. At first glance, it
appears to be a tribute to the pack, until one reads the statue's
brass plaque:

The monument commemorates the town founders for
"redeeming Lancaster from the wilderness." From a wolf's
perspective, it's hard to get one's mind around the wording in that

dedication. It means the townspeople believed their ancestors literally *saved the town from the wilderness.* They didn't say carved it out of the wilderness but, rather, saved, recovered or rescued it from wilderness. Obviously, the pack symbolized the wilderness they saved or rescued it from.

---

**1763-1913**

"To honor the brave men and women who redeemed Lancaster from the wilderness, this memorial was erected by their loyal sons and daughters on the 150th anniversary of the founding of the town, July 6, 1913."

---

Wild animals were viewed by the Euro-Americans as valuable only to the extent they served man's needs. The word "vermin" originated in England—what was not game, was considered vermin or varmints, especially those animals that competed with man. The pack was declared to be the worst of all vermin, a scourge. What continued to play out as a result, from the pack's viewpoint, was a form of ecological chaos.

In 1885, the federal government had established the U.S. Bureau of Biological Survey, not ostensibly to kill predators at first but, rather, to research birds and insects. As wealthy livestock owners demanded more grazing ranges and extended their influence over policy makers in Washington, D.C., the bureau's primary role became shifted to predator control. By the twentieth century, a new office of the Survey had been created, the Predatory Animal and Rodent Control Branch, later renamed the Bureau of Animal Damage Control; and again, later, Wildlife Services. The bureau advertised itself as the "predator's nemesis."

We wolves were targeted in particular. Stock owners complained the ranges were "infested" with our kind. Even Theodore Roosevelt, whom people applaud as a leading conservationist of the time, declared us to be "the beasts of waste and destruction." The Biological Survey proclaimed the elimination of the wolf was "the paramount objective of the government." The U.S. Forest Service jumped into the fray to appease its livestock-grazing permittees and rural community leaders and, not so altruistically, to line their organization's budgets with monies western congressmen were generously allocating for predator control.

The fledgling Forest Service teamed up with the Biological Survey to remove the pack from millions of acres of national forest and range lands. The Forest Service issued leghold traps to their rangers, and they published and widely distributed *Wolves in Relation to Stock, Game and the National Forest Reserves*, a 31-page booklet on how to trap, poison, and hunt my kind; and how to find and excavate the dens where our pups were hidden.

At the 1899 Annual Convention of the National Livestock Association held in Denver, the need for the destruction and extermination of the pack headed the list of topics. In the opening invocation, Reverend Dean M. Hart, urged attendees to "use the forces of nature to their benefit" and to "subdue the Earth." The ranchers hardly needed the reverend's blessing. Any livestock found dead by ranchers in those days were baited with strychnine; the bounties the agriculturist's collected on my kin's scalps compensated them for any of their losses.

Human beings' irrational hatred for my kind had no bounds, nor did their cruelty. If similar atrocities had been directed at a race of people instead of our species, it would have been labeled genocide by historians. We were persecuted beyond belief. A massive campaign was mounted, not just intended to control the pack, but to eradicate my species. Wolfing—the killing of wolves—was elevated to a profession; bounties reached their zenith; strychnine-poisoned meat lines up to one-hundred-fifty miles long were laid out. My kind were poisoned, shot, trapped (the No. 4 1/2 Newhouse trap came with a booklet on "How to Catch Wolves"), clubbed, torn apart by packs of dogs, blown apart by set guns, dug from our dens, had our dens dynamited, were roped from horses, had our jaws wired shut and then turned loose, set on fire, and were inoculated with mange and turned loose with the intent that we would spread the disease to other members of the pack. From a wolfish standpoint, it was a singularly shameful blot on human nature and the country's character.

Government sponsored elimination of my kind was effective. Based on paid bounties, in the state of Montana from 1883 through 1918 alone, 80,730 pack members were destroyed. By 1914, western states were paying over a million dollars a year in predator bounties. In 1923, the Biological Survey spread strychnine-laced fat balls across thirteen million acres in Arizona alone. Bounties of up to $150 were offered by Stock Growers Associations, a huge amount of money in those years. It is obvious in retrospect that something more than economics—something, as one person termed it, in "the spooky regions of the human psyche"—appeared to be driving human beings in their single-minded efforts to destroy my kind.

There was a lot of monetary incentive and local prestige for hunting and killing wild canines. Many amateur hunters and trappers attempted to take advantage of the "easy money" only to find the last of my kin had become extremely wary. Someone invented the name "super wolves" for our legendary survivors. We were attributed supernatural powers, and human beings began to gain some appreciation for our intelligence and adaptability. In the face of the relentless persecution, some might characterize our fight to hold on as heroic.

T.B. Bledsaw and other government hunters for the U.S. Forest Service pose with their January 1914 catch of wolves from Arizona's Kaibab National Forest (photo courtesy of the Arizona Historical Society, Barnes Collection, AHS-5929).

The famed professional wildlife bounty hunter Ben Corbin justified his actions against us by labeling the pack "the enemy of the state." He claimed to have killed more wolves than any man alive. Our final destruction was orchestrated by a combined and concerted effort of the federal government, livestock growers, sport hunters and professional bounty hunters; people termed it an "anti-vermin alliance."

From 1915 to1925, more than 5,000 wolves were reported "killed and scalped" by just government hunters alone. The last pack member inside Yellowstone National Park was killed in 1926. Two of my kin still roamed Jackson Hole in 1928, but they soon disappeared. From 1900 through the1940s, the wolfers wiped out my kind from nearly every region in the conterminous U.S. The so-called "greatest wolfer of all times," Bill Caywood, was lauded in *Outdoor Life* magazine as being "so good at his job that there's almost no job left."

In the end times, in 1929, the chief of the Division of Predator and Rodent Control in the Bureau of Biological Survey, Stanley P. Young—later referred to by one writer as "the high priest of obliteration"—who had begun his career with the bureau as a government trapper, and Arthur Carhart, ironically best known for his wilderness recreation advocacy, published *The Last Stand of the Pack*. The book was a compilation of embellished tales, romanticizing the hunting and destruction of the last wolves and the professional bounty hunters who pursued us. Based on its sales, the book produced a yawn for most people at the time. By then, the majority of people lived in cities, and for the most part, they were not personally engaged in or even aware of the ongoing predator wars; although they were financially supporting it through their taxes.

### Roll Call of Legendary Wolves in Random Order

Old Three Toes–Harding County, South Dakota
Two Toes–North Park, Laramie Range, Colorado
Custer Wolf–Custer, South Dakota
Rags the Digger–Cathedral Bluffs, Colorado
Old Lefty–Burns Hole, Colorado
The Syca Wolf–Southern Oregon
The Queen or Unaweep Wolf–west-central Colorado
The Ghost or White Wolf–Judith Basin, Montana
Spring Creek Wolf–Club Ranch, Colorado
Spring Valley Wolf–northern Arizona
Old Aguila–Arizona
Old One Toe–north of Wickensburg, Arizona
The White Lobo–Texas
Las Margaritas–northern Mexico
      (a last outlaw wolf, taken in 1970)
Bigfoot–Lane County, Colorado
Cody's Captive–Cheyenne, Wyoming
The Greenhorn Wolf–Pueblo, Colorado
Mountain Billy–Medora, North Dakota
Old Whitey–Bear Springs Mesa, Colorado
The Pine Ridge Wolf–southeast South Dakota
Pryor Creek Wolf–southeast Montana
Split Rock Wolf–west-central Wyoming
Three Toes–Apishapa, Colorado
The Traveler–Arkansas
The Butchering Wolf–Colorado
The Truxton Wolf–Pine Ridge, South Dakota
Bearpaw Wolf–east of Glacier National Park, Montana
      (another last outlaw, taken in 1981)

## A Sampling of Celebrated Wolf Bounty Hunters

William Casto
William Caywood
Ben Corbin
Roy T. McBride
S.A. McIntyre (Rattlesnake Jack)
Albert McIntyre (Rattlesnake Jack Jr.)
Hegewa A. Roberts
Roy C. Spangler
Monte Wallace
Harry P. Williams
Stanley P. Young

Carhart and Young's *Last Stand* tales mirrored naturalist Ernest Thompson Seton's "Lobo, the King of Currumpaw" story. In their accounts, outlaw wolves became anti-heroes who achieved a kind of legendary infamy. Seton wrote, "They seemed to possess charmed lives, and defied all manner of devices to kill them." After my above recounting, would you truly consider any wolf's life "charmed"?

Humans' romanticized stories about the last of my kind were self-serving, a form of advertising and lobbying. The narratives justified and celebrated federal predator control; they impressed western livestock owners, congressmen, and bureaucrats, which helped to assure that the Biological Survey's budget requests were met. But the "last wolf" stories backfired in an unintended way as we shall explain.

When the pack was nearly vanished, only "lone wolves" were purported to remain. These "super wolves" made the Survey's work seem even more imperative. While entire communities pursued the "renegade wolves" by any and all means, stock growers became convinced running down the last of the wily marauders was a fulltime job for professionals, not part-time amateurs. It was true, the last of my kind were remarkably cagey and savvy. Admittedly, amateur hunters in those days posed a relatively minimal threat to them.

Hunting down the last "outlaw wolves" assumed the overtones of the era's FBI fight against gangsters. Like John Dillinger, Dutch Shultz, and Bonnie and Clyde, the last of my kind were played up as doomed, yet heroic, outlaws. Humans celebrated them, but fatalistically acknowledged they were all damned to perish as the government agents closed in and hunted them down. The *Denver Rocky Mountain News* headlines read: "U.S. Agents Stalk Desperadoes of the Animal World."

A South Dakota newspaper described one particular kin of mine—the Custer wolf—as "the cruelest, the most sagacious and most successful animal outlaw... the master criminal of the animal world." For nine years, the Custer wolf managed to survive and outwit the hunters and trappers who pursed him. By that time, people attributed him "all the qualities of the werewolf of Old World legends." Government hunter Harry P. Williams was finally enlisted. It took Williams nearly eight months to run the "renegade" down. The headline on a January 17, 1921 U.S. Department of Agriculture four page press release describing the end of the chase read: "Master Criminal of the Animal World Dead." A South Dakota newspaper likewise announced: "World's Greatest Animal Criminal Dead." Larger in life, he weighed only ninety-eight pounds.

The last ragtag remnants of my kind resembled a defeated force. They exhibited in their scars, wounds and behaviors, a prolonged history of surviving adversity. One of my kin, the Greenhorn Wolf, for example, had managed to escape from traps on both her front feet, had disgorged poisons, and survived being shot, before finally being fatally poisoned from baits carefully laid by government hunter Bill Caywood. Humans reported she was eighteen years old and toothless. The word survivor is from the Latin *supervivere*, meaning to live a "super-life." But in reality, my kind only lived the life of a wolf; it is the only way we know, it is the way the creator intended for us to be.

The social structure of the packs was destroyed. The final survivors had all experienced narrow escapes with death; nearly all had been maimed by traps, bullets or poisons; they were missing toes, paws, teeth or tails. All were accused of unforgivable misdeeds and were allegedly responsible for vast numbers of livestock deaths and huge financial losses suffered by ranchers. Some people would later recognize we preyed on livestock because most of us were no longer physically capable of catching wild prey, if there were any wild prey to be found at all. The ranges were invariably monopolized and overgrazed by domestic livestock, and literally all wild animals had been methodically removed.

You might think in telling this story from my perspective that I exaggerate, but even potential small prey were cleared from the land. The agriculturists and Biological Survey declared them "pests." In 1924, the Survey reported farmers and stockmen cooperated in organized poisoning, trapping and gas attacks to clear 12,000,000 acres of federal and 105,000,000 acres of state and private lands of all "disease carrying rodents and pests"—prairie dogs, ground squirrels, pocket gophers, jack rabbits, woodchucks, field mice, and cotton and kangaroo rats. In Utah alone, cooperating ranchers systematically covered 128,220 acres with poison and reportedly eliminated 340,500 jackrabbits in what was termed "the greatest rabbit war yet staged." It was a biological holocaust. As you might imagine, there were unintended ecological consequences. One of those was the near extinction of the black-footed ferret.

The last of my kin were beleaguered, harassed and relentlessly pursued. Contrary to the colorful tales, the last of us wolves were a bedeviled and besieged lot, desperately trying to evade being killed. We displayed an extraordinary tenacity for life. Death was not enough; many of the last wolves were tortured regardless of the submissive behaviors they showed their captors. Humans mistook our behavioral communications of submission as a sign of cowardice. They sparred none of us. As a final epitaph, Bureau Chief Stanley Young proclaimed, "There is no place in today's civilization for the gray wolf except in fur shops, museums and zoos."

Oddly, no sooner was the last "cunning, but doomed renegade" brutally sent loping across the great divide than some people experienced regret; they realized an era had passed. The destruction of the pack and the killing of the last wolves in Colorado and Wyoming in 1943 produced nostalgia. Vanished from the mythical West were not only wolves, but the bison, Indians, wilderness and the tough men that had been required to master them. Of course, at the time, it was not necessarily the pack itself that people missed but, rather, all we symbolized.

Around this time, a hopeful ray of enlightenment appeared within the National Park Service in the personage of a young biologist, George M. Wright. We wolves applaud Wright's contribution: he recognized the importance of all wildlife in the National Parks. Like Joseph Grinnell, years earlier, he proposed the restoration of predatory species. Not that American citizens and the government bureaucracy reversed their mindset and overnight jumped to implement his concept, the idea was revolutionary and counter to all that had come before.

Wright was among the first humans to champion the pack publicly. Unfortunately, for us and the American people, he suffered an untimely death in an automobile accident in 1936. Without his energetic personality and leadership his wildlife programs and ideas languished. However, along the way, Wright had hired a biologist by the name of Adolf Murie, who also proved himself a maverick when it came to conventional wisdom.

Our species is indebted to Adolf for his studies in Alaska's Denali National Park, *Wolves of Mount McKinley* (1944). Murie was the *first* human being to study us in our natural habitat. You might say, he was a type of lone wolf in his field. We would make him an honorary pack member, if posthumously, we wolves could. Changes in America's attitudes and tolerance towards the pack that exist today, took root from seeds of biological wisdom sown by him. As a scientist he was objective and conscientious, and he possessed professional integrity.

Adolph discovered and published the fact that the Dall sheep we preyed upon were mostly the weak and least fit animals, and that we actually helped to regulate the health of ungulate populations. It was contrary to the prevailing orthodoxy; it outraged sport hunters. They denounced Murie and his research findings, and they further cursed the pack, too. But Adolf persevered and the pack is beholden. His work ultimately led to the termination of predator control within Denali and Yellowstone National Parks.

Aldo Leopold was a forester twice employed by the U.S. Forest Service. In his early years, he was an enemy of predators. As Aldo matured intellectually, he found himself at odds with his stubbornly utilitarian agency and resigned. In 1949, he wrote *A Sand County Almanac*. His "Thinking Like a Mountain" essay in the *Almanac* was an allegory about the pack and his predator control days within the Forest Service in Arizona and New Mexico. In the essay, he described watching the "fierce green fire" dying in one of my kin's eyes after she had been shot. He wrote, "... there was something new to me in those eyes—something known only to her and to the mountains."

Leopold's essay at first glance appeared to be another "last of my kind story," but it went deeper, it was also "a truth recognized." Out of the ashes of the pack, the green fire of Leopold's wolf's final gaze ignited people's nostalgia, their sympathy, and the science of ecology into an environmental movement that spread across America. We wolves stand as the movement's symbol. Perhaps it is possible yet that someday people will view us not as evil and symbols, but more for what we are: wolves, a natural part of a functioning ecosystem—a creature who is precisely how the creator intended for us to be.

## Part II - Afterward

*This call to arms against [the wolf] is in part a fear of letting the wild back into Western lands.*
—Timothy Egan, 2009

The continuing extinction of North America's living things— the Carolina parakeet, eastern cougar, eastern elk, passenger pigeon, and others—spurred the 1973 passage of the Endangered Species Act. The gray wolf, *Canus lupus,* had the dubious distinction of being foremost on the endangered list. It opened a new chapter for the wolf in the conterminous United States; a chapter whose outcome has yet to be fully determined.

At the time, wolves persisted only on Isle Royale, the Upper Peninsula in Michigan, and in northern Minnesota in the lower-48. In the Northern Rockies, the closest wolves were believed to reside two hundred miles to the north in Jasper National Park, Canada.

In 1980, a wolf showed up near the Bear Paw Mountains east of Glacier National Park—undoubtedly a dispersing Canadian gray wolf, a lonely vanguard attempting to reoccupy ancestral habitat. He was named the Bear Paw wolf; allegedly he killed some livestock.

A wolf pack on the move across the Yellowstone National Park landscape (photo by Judy Wantulok).

For over a year, Bear Paw displayed an uncanny ability to evade traps and hunters. He was a virtual reincarnation of a lone "renegade" from out of the past. There was concern that Bear Paw could derail plans for wolf recovery in the lower-48.

The U.S. Fish and Wildlife Service called in the Biological Survey's Branch of Animal Damage Control—since renamed Wildlife Services—to deal with Bear Paw. To discourage any claims of impropriety, the Fish and Wildlife Service disingenuously declared him not to be a wolf, but rather, a "wolf-dog hybrid," so that he was not protected by law. Government agents located his tracks and pursued him by aircraft across snow-covered terrain for fifteen miles before killing him. Laboratory analysis confirmed he was a male wolf, not a hybrid.

While there are many opponents of the Endangered Species Act, there are also others who would like to see it made stronger. They criticize it as being a "last-ditch approach." A species must be in serious trouble before anything is done to protect it, and then it is generally a piecemeal, single-species effort, not a holistic ecosystem approach.

Nevertheless, listing the wolf did dampen its relentless persecution. In 1994, twenty years after the Act's passage, forty-eight wolves comprising six different packs had returned to their old hunting grounds in northwestern Montana.

Conservationist and writer Renee Askins was a fierce advocate for wolf restoration in Yellowstone. She was helped by another driving personality behind wolf restoration, biologist John Weaver. Askins was an otherwise gentle spirit and compassionate person, who bravely championed the wolf. In her own words, "she gave her heart to working for wolves and the wild."

Askins founded the Wolf Fund in 1986 and traveled and lectured extensively on behalf of wolf restoration. Her campaign was very popular with the American public, but it aroused incredible rage among anti-wolf factions. Despite having to endure political manipulation and death threats, she and her colleagues successfully completed their mission.

In 1995-96, seven decades after the last wolf had been banished from Yellowstone National Park, and after years of intense controversy, litigation, and intrigue, sixty-six gray wolves were captured and transported from their Canadian homes to the unoccupied former haunts of wolves within Yellowstone, and the Frank Church River of No Return Wilderness and Nez Perce Indian Reservation in central Idaho. The environment statement for wolf recovery had received 160,000 public comments, the majority of which favored the wolf's reintroduction.

Regardless, the Wyoming Farm Bureau Federation, affiliated organizations, and others, such as the Wyoming Wolf Coalition, have doggedly continued to litigate and demand reversal of the wolf's reintroduction. They argue, among other things, that the introduction of "non-native Canadian gray wolves" violated requirements of the Endangered Species Act. Fifteen years later those opponents of the reintroduction are still insisting the wolves be euthanized or somehow rounded-up and removed.

On-the-other-hand, the Nez Perce held a welcome ceremony for the wolves. Tribal Elder Horace Axtell gave a blessing: "We ask the Creator that wolves may be allowed to run free again, that they be able to live, to be a part of us, to be a part of the land, to be a part of the creation for which they were intended." Wolf packs could be heard howling their applause in long and graceful choruses.

Being captured in snares, tranquilized and transported was no doubt a harrowing experience for the wolves. In Yellowstone National Park they were first held in enclosures to acclimate them—"a soft release." When they were released, the wolves found themselves in unoccupied historic habitat filled with natural prey that had become naive and unsuspecting. Initially, it was as good as it gets for wolves—a virtual paradise for them.

By 2009, the wolves' numbers in Wyoming, Montana, Idaho, including pack members that dispersed into Washington and Oregon, had grown to 1,706 in 115 breeding packs. But also by 2009, a self-regulating mechanism appeared to kick in. Their population growth had slowed to less than 4 percent, indicating a leveling off in respect to available habitat.

The adaptability, intelligence and biological fitness of wolves once again proved impressive, so much so, it alarmed and frightened some people. The drumbeat for their control began to be sounded loudly. However, Montana Senator Conrad Burns' earlier fear mongering, "Mark my words ... there'll be a dead child within a year," had not come to pass.

Since the wolf reintroduction some people have fearfully worried about being attacked—"gobbled up" as one distraught person put it. However, there is no record of anyone ever being attacked or killed by healthy wolves in the western United States. Conversely, dogs reportedly bite about 5 million people and kill 10 to 15, usually small children, in the United States annually. Likewise, feral dogs also kill large numbers of wildlife and livestock. The federal Wildlife Services wiped-out 87,000 coyotes in 2006, but they killed only 512 dogs. Incongruently, offending dogs are apt to be simply captured and placed in animal shelters, whereas, similar wrongdoing by wild canines makes major news and their eradication is pursued by all means.

The lives and behaviors of different pack members have been closely monitored since their homecoming. A great deal has been learned, including even the detailed history of some individual wolves' lives. We could assemble another roll call of legendary wolves since their reintroduction, but this time the reasons for them achieving distinction are different from the past.

Historically, wolves achieved notoriety and condemnation for killing livestock for their cunning ability to avoid being killed or captured. This time, however, more than seventy years later, they are frequently characterized in more positive and heroic ways, earning reputations and fame for distinguished behaviors contributing to the success of the restoration and recovery program. In the words of Yellowstone Park's chief wolf biologist, Douglas Smith, wolves have "an incorrigible and incorruptible spirit." That characterization reflects a marked change in many people's perceptions and attitudes.

If we were to designate legendary nominees, certainly deceased wolf R10, a dramatically "bold, authoritative and confident" black alpha male, and his inherently "very cautious" mate, alpha female R9, would be among the first to be considered for a contemporary roll call of famous wolves.

In April 1995, not long after R10 was released in Yellowstone National Park, Chad McKittrick senselessly shot and killed him near Red Lodge, Montana. The alpha male and his mate were seeking a denning site at the time.

Biologists had high expectations for R10 in the recovery effort. He was an impressive example of his species. McKittrick testified he killed R10 with a "borrowed rifle," apparently so that his weapon wouldn't be confiscated.

Publicity surrounding the alpha male's wanton destruction resulted in a public outcry; R10 achieved a type of martyrdom. McKittrick received a six-month jail sentence, a $10,000 fine, and had his hunting privileges revoked for two years for his singularly reprehensible act. It was unprecedented and sent a message that the federal government would indeed protect our presence under the law.

The Farm Bureau Federation jumped on-board the McKittrick hearings, too, using the opportunity as an intervener essentially to again argue the illegality of introducing non-native wolves from Canada and making a show of demanding the removal of the reintroduced wolves.

Was McKittrick's sentence justice? Not entirely. The court recognized he was indigent, so he never paid his fine; supposedly, he did serve three months of his jail sentence. Afterward, McKittrick had the audacity to ride horseback in Red Lodge's Fourth of July parade, flaunting his killing of R10 and breaking of the law, while unsavory cronies cheered him as a celebrity.

Between 1995 and 2004, at least thirty more pack members, which were supposedly protected under federal law, were illegally killed. Some people say wolves are not to be trusted, but those same people proved that they themselves could not be counted on to obey their own laws. The McKittrick incident is not without irony, since it generally has always been the wolves that are labeled "outlaws."

Author Steve Nicholls' in *Paradise Found: Nature in America at the Time of Discovery* characterizes such people as "misfits who are frustrated by the world around them," and that "their ancestors obtained the land by slaughtering the bison, Indians, and wolves, in the first place, and they appear to believe more killing can maybe get it back for them." For them, killing wolves is a type of "redress for other problems." Bumper sticker's boast: "Wolves–Government Sponsored Terrorists" or "Smoke a Pack a Day." While it is true, wolves prey on other animals, they are not motivated by hate.

Nature's retribution for McKittrick's unlawful act occurred that spring when R10's mate gave birth to a litter of eight puppies. What happened to R10's progeny? Four years afterwards, genetic studies showed 79 percent of all wolves in Yellowstone at that time were related to the alpha-female R9.

No one ever predicted that observing wolves in their natural habitat—"wolf-watching"—would become such a popular activity.

Tens of thousands of people have enjoyed the activity, observing the interaction of wolves with their natural habitat and other animals. During the fourteen years the Druid Pack inhabited the Lamar Valley in Yellowstone National Park more than 100,000 people viewed them.

At its peak, the Druid Pack boasted thirty-seven members. People were in awe of them. Several film documentaries were produced about the Druids. Their presence has had significant economic benefit for the gateway communities surrounding the park. It's reported that visitors who specifically want to see wolves have generated $35.5 million in annual revenue for the three states surrounding Yellowstone National Park. People have traveled from all parts of the world for the opportunity to watch, photograph, and study them. There's obviously a great divergence between those people and persons who think and act like McKittrick.

People observing the Druid Pack recorded complex social interactions between wolves that had never been seen before. For example, in one unprecedented case, the Druids allowed researchers to witness a "six-hour-long ritual song and dance" that they performed, culminating in a new wolf's acceptance as the breeding alpha-male. The wolves continue to reveal sentient and social behaviors that previously were not fully appreciated by mankind and science.

It is believed that wolves generally self-regulate their populations based on territory, available prey, and other natural phenomenon. Their numbers within Yellowstone National Park have declined for the past two years in a row suggesting the population may be stabilizing in relation to the existing prey base. But dispersing pack members are frequently thwarted in their attempts to find new territory. With the march of "human progress"—the ever-burgeoning human population, expanding residential subdivisions, more highways, farms, ranches, and towns—there is simply less potential habitat.

One wolf made a remarkable roundtrip journey from Yellowstone to Colorado, searching historic haunts for possible territory. In that entire solitary reconnaissance, presumably he encountered little suitable habitat, no other pack members, nor a potential mate. Had he found any of those, it's unlikely he would have returned to Yellowstone.

Generally, at least one member of a pack is captured by wildlife agents and fitted with a radio collar; he or she is then becomes known as the "Judas wolf." In that way, it is possible to locate and keep track of the pack's movements and activities. Askins termed the collaring and electronic tracking practices "the need to control what we set free." Pack members assist one another in chewing the collars off, but wildlife agents keep replacing them.

Few people are aware of the numbers of wolves killed annually by government agents, often entire wolf packs are obliterated. Generally, around 20 percent of the wolf population in the Northern Rockies is wiped out each year by state agents or federal Wildlife Services' SWAT-team-like aerial gunning. In 2009, 270 pack members were destroyed by "government agency control actions."

The SWAT-team approach is employed when it is decided wolves are encroaching on or even *potentially* endangering people's property; especially if livestock and pets are being threatened or killed. The problem is exacerbated when wild prey is scarce. One high-ranking wolf biologist's mantra has been: "Wild wolves cause real problems that need real solutions." That person has been politically astute enough to avoid saying much about how, from a wild canine's perspective, postmodern society and people living in rural areas carelessly or unknowingly contribute to those "real problems." People have a malicious way of starting rumors and projecting blame, so that wolves are held responsible and judged guilty, not people or the circumstances they set in motion.

A recent case in point has been when mountain lion hunters run their dogs within a pack's territory, the wolves defend their territory against the trespassing hounds. They instinctively attack and drive the invaders from their hunting grounds; it's the only way they know. The outfitters who run their hounds within a pack's territory knowingly risk creating problems for themselves and their dogs, yet the incidents where dogs are killed are reported as if it is entirely the fault of the wolves. The cougar's territory and the pack's may overlap and is shared, but man assumes it all to be his alone.

In the Southwest, there is another example. The Mexican or lobo wolf, *Canus lupus baileyi*, is a smaller, genetically unique, and imperiled subspecies. While the name "lobo" is historically associated with a menacing presence in Western myth, the Mexican wolf actually weighs only fifty to eighty pounds, not much more than the coyote-wolf hybrids found in the northeastern United States. To date the recovery of the southwestern species has not fared well. Prolonged drought, a century of overgrazing the desert ranges, and a decline in livestock prices, has put pressure on the ranching industry there. Some are going out of business; they are angry. A Catron County, New Mexico, commissioner claims, "I've had ranchers' wives come to me just bawling because everything they and their parents have worked for is going down the drain." When those irate people look around for something to blame, they invariably project their anger and frustrations at the program for the lobo's restoration.

The gray wolf was declared "recovered" in the Northern Rockies on March 15, 2009; many people have mixed feelings about it. It was announced wolves would be removed from protection under the Endangered Species Act, and the states would assume management. For that to happen, each state was required to develop a sound management plan. The states straight away unveiled plans for hunting and reducing the number of the wolves. The amnesty wolves had enjoyed since their return to the northern Rockies was over.

The management method used by the states is regulated hunting. Properly employed it is an accepted and primary tool in modern wildlife management. For the wolves at this point, however, it is controversial. Given the history of predator control in the United States, not all people trust the process, believing it equates to little more than a license for killing; a return of the wolf-wars. Events shaping the tone and timbre of what some were to call "the modern wolf wars," began to be chronicled in the media almost daily.

It is a little publicized fact that the states were originally offered the chance to manage the wolves at the time of reintroduction, but they refused. The politicians and officials were intimidated by the outraged rhetoric of their rural constituencies. Wolves were a political hot potato that local officials were afraid to touch. Since then, it has served the political ambitions of such people to do a great deal of howling, posturing and bashing. None of it encourages trust. It's clear, though, certain elements of society had been salivating, waiting for the chance to "legally harvest" pack members.

The Idaho Anti-Wolf Coalition and state's Governor C.L. "Butch" Otter enthusiastically announced they wanted to reduce the wolf population in their state by 85 percent; from 650 down to 100, the "minimum recovery figure" originally set by the U.S. Fish and Wildlife Service for their state. Governor Otter set the tone by publicly announcing: "I want to be the first to shoot a wolf when they are delisted."

The Idaho Fish and Game Department, however, crafted and promulgated a more conservative plan and regulations for hunting than the governor called for. Still, in 2009, Idaho sold over 21,000 wolf tags. At first glance it appeared a small army was eager to kill wolves, but in reality it represented only 1.4 percent of the state's total population.

For some, purchasing a wolf permit was a symbolic gesture in support of the hunting program; others, in an attempt to save wolves, also bought licenses. The latter intended to tag any unretrieved road kill or government agency kills, so they could be counted toward the state's quota. Idaho game officials rejected the idea. They confiscated a former alpha-female that was destroyed in a government control action near Ketchum, after an advocate found the dead wolf and attempted to use her tag.

In Idaho, resident wolf tags were priced at $11.50, the same amount as for bear and cougar. Interestingly, wild turkey permits fetch $19.75. It seems odd that a license to hunt turkeys should be valued more than that for a wolf, bear or cougar—animals that potentially represent lifetime trophies. It does suggest those three species still suffer from their past categorization as varmints; a holdover from the belief that "what isn't game is vermin." If the cost of a permit to hunt wolves better reflected the unrivaled and unique once-in-a-lifetime hunting experience they potentially represent, not to mention the efforts and costs invested in their restoration, it might help send a different message to conservationists, hunters, and the wolf's protagonists alike.

Hunting in its purest form consists of sensory immersion into one's environment. It involves employing knowledge about the prey, its habitat, and tactics. This has always been the way of predators, and once it was true for human hunters, too. But hunting today can be much different than it was in the past. Nowadays, there is improved access and equipment, and instead of the senses, hunters are more apt to rely on technology, including: scouting from roads, 4-wheelers and snowmobiles, camouflage clothing, scents, two-way radios, cell phones, motorized and other types of decoys to simulate an injured prey animal, portable lightweight digital (electronic calls are currently banned in Idaho and Montana) and cassette calling devices, as well as mouth calls that mimic prey or other wolves, all to lure the animal within range of accurate high-powered weapons such as AR-style rifles—the semi-automatic rifles which are popular with "varmint hunters" and that are styled after military weaponry.

There are also how-to-books and web site information available for the neophyte hunter, and technological gismos, such as geographic positioning systems, night scopes, spotting scopes, range finders, and motion sensory cameras to track the animal's coming and going. And some biologists, who electronically monitor the wolves and have knowledge of their whereabouts, are not above leaking that information to hunters. In addition, there are national and state predator hunter organizations, which network and share knowledge among members. The idea of applying "fair chase" to wolves is apt to cause a raised eyebrow among many sportsmen, but in modern wildlife management, it is the ethics of the chase that distinguish "hunting" from simply a license to kill.

Additionally, as was pointed out earlier, today there is also less backcountry habitat in which wolves and other large cursorial wildlife can hide. Recent studies by University of Wisconsin scientists quantitatively corroborate that there is continually less and less wild country or habitat available for the likes of wolves. In their study of residential development surrounding national parks, national forests and Wildernesses, they found that in 2000, there were 38 million residences within fifty kilometers (~ 30 miles) of those conserved lands, compared to 9.8 million in 1940, and current housing developments are growing faster inside that fifty-kilometer belt than outside of it. They projected that by 2030 residential development will have grown another 45 percent (10 million units) adjacent to Wilderness areas and 52 percent within one kilometer of national forests. Human beings are in direct competition with large carnivores not only for prey, but also for space.

What takes place right outside and near the boundaries of conserved wildlands not only affects wolves and other "wilderness species," but all wildlife and biodiversity in general. Lines on maps alone do not provide protection for nature, what happens outside those boundaries also affects what happens within.

On September 2, 2009, the first wild wolf was officially harvested on Spirit Revival Ridge along the North Fork of the Clearwater River in Idaho under the state's management plan. The hunter who lived in Kamiah was quoted in *Field and Stream* saying, "I felt it was my duty to help predator control." It suggests from his remark that the hunter thought of his wolf primarily as a "predator," not as a trophy game animal. It is possible to be both. However, to his credit, the hunter later confessed his "excitement was tempered with a measure of remorse." To the anti-wolf contingent he became an instant hero.

But instead of receiving unanimous congratulations, it was surprising to learn the hunter was angrily harassed by people who sympathized with the wolf. It was an unprecedented example of changing attitudes among the America populace.

Sport hunters and game managers frequently use the bureaucratic euphemism "harvest" to officially sanction or justify the legal killing of wild animals. Use of that word attempts to impart emotional detachment. It implies it is "the result of conditions or operations." But killing wild animals is far different than harvesting crops. The difference is underscored by the double standard of its usage. Sport hunters say they "harvest" game animals, but they turn right around and say wolves "prey on, kill, and slaughter" those same animals. It seems consistent to say wild predators harvest game, too.

By mid-November 2009, hunters in Montana killed seventy-five pack members, the state's planned quota. A state biologist declared the hunt demonstrated they can manage wolves "appropriately." Obviously, "appropriate" is a charged concept. There is not consensus on what constitutes "appropriateness" in wolf management. It is not science, but rather a moving, highly-disparate and disputed objective; a guess, or maybe a heuristic or theoretical number at best.

In Idaho, 113 pack members were taken as of November 24, 2009, representing a hunter success rate of about 0.05 percent. Idahoans extended their season in some areas to try to kill 220; 34 percent of the population, their full quota. However, by the end of January, 2010, the Deputy Chief of the Idaho Department of Fish and Game, in a meeting with the state senate, was only able to report 142 wolves had been killed. Open season was extended through March, right up to the beginning of denning season. After Idaho's seven month season came to a close, a total of 185 wolves had been dispatched. But that is not the complete picture; in addition and less know, wildlife agents wiped-out another 138 wolves. It seems reasonable that wildlife agent kills should be applied toward satisfying quota numbers, but under the state's current systems they are not.

In November, a pack near Stanley, Idaho, was allegedly wrongly accused of killing sheep. In spite of some people's protests, the pack was hunted down by helicopter in full view of the town and destroyed. Federal and state wildlife control agents respond quickly to rancher's complaints and are single-minded in their approach; it is their job. They act to build a case against a pack and then unilaterally serve as judge, jury and executioner. Their tactics are militant, and some believe "heavy-handed." While it recalls the U.S. Fish and Wildlife Service official's slogan: "Wild wolves cause real problems that require real solutions," it also raises the question: who and what really motivates and controls the government agents? Because of the authoritative urgency the control actions assume, there is little or no public transparency built into the process.

It is curious that Idaho officials set a quota of five wolves for the agricultural and developed area within the southern-half of the state. No wolves were believed to exist there. That being the case, it guaranteed the state's total quota would not be met. It also appeared to encourage abuse of the system. On December 28, a wolf was reported killed in southeastern Idaho at a place where it is thought unlikely any existed. Idaho Fish and Game enforcement officers are investigating if the kill actually took place in the zone where it was reported.

The administration of quota systems can be less than straightforward. For instance, a Montana man shot a wolf on October 18, near Lewis and Clark Pass after the 2009 hunting season had closed. He said he thought the season was still open. Another wolf was road killed on highway I-90 around this time, too. And in a government agency control action on November 25, 2009, a government trapper—déjà vu the nineteenth century—destroyed nine more wolves after they allegedly "repeatedly attacked cattle" in the Big Hole Valley.

Montana's harvest quota was set at seventy-five, but control agents, ranch workers, and poachers actually destroyed no less than 145 more wolves—nearly twice that of the 2009 hunt quota. How did Montana account for this additional unplanned mortality in their claim of "appropriate management?" It raises the question does "appropriate management" serve science, an ideology, prevailing sentiment, or simply immediate contingencies?

Despite of the number of pack members destroyed, for some people it was not enough. A Sula, Montana, rancher, sounding uncannily like the early twentieth century call to arms against the wolf, was enthusiastically cheer leading the state to do more than just the regulated hunting: "They're going to have to do something drastic—poison them or trap them. They're too smart a critter to be hunted; [the hunt] wasn't enough"

Likewise, an Idaho Outfitter who believes the wolf's presence has doomed elk herds in the Northern Rockies, and has outspokenly called for trapping, poison baiting, and use of electronic calls. He declared, "You can't manage wolves through incidental hunting in [wilderness] country. Come on."

For decades ecological balance has been an ongoing issue in Jackson Hole, Wyoming, where ungulate herds have continued to remain above the state's population objectives. In December 23, 2009, *JH Weekly* reporter Brigid Manderm, in doing a story about the National Elk Refuge, wrote, "If natural predators regain their traditional hunting grounds and help control the elk [in Jackson Hole on the Elk Refuge]... wildlife officials will be more than happy to have their help." But if wildlife officials in Jackson Hole, and in Wyoming in general, agree, they have failed to convincingly communicate that message to local sport hunters, outfitters, and the agricultural community.

To date Wyoming has resisted preparing a plan for the management of wolves that is acceptable to the U.S. Fish and Wildlife Service. They want to classify wolves outside of the northwestern part of the state as predators to be killed anytime by any means. The proposal is not acceptable to the U.S. Fish and Wildlife Service, to whom the state must defer on scientific questions related to the wolf's management. But Cowboy State officials have made it a point *not* to show deference, instead they have joined with the Wyoming Farm Bureau and Wolf

Coalition, in continuing to challenge the legality of the 1995 wolf transplant and demand removal of the introduced "Canadian gray wolves," using those groups and others to politically leverage their position.

In Cheyenne, Wyoming, on January 2010, attorneys for the state, Park County, and the Wyoming Wolf Coalition, argued for the court to uphold the rejected state plan. Sport hunters, ranchers, outfitters, and wolf protagonists gathered and marched to the capitol to demonstrate their support, while officials representing Wyoming's Association of Conservation Districts, the Farm Bureau, and Stock Growers associations, and outfitters, testified in organized support of the rejected plan.

In March 2010, in Jackson, Wyoming, two hundred outfitters, ranchers, and sport hunters gathered on Center Street to "rally against wolves;" the participant's rhetoric sounded eerily like a throwback to the wolf wars of a century or more ago. One of the event's organizers, an outfitter, set the rally's tone by disjointedly and angrily denouncing wolves and the federal government, shouting: "The wolf has no place on the endangered species list. They back us into a corner and, by God, were ready to fight ... we have no ability to keep the wolf from our door."

Another outfitter from Teton Valley ranted, "The elk don't have guts enough to go back into the timber ground or up into Yellowstone for fear of their lives. You wouldn't go home either if your neighborhood was filled with rapists, murderers and thieves."

Inflammatory stories were shouted-out detailing how wolves chase down and kill elk, household pets, and livestock, almost as if to serve as an exorcism of the beast. One person claimed he "worried about children getting gobbled up." Photographs of dead and bloody animals allegedly killed by wolves were pictured in a paid advertisement in the local newspaper.

From a historical perspective, the only thing missing was for participants to engage in an eighteenth century "circle hunt." The rally's rhetoric demonizing wolves appeared over-the-top and ridiculously exaggerated. It also appeared astonishingly similar to the language and attitudes characteristic of the wolf wars centuries ago.

An Afton, Wyoming, resident who outfits hunters in the Teton Wilderness south of Yellowstone National Park struck a more measured tone: "We know we're stuck with them. We just need to be managing the damn things."

The ongoing vexation of these people over not being able to hunt and kill wolves in Wyoming appeared misdirected. The protests should have been directed at the Cowboy State officials and those organizations that have frustrated everyone by stubbornly thwarting the preparation of a reasonable and acceptable management plan.

Law professor Elizabeth C. Brown, in the *Boston College Environmental Officers Law Review,* has remarked, "It would be far more productive if the Farm Bureau and Fish and Wildlife Service worked together on solutions that will save the wolves and give ranchers the protections they are seeking." To that, we can all say "Amen."

In Idaho and Montana's plans, a hunter is required to obtain a permit to kill a wolf, follow required regulations, and to report their kills in accordance with the management plan quota system. None of that would be a necessary part of Wyoming's proposed plan.

Wyoming's unacceptable approach proposes to reduce the twenty-one breeding pairs that currently exist outside of Yellowstone National Park down to seven; a reduction of nearly 70 percent. The proposal, like their proposed and also unacceptable plan for grizzly bears, would bring the populations down to or below the minimum originally determined for recovery. There are no allowances for error and little or no concern about requirements to ensure a sustained minimum viable population. Also, by virtue of allowing uncontrolled hunting and trapping, it potentially limits the wolf's dispersal into other existing suitable habitats within the state.

If Wyoming had participated in the wolf hunting in 2009-10 with their approach, the total mortality of wolves in the Northern Rockies would have far exceeded 30 percent. As it was, wildlife agents still killed thirty-two pack members in the state; another nine died of unknown causes, some of which are currently under law enforcement investigation. Mortality in Wyoming without a hunt amounted to 15 percent of the state's wolf population outside Yellowstone Park.

Wyoming has some very capable wildlife biologists, so you might ask who or what is driving them to treat both grizzly bears (see Discussion section for Chapter 1) and wolves in this manner? Presumably, the state's biologists are carrying out orders. Those who are pulling the biopolitical strings have been reported by journalists to be: "Wyoming officials, outfitters and agricultural producers anxious to end federal protections so the state can start killing more [wolves]."

A 2010 Wyoming gubernatorial candidate has stated, "[we] were told they [the wolves] would stay in Yellowstone... I think it's great they are there. But when they impact the rights on your land, that's a problem." The candidate's grandfather years ago had launched his political career in Wyoming by stormily opposing the establishment of Grand Teton National Park.

To become an alpha-male, a wolf must demonstrate integrity, strength, courage and leadership. However, it seems that to become local or state officials in the western states, one must characteristically be "anti"—anti-wolf, anti-grizzly bear, anti-bison, anti-wilderness, anti-regulation, and so forth. Not only no, but hell no. Wouldn't it be better to earn resprect through acting for things, rather than against?

Meanwhile, in contrast to the ongoing state's hubris, in an attempt at a more humane control method, the federal wolf biologist assigned to Wyoming has been issuing firecrackers and rubber bullets. The use of rubber bullets is one non-lethal, preemptive way to educate wolves against violating human territory and property and to remind them to fear humans.

In addition to the mortality from the different state's regulated hunting, control actions, and other causes, the famed and once powerful Druid Pack within Yellowstone National Park, which numbered eleven members at the start of the 2009-10 winter, was decimated by natural causes—killed by other wolf packs and mange. All but one member died.

In the end, 2009 was not a good year to be a wolf in the Northern Rockies. Over five hundred were destroyed. Of those, more than half were killed by government agents, ranch workers, poachers, and natural causes. Some people, though, just like in the past, would prefer that there were no wolves left at all.

After the extent of the wolf population extinguishment was tallied, biologists claimed "the region's total wolf population remained stable." And the federal government assured that "the wolves are doing just fine." Montana's leading wolf biologist claimed, "This puts a few things to rest, first and foremost that hunting was going to hurt the population." Perhaps, but the results after one year of hunting are hardly sufficient to make that determination, especially when government agency control actions continue to be a wild card.

It has also been reported that wildlife officials in Idaho and Montana "encouraged by this year's hunt, are already making plans to expand quotas for next season and giving hunters more advantages for tracking and killing wolves." At this point, it appears to amount to little more than an uncontrolled experiment in wildlife control and management.

Among the pack members killed adjacent to Yellowstone National Park in Montana's 2009 hunt was another legendary wolf. Identified as "Wolf 527," she was more than a number, she was an alpha-female considered to be "a genius at survival strategy," her history was well-documented. Wolf-watchers named her "Bolt". Wolf 527 originated from the Druid Pack in 2007. She was made famous by the PBS documentary *In the Valley of the Wolves* For awhile she joined the rival Slough Creek pack. Then she and her mate split off and formed their own Cottonwood Creek Pack.

Regardless of the many sentimental expressions over Bolt's demise, she was very much a wild wolf possessing all the instincts and territoriality of her kind. In spring, 2006, she encountered another denning young female wolf. Brutally Darwinian, Bolt and her mate killed her in her den and then killed and ate the young female's pups.

What the repercussions of Wolf 527's death may have on the social structure, territory, and hierarchy of the packs that inhabit the Lamar Valley and adjacent areas isn't fully known yet. Or, for that matter, what the wide-spread killing of wolves across the Northern Rockies will have on wolf behavior, dispersal, reproduction, and the overall recovery effort. It is something biologists, and wolf-watchers alike will be monitoring.

Conservationists and wildlife advocates are concerned the states in combination with government hunters have the wherewithal to drive down wolf numbers to minimal levels. Extremist opinions on both sides have raised trust issues for people and organizations. Some watch-dog organizations and wildlife advocates are intervening; they have filed a lawsuit to put wolves back on the endangered list.

Under the circumstances, with the false information and prevarication on both sides surrounding the wolf, most sport hunters and outfitters have been influenced to come out strongly in support of reducing wolf numbers. They claim predation by wolves has impacted the well-being of elk and deer herds throughout the Northern Rockies and lowered chances for human hunter success; many are incensed over it, and their views carry a lot of weight in the respective states. But to date, the data hardly justifies their strong reaction.

*Field and Stream* and *Bugle* report that *overall* elk herd populations generally remain stable, at or above statewide management objectives, in both Wyoming and Montana. Wyoming, in fact, remains 12 percent above their overall elk population objective; hunter success in 2008 was 37.1 percent. Compare that to Colorado's 20 percent, where there are no wolves.

Sport hunters argue that is misleading. The Rocky Mountain Elk Foundation says, "Pro-wolf groups like to cite statewide numbers because it glosses over the ongoing annihilation of local elk herds." They say elk herds are only expanding or stable where wolves are not present. Where wolves occur they insist elk numbers have declined. At places where wolves are concentrated in localized areas with limited habitat and prey, and human being's traditional harvest of game also continues to be high within those same areas, it undoubtedly does put pressure on deer and elk populations. Perhaps another way of looking at it is it indicates a need for a timely reexamination of traditional game management and harvest levels for both wild ungulates and predators in those places, so that overtime a realistic balance might be achieved. Sport hunters currently appear to have little patience for that idea. And, historically, some people have always begrudged all wild hunters their take and place in nature.

The northern Yellowstone herd is invariably cited as an example of where the pack has caused a drastic decline in the elk population—reportedly from 19,000 in 1995 to 6,000 in 2008. But it is a commonly known fact that Yellowstone's northern elk herd had grown beyond the carrying capacity of its range. Wolves have contributed to restoring ecological balance on the northern range; indeed, aspen, willow and beaver are returning where they had been in decline from years of heavy ungulate grazing as was illustrated in *National Geographic*, March 2010. Many people believe this is a good thing, but it's not something everyone agrees with or understands. Earlier it was pointed out the wolf is often blamed for conditions humans set in motion—the northern range is another case where wolves are being singled out as the sole scapegoat.

The ecological consequences from predator removal on Arizona's Kaibab National Forest deer ranges a century ago has been recounted by author Peter Matthiessen in *Wildlife in America,* and by others, too. The Kaibab's deer population explosion, habitat destruction, and eventual dramatic crash in the deer population, are lessons that seem to be mostly forgotten today.

It is also recognized that elk behavior has changed at places as a result of predation by wolves. The elk appear more wary and alert, they keep on the move, and they tend to occupy rougher terrain and thicker cover. Scientist Joel Berger, in *The Better to Eat You With*, describes this phenomenon in his studies on predation and ungulate behavior. Maybe it is not all bad. It makes hunting more challenging for both wolves and sportsmen. For some, it is another irritation for which the wolf is held responsible.

Some believe if careless or habituated wolves are destroyed in hunts, and the survivors are sufficiently traumatized, we might expect an encore of the super wolf. But, realistically, the idea of super wolves fades in the face of modern technology, aerial control methods, and today's restricted habitat. It is little more than myth.

In the end, it appears those who are outspokenly calling for the wolf's hide comprise the same hegemony of local and state officials, sport hunters, and agricultural producers who were originally responsible for its eradication. Having that group in position to determine the wolf's fate again does raise the specter of the age-old wolf wars cloaked in the guise of state management. What gives one further pause is knowing that if the ancestors of many of those people who are calling for the destruction of the wolves and grizzly bear had gotten their short-sighted way on earlier conservation issues, none of the national forests, Teton National Park, or most Wildernesses, would exist today.

Not to be outdone by Wyoming, in January 2010, a Utah State Senator introduced a bill that would require state wildlife officials to capture or kill any and all wolves that might disperse into Utah—ignoring the mandated protection under the federal Endangered Species Act. The senator says he "worries that wolves ... could eventually decimate Utah's elk and deer population and hurt the livestock industry." In addition, he made the odd statement that "the lifestyle of wolves isn't compatible with ours." I'm sure we would all be curious to have the senator describe the wild animal "lifestyles" that he thought were compatible with Utahans, just for a frame of reference.

Wolves have already made reconnoiters through parts of the senator's state. In 2002, a male wolf was caught in a leghold trap set for coyotes in Utah. The wolf was released and it returned to Yellowstone and joined the Druid Pack. Utah already has a management plan in place that allows wolves into the state, compensates livestock owners for losses, and allows pack members to be killed if they attack livestock or drive down game numbers.

If the senator's bill were to be enacted, it would be unconstitutional, violating the supremacy clause wherein federal law supersedes state law. The senator's bill appears to be more inane, but divisive, bio-political posturing at the expense of tax payers in order to gain a certain constituency's attention and approval. It is sobering but true, such people get elected because they share the majority of their constituency's views.

Given the wolf's history with mankind in Part I, the above overview of the wolf's management status, and ongoing protracting events such as rallies, continuing litigation, outrageous state and local official's political posturing, and dogmatic attitudes, it becomes understandable why some groups and people might distrust the different state's motives, credibility, and ability to "scientifically manage" wolves. Having western state officials, agriculturalists, and sport hunters with an axe to grind making the decisions, while they simultaneously renounce the wolves with nineteenth-century rhetoric, does not exactly engender confidence, collaboration, or the assurance of good faith.

The states are going to be required to monitor their wolves and management programs and make annual reports to the U.S. Fish and Wildlife Service for at least the next five years. The requirement further justifies the biologist's penchant for keeping tabs on the packs and monitoring our behavior. At what point does manipulation and control raise a question about what it means for wild animals to be truly wild and free?

It is a complex, emotional, social, and wildlife management issue, invoking centuries of misunderstanding and hatred for the wolf. If our society supposedly representing one of the most advanced civilizations on Earth is not capable of progressing beyond a seventeenth to early-twentieth century mindset toward wild animals, what does that say about *Homo sapiens'* chances for successfully resolving much larger complex issues facing our kind worldwide?

While wolves struggle to adapt and evolve in response to changes in prey species, habitat, and coexisting with people in today's world, their challenges pale in comparison to that of man's for continuing success as a species. Mankind is faced with the unprecedented need for continual and rapid evolution: adaptation to burgeoning populations worldwide, adjusting to limitations imposed by finite resources, dealing with rapidly changing technologies and the digital revolution, addressing increasing economic disparities, and the necessity to resolve differences in widely-conflicting ideologies.

Some people are searching for a new and sustainable way for mankind to relate to nature. They are proposing to adopt a "new ecological paradigm" that would diffuse human's destructive attitudes and unsustainable practices and be based on the interconnectedness and shared character of Earth's natural resources. To this end, some conservation organizations have instituted "human-carnivore conflict reduction" projects with the cooperation of a few livestock producers. The goal of these pilot projects is to find ways to make it safer for large carnivores to coexist with people. In April 2010, the U.S. Fish and Wildlife Service announced it would allocate one million dollars to help livestock producers take non-lethal steps to reduce conflicts with wolves—Idaho, Montana and Wyoming will receive the most money among the ten states in the United States with wolves.

However, for man to forge a new future for humanity in nature, understanding and dealing with the centuries' old mindsets of fear of the beast (theriophobia) and blind hatred will be necessary. Author Steve Nicholls wrote, "it is in man's attitude towards the ultimate symbol of untamed nature [the wolf] that mankind can gauge its progress toward this vital understanding."

To paraphrase conservationist and writer Todd Wilkinson, "Wolf Rhetoric Makes Some Folks Look Silly" in his March 31,

2009-2010 Gray Wolf Pack Distribution within the Northern Rockies in the United States.

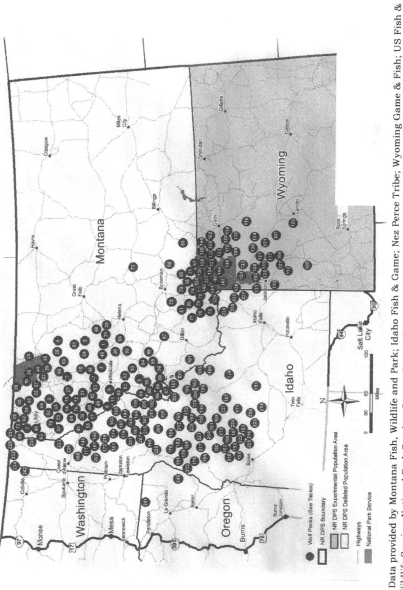

Data provided by Montana Fish, Wildlife and Park; Idaho Fish & Game; Nez Perce Tribe; Wyoming Game & Fish; US Fish & Wildlife Service; National Park Service; Oregon Dept. of Fish and Wildlife; and Washington Dept. of Fish and Wildlife. All other data layers from Montana, Idaho, Wyoming, Oregon and Washington data clearing houses.
Montana Fish, Wildlife and Parks; 1420 E. 6th Ave. Helena, MT 59620. AnnualProject/WolfReport/2009 Season - 2/19/2010.

2010, *Jackson Hole News and Guide* column *The New West* —"Wolves have a place in this region... The Greater Yellowstone, the central Idaho Wilderness, and the Crown of the Continent ecosystems are sources of pride, inspiration, and wonder for the American people. They are examples in wildlife and wildlife conservation for the world. The presence of wolves contributes importantly to those natural systems and to the fascination and wonder of those places for people from the world over."

Many people are conscious that the wolf's presence puts "the wild" back into wild lands and believe that is a good thing; they value the wolf's presence. Such enlightenment goes hand-and-hand with man's recognition that he is a part of nature, and not apart from it.

There's a chance mankind will have the wisdom to get it right this time around and recognize the pack is not evil, but a natural part of a functioning healthy ecosystem. Most remain hopeful that common ground can be found, but there is much history to overcome and to avoid repeating.

# IV
## Discussion and Source Materials

Readers frequently ask three questions: "What gave you the idea or inspiration to do this story? What is your experience, expertise or background on the subject? What research and sources did you consult?" This section attempts to answer those questions.

Some of the author's background, interests, and experience related to each story are given and an accounting of the source materials that were researched for each story is provided. The listing of sources might also be used as an additional reading guide for each animal or story. Also included is additional discussion and author's commentary on ongoing studies, issues, or other asides that may not have been detailed within a particular essay.

Some of the animals and the associated issues treated in this book are at the forefront of ongoing controversy and contentiousness in today's management of wildlife, wildlife habitat, endangered species, and predator control in the western United States. As a consequence, there are continual and ongoing newspaper reports, organizational newsletters and stories, magazine articles, and research publications about those animals.

For a book of this kind, it can address, analyze, or include the latest of those items only up until a point before it goes to press; otherwise, as I have discovered, it will never get to press. In those cases, the progression and true ending to the story may remain to be discovered in the future.

While the essays provide valuable historical and natural history context and benchmarks, they are more than snapshots. Whether you disagree or agree with the perspective or opinion presented, the stories can stimulate and assist learning about the species and habitat issues. There are valuable lessons and insights to be learned from the past, too. Knowing the past is important; it can help explain the present and perhaps help prevent repeating undesirable practices and outcomes.

## IV-1
## The Spirit of Tosi

Through independent research in the late 1960s and early 1970s, I provided the first published documentation establishing the fact occupied grizzly bear habitat existed in the southern Selkirk Mountains within the United States. My findings were published in *Northwest Science,* Vol. 52, No. 2, 1978.

Later, I was employed by the U. S. Forest Service in a position that, among other things, involved the delineation of critical grizzly bear habitat on Wyoming's Bridger-Teton National Forest, as well as coordination of the Forest's resource management programs with various agencies involved in bear management. Still later, as a private consultant, I prepared biological assessments under the Endangered Species Act for projects potentially affecting grizzly bears at various locations throughout the Greater Yellowstone. Those jobs and experiences gave me some knowledge about the bears and an insider's view of agency programs and attitudes at that time.

In the mid-1990s, grizzly bears appeared to be actively dispersing into unoccupied historic habitat. Some people were quick to proclaim this demonstrated a successful bear recovery and was reason for delisting. But there was a flip side. There were also reports of record numbers of bear conflicts, removals, and mortality.

I kept a file of newspaper stories on those incidents. For instance, in 1994 ten grizzly bears were reported killed, in 1995 seventeen, and in 1996 fifteen. A rash of livestock depredation incidents were also reported; for example, in 1996, three bears were removed from the west slope of the Tetons in the Jedediah Smith Wilderness and at least four bears from outside of designated recovery zone in the upper Green River at Tosi Basin. Those removals were "preemptive" because the bears were close to sheep allotments. Depredations were also reported, such as those on the Walton Ranch's Togwotee cattle allotment in the Absaroka Mountains south of the Teton Wilderness, which resulted in bear removals, too.

The number of bears euthanized and removed from the Upper Green and elsewhere in the Greater Yellowstone Ecosystem, because of conflicts with livestock, especially sheep, at that time, was distressing. If we as a society want grizzly bears, isn't it asking for trouble to knowingly run livestock on Wilderness grazing allotments within occupied bear habitat? Author Harley Shaw, in *Soul Among Lions*, likens it to "a person who parked his car on a railroad crossing, then sues the railroad company for the vehicle's destruction." It raises the question: do we want bears or livestock in our Wildernesses?

In more recent years, it seems the press reported relatively fewer bear incidents. The last I noted from Tosi Basin was in 2002, when a large male grizzly was destroyed for killing sheep. Grump, perhaps? I have a suspicion fewer reports for awhile after that time period were not because depredation incidents and bear removals diminished but, rather, that the internal political climate within government agencies during that time had changed. The agencies may simply have been less open and forthcoming.

The bears were delisted in 2007. Some officials immediately began pressing for a bear hunting season. In 2008, mortality in the Yellowstone ecosystem was seventy-nine bears, about 15 percent of the total population, a record amount. The total population estimate for the Yellowstone region was about 580 in 2009. In September 2009, U.S. District Judge Donald Molloy ruled the U.S. Fish and Wildlife Service had acted too hastily in removing the bears from their threatened status. But in a 2009 written report to the state legislature, Wyoming biologists continue to resist that determination, insisting "the grizzly population is biologically recovered." Some politically connected people in Wyoming want fewer bears.

In 2009, there were twenty-six grizzlies captured in Wyoming alone; four of those were killed, two were sent to zoos, and twenty-two "trauma conditioned" bears were relocated. The Wyoming Game and Fish bear management program supervisor has justified the active relocation program by saying, "getting caught and transplanted via a steel cage is traumatic for a bear, so they become much more wary of humans."

This proved to be a false assumption in June 2010, when an enraged grizzly bear killed a Wyoming man just hours after researchers had trapped and tranquilized the animal.

At this time, there is biological basis for *not* delisting the grizzly bear. Jackson Hole biologist and activist Franz Camenzind, in a December 16, 2009, *Jackson Hole News and Guide* editorial, "Grizzly bears still need our protection," points out that although the bear population has increased to nearly 600 from 250 in the 1970s, there have been unfavorable changes to the bear's habitat in the past decade: the widespread decline of whitebark pine, collapse of the Yellowstone cutthroat population, more people in the backcountry, the bears occurrence outside of the primary recovery area where if it is delisted its welfare will suffer, a conflict with black bear baiting and hunting, and the State of Wyoming's desire to manage for fewer bears, all of which collectively and individually have potential to negatively impact grizzly bears.

Tosi Basin at the head of the Green River is obviously historic and preferred habitat for grizzly bears, regardless that it is not identified "recovery area." This is evident by the bears' continual attempts to reoccupy it. Can there really be "recovery" if dispersing bears can not reasonably expand their ranges and reoccupy suitable historic habitat within congressionally designated Wildernesses on public land without continually being subject to capture and relocation?

To compose my fictionalized and metaphorical account of Grump, I drew upon personal experiences and knowledge, as well as bear incidents and happenings reported by newspaper journalists and editorials, such as those by McCrystie Adams, Angus Thuermer Jr., Tom Hacker, Deanna Darr, Barrie Gilbert, Pam Lichtman, and others, in the *Jackson Hole News and Guide, Bozeman Chronicle,* and *Casper Star Tribune,* over a period of years in the mid-1990s; and also more recently, other AP news releases.

The County Commissioners, Wyoming Stock Growers Association, and Wyoming Game and Fish statements quoted in this story and discussion are not fictional. They are taken from the above various published newspaper articles, interviews, and other sources.

The Wyoming Game and Fish Department has recently provided a Web page that provides up-to-date information on grizzly bear management activities in Wyoming, it also links to the State's grizzly bear management plan and other technical documents, at http://gf.state.wy.us/wildlife/grizzlybearmanagement

The construct describing the guest ranch owner's hair-tingling edginess in knowing the great bear was out there somewhere, perhaps nearby but unseen, touches on the fundamental nature of the grizzly bear's presence to a true wilderness experience. One strongly remembers the feelings that an encounter brings or the enhanced sensory attunement and awareness experienced when one is within occupied grizzly bear habitat. A wilderness devoid of its native compliment of carnivores was rightly described by Thoreau as having been "emasculated."

## IV-2
## Castor the Snake River Beaver

In 1980, a friend living along the Snake River north of Jackson, Wyoming, asked for my help in removing some beavers from a spring creek on his property. The beavers were doing what beavers often do: damming culverts and ditches. They kept flooding his access road. Like many in my generation who grew up in a rural area, I had experience trapping, including for beavers. It was one of the few ways I had to make any money as a kid; and like many boys in rural areas back then, I grew up dreaming of the fur-trade era.

I agreed to help the friend out. One of the beavers I caught turned out to be a very large, old, and battle-scarred veteran. It made a deep impression. It was the last beaver I ever trapped. Afterwards, I tried to write a story about the venerable old rodent;

a type of catharsis, I suppose. The unpublished hand-typed manuscript sat in a file drawer for all these years. With some additional updating, research, revision and literary liberties, it was resurrected into the Snake River beaver story appearing in this book.

A general reference for beaver that I used was David Macdonald's 2006 ed. *Encyclopedia of Mammals*, pp 590-595. There are also a number of Web sites that describe the natural history of beaver that I consulted, including www.beaversww. org/beaver and www.wikipedia.com.

Ken Mitchell's 2008 *The Beaver Fur Trade* was one source I used for an overview of the fur trade at www.bell.lib.umn.edu/Products/beaver, and also F.L. Graves, *Montana's Fur Trade Era* (1994), Unicorn Publishing, Helena, MT. Another accounting of the history of the fur trade and the beaver's natural history which I referred to was in Steve Nicholl's *Paradise Found: Nature in America at the Time of Discovery*, University of Chicago Press (2009), pp 171-191.

The process for making beaver hats is detailed online at www.whiteoak.org/learning/furhat.

Recent information and photographs of beaver dams on North Horse and Mill Creeks, Green River tributaries in Sublette County, Wyoming, have been posted on the Web by O. Ned Eddins under the title *Traders and Indian Trappers of Beaver Pelts*, they can be found at www.thefurtrapper.com/images/Beaver.

Historic and current information on "The Beavers of Yellowstone" may be found in Douglas Smith and Dan Tyers' featured article in *Yellowstone Science,* Vol.16:3 (2008).

Another article with useful historical information was Kevin Taylor's "Voyage of the Dammed" in *High Country News*, June 2009.

Michael Punke in *Last Stand* (2007) records some early-day arrests made for illegal beaver trapping in Yellowstone Park.

Sources for information on Jackson Hole's notorious poacher Charles "Beaver Tooth" Neal are: Fern Nelson's *This Was Jackson's Hole* (1994), pp 258-267, and Kenneth and Lenore Diem's *A Community of Scalawags, Renegades, Discharged Soldiers and Predestined Stinkers* (1998).

## IV-3
## Ghosts of the Forest

From 1967 to 1972, except for a year out of that time to complete my Master of Science degree, I was employed by the U. S. Forest Service in northeastern Washington. During the winter months in those years, I spent a significant amount of my own time researching mountain caribou and on snowshoes in the backcountry looking for caribou. I knew little about snow avalanche hazards, and that I managed to avoid triggering any avalanches was due to the benevolence of the mountains, rather than any skill on my part.

In those years, I made a few memorable overnight snowshoe treks into the Salmo Guard Station cabin, which was hidden deep in the Salmo Basin's old-growth forest. On one of those occasions, in which I was accompanied by Washington state biologist, Jerry King, just the peak of the cabin's roof was showing above the snow. We had to tunnel our way onto the covered porch to gain access into the cabin. The passage of time was strongly brought to my attention about ten years ago, when I returned to the Salmo Basin to discover only a shell of the old cabin remained.

On one of my snowshoe forays off of Salmo Pass in British Columbia, I managed to track down and photograph caribou. Aerial observation in winter proved to be a much more efficient means to locate and observe the caribou, even without the benefit of telemetry.

The results of my research on mountain caribou were published in a monograph entitled "A Review of the Mountain Caribou of Northeastern Washington and Adjacent Northern Idaho," *Journal of the Idaho Academy of Science*, Special Research Issue No. 3, June 1974. 63p.

The caribou were not a popular issue with everyone. They still aren't. My monograph was actually completed much earlier, but through no fault of mine, it sat waiting "in-press" for three years before it was finally published and made available.

For this story, I drew upon my field experience, material in my monograph, recent research findings and publications posted online, press reports, and personal correspondence with biologist Timothy Layser. Tim kindly provided information on "caribou 109." Caribou 109's story encapsulates some of the hope and frustrations efforts for caribou recovery have experienced.

There is a great deal of information available on climate change today. At the time I was working on caribou, there was not. I first suggested there may be a correlation between the decline of caribou and climate change in my article "Forestry and Climate Change," published in the *Journal of Forestry* (1980). Shifts in occupied caribou range corresponding to climate changes overtime is a theory I first proposed in that article. Climate change, however, is only one contributing factor relating to the decline of woodland caribou over the past century, as I try to explain. Catastrophic wildfires, habitat fragmentation, hunting, poaching, road kill, and predation have all converged to impact them.

A recent Associated Press report, "Glacier Ice Fields May Be History by 2020," published in the *Jackson Hole News and Guide,* June 15, 2009, provides a summary of recent research on Glacier National Park's retreating glaciers. The history of retreating glaciers, in close geographic proximity and similar latitude to where the caribou occur, is one example demonstrating potential for continuing and ongoing habitat changes from warming climate.

There is a great deal of material that has been published on the Selkirk caribou since the 1970s, as well as the formation of an International Mountain Caribou Technical Committee and the initiation of the Selkirk Ecosystem Project. Much of this information has been posted online at www.imctc.com.

Three government publications I referred to in writing my story are the "Mountain Caribou Recovery Plan" (1985); "Habitat Use by Woodland Caribou in the Selkirk Mountains" (1989); and the updated "Selkirk Mountain Woodland Caribou Recovery Plan (1994)."

Other recent works I consulted are: "Selkirk Mountains Woodland Caribou Herd Augmentation in Washington" (January 1996); and, J. A. Almack's "Recent Augmentation of Mountain caribou to the Southern Selkirk Mountains of Northeastern Washington, Northern Idaho, and Southern British Columbia" in *Proceedings of a Conference on the Biology and Management of Species and Habitats at Risk*, Kamloops, B.C. (1999).

David Tallman's "Population Viability Analysis of the Selkirk Mountain's Woodland Caribou," University of Montana, Department of Biological Sciences (1994), presents a population model that predicts the caribou's extinction within twenty-two to twenty-nine years in the southern Selkirks. "Factoring in ongoing logging," in his words, "will decrease those estimated times to extinction." In the worst case scenario, Tallman predicts extinction before the year 2016.

In 1995, the Biodiversity Legal Foundation and the Selkirk Ecosystem Alliance sued the U.S. Fish and Wildlife Service to force them into designating "critical habitat" for the caribou as per the Endangered Species Act. As far as is known, the U.S.

Fish and Wildlife Service still have not made a determination of critical habitat, although, as of 2009, with the change in the administration, that work may be in progress.

The snowmobile issue was reported by Associated Press writer Nicolas K. Geranios in "Caribou Struggling for Survival," February 2006. The article also contains information on British Columbia's efforts to protect the caribou and the fact that the Canadian provincial government may abandon recovery efforts for some smaller herds.

Additional information on the snowmobiling issue and the court case ruling for limiting snowmobiling within the caribou recovery habitat can be found in "More Protection Granted for Mountain Caribou" (2007) at www.conservationnw.org/pressroom.

Journalist Kevin Taylor in "Ghosts of the Selkirks Fading Fast," *High Country News,* March 4, 2002, summarized the status of caribou recovery efforts, costs, and its failures. After the transplanting of 103 animals and the resultant unnaturally high mortality, British Columbia opted out of the program and withdrew its funding participation. Over time the caribou recovery program has cost millions of dollars but, unfortunately, it does not, at this time, appear to have attained the goal of achieving a viable and sustainable population in the southern Selkirk's within the U.S. In no way has this been a direct fault of the dedicated biologists that have been involved in the program. One can conclude the complex variables involved in the caribou's decline are not controllable through the efforts of field biologists alone.

The most recent "Caribou Status" report can be found in the Spring 2010 Selkirk Conservation Alliance newsletter, *Sightlines,* pp 1&5.

## IV-4
## The Undine and the Merle: Why the Ouzel Curtsies

My whimsical story on water features and the water ouzel stems from an interest I developed on waterfalls within the Greater Yellowstone region in the early 1990s. It is about the magic of flowing waters as much as it is about the ouzel. At that time, Rubenstein, Whittlesey and Stevens' *Guide to Yellowstone Waterfalls and Their Discovery* (2000)—the first definitive work on waterfalls in the park—was not yet published and I was unaware it was a work in progress at the time.

Searching out and photographing waterfalls in the backcountry of the southwestern part of Yellowstone National Park—originally named "Cascade Corner" by Superintendent Horace Albright because of the number of waterfalls concentrated there—and also elsewhere throughout the region, was an enjoyable experience. Hard to believe that in such recent time there were still undiscovered waterfalls. Many had never been mapped and some major ones not even named. The literature that existed on the park's waterfalls up until the above 2000 *Guide* was skimpy at best.

But even more astonishing, in the early 1900s, the southwest corner of the park was shown on maps as "swamp." Under the Swampland Act of 1850, wetlands could be turned over to a state by the federal government. The state could then sell the land to a private entity, who would agree to turn "worthless swamp" into a productive agricultural enterprise. It's a little known, but important, conservation story that had it not been for the lobbying efforts of a few individuals, led primarily by William Gregg, and supported behind the scenes by Superintendent Albright, the entire southwest corner of Yellowstone National Park would have been flooded by the dams proposed by southeastern Idaho irrigation interests. Gregg and his colleagues explored the area and published an article, illustrated with waterfalls photographed for the first time, entitled: "The Cascade Corner of Yellowstone Park," in *The Outlook*, November 23, 1921. It extolled the previously little known water features and waterfalls occurring there. Gregg's article was important for lobbying and informing congress of the issue and of the water features present; and, most importantly, in defeating the proposed dams.

Yellowstone's little visited waterfalls hidden in backcountry canyons with difficult access captured my imagination. My field research and photography allowed me to publish two pieces on waterfalls. One appeared in the summer-fall 2000 issue of *Jackson Hole Magazine*, entitled "Waterfall Country" (with the magazine presumably mislabeling the names of the pictured falls to discourage people from flocking to them); and the other, in the summer 2002 issue of *Yellowstone Country Magazine*, entitled "The Magical Waters." I also taught a course on Yellowstone's waterfalls for the Yellowstone Association for a few seasons, too. As John Muir said, "Where the great rivers take their rise, there is a region full of wonders." The waterfalls are certainly a part of those wonders.

While exploring and photographing the pristine waterways (and also when wielding a fly rod), I invariably encountered water ouzels. The birds were fun, interesting, and curious companions. I was also sparked by Olaus Murie's essay "Whetstone Canyon" in *Wapiti Wilderness* (1985), about places of enchantment and the water ouzel: "Here lives the real proprietor [the ouzel] of Whetstone canyon." Since Olaus's time, the shale canyon below the falls was scoured to bedrock by a mud flow, but the ouzel still occupies the canyon.

In 2001, I published an essay, "Secrets of the Ouzel," in an anthology entitled *Stories of the Wild."* The anthology was a Jackson Hole Murie Center project. In my story, I described discovering an unnamed and unmapped waterfall pouring out of a limestone cliff in the Gros Ventre Wilderness (it is still unnamed and unmapped), and how by working my way along the plunge wall on a narrow ledge I was, like the ouzel, able to go behind the falls. The effect of peering through the thundering cascade was kaleidoscopic. It was enchanting and restorative, a place of special power.

After I had drafted the ouzel story appearing in this book, I discovered John Muir had published an essay about the bird in the Sierras a century earlier in the *San Francisco Bulletin*. Muir's piece can also be found in book which is a compilation of his essays entitled *John Muir: Nature Writings* (1997), pp 486-499.

The above field experience and reference works combined with additional library and World Wide Web research on the natural history of the water ouzel provided the inspiration and basis for this piece.

## IV-5
## The Nutcracker and the Whitebark Pine's Covenant

In this story, I am hopeful the liberties I have taken in anthropomorphizing, as well as the literary device of having the animals and tree talking amusingly to one another, will contribute to conveying the underlying scientific, natural history and informative content of the story.

Perhaps it is a stretch for some to think of trees as "wildlife." But it is not uncommon to categorize native flora under "wildlife" nowadays. Forester Aldo Leopold was probably the first to do so in practice.

As a forester and outdoor enthusiast, I consider the whitebark pine to be my favorite tree in the northern Rocky Mountains. While it has little commercial value, it tops the list for aesthetics and inspirational qualities. I associate the tree with the rarified and glorious high-elevation ridges, crags, and summits. The autumn chortle of the nutcracker is inextricably linked to my sensory images of the tree.

I first noticed whitebark pine dying from white-pine blister rust, *Cronartium ribicola,* on Crowell Ridge in northeastern Washington around 1967. Since then, in my lifetime, I've witnessed the widespread catastrophic loss of whitebark pine across much of its range in the northern Rockies. Ancient, gnarly and lightning-scarred veterans that were old friends along favorite hiking routes now sadly exist only as bleached skeletal snags.

Life at high-elevation is tenuous. Subalpine and alpine organisms and ecosystems are fragile. While whitebark pine is a sturdy, tenacious, and admirably tough species—it's normally able to survive for centuries in some of the most austere environments that exist in the Rocky Mountains—it has little or no resistance to the microscopic blister-rust fungus; an introduced, nonnative pathogen.

In the past, the severe climate where whitebark pine normally grows prevented bark beetle infestations. The beetles could not complete their life cycle in the cold environment. Warming climate—the past eleven years are reportedly some of the warmest on record within the tree's range—has allowed the beetles to expand their range into higher elevations. Whitebark pine trees weakened by blister rust, and warming climate and seasonal drought, fall prey to beetle attacks. And the dead and dying trees have set the stage for potentially large, catastrophic wildfires.

On December 15, 2008, the U.S. Forest Service held a workshop in Billings, Montana, to educate their employees about changing climate and its ramifications. Experts there warned "we're almost on the cusp of an ecosystem shift." In short, whitebark pine's die-off is a warning or indicator of potentially larger problems or consequences to come in our mountain ecosystems.

In view of these circumstances, in 2008, the Natural Resources Defense Council petitioned to protect whitebark pine under the Endangered Species Act; see "Greens Move to Save Tree Bears Depend On," in the *Jackson Hole News and Guide,* December 10, 2008, p 2A.

In March 1989, I participated in a "Symposium on Whitebark Pine Ecosystems: Ecology and Management of a High-Mountain Resource," *USDA Forest Service Intermountain Research Station Technical Report*, INT-270, 396p. In writing and researching the subject piece, in addition to my own professional observations, I drew upon information presented at that symposium; and also a more recent Forest Service research publication by Teresa J. Lorenz, et al., "A Review of the Literature on Seed Fate and the Life History Traits of Clark's Nutcracker and Pine Squirrels," *USDA Pacific Northwest Research Station Report* GTR-742, April 2008.

## IV-6
## The Bellwether in the Rock Pile

I have always thought it was a delightful experience to see pika when hiking in subalpine and alpine areas of the Rocky Mountains. In the northern part of Jackson Hole, pika colonies have been discovered to occur in rocky habitats at places as low in elevation as the valley floor. The side canyons in Grand Teton National Park, such as Cascade, Death and Paintbrush Canyons, and the Sheep Steps above Alaska Basin in the Jedediah Smith Wilderness, provide more typical habitat and are good places to observe pika. The little lagomorphs also occur elsewhere along the Greater Yellowstone cordillera, such as in the Absaroka and Wind River ranges; and elsewhere, northward along the Rockies to Alaska.

I've watched people walk right past pika colonies—complete with haystacks, while the animals were making their characteristic vocalizations—and observed that many folks don't have a clue the little critter even exists or that the pika were there watching them.

An excellent general reference for pikas is David McDonald's *The Encyclopedia of Mammals* (2006). Professor McDonald refers to them as: "denizens of high, remote mountains and wild country, serving as symbols of untamed nature."

Other sources I consulted include Darwin Wile's *Identifying and Finding the Mammals of Jackson Hole,* and World Wide Web sites, such as those of the Canadian Museum of Nature, Nature Works, and Wikipedia, for the natural history of the pika.

Usha Lee McFarling's *Los Angeles Times* February 26, 2003, article, "A Tiny Warning of Global Warming Effects" describes the potential impacts of a warming climate on pika. Likewise, The Center for Biological Diversity's October 4, 2007, Federal Endangered Species Act petition to list the pika, details the animal's life history and the threats to them from global warming.

A story by Cory Hatch in the *Jackson Hole News and Guide,* December 23, 2009, informs of an ongoing pika Teton Science School study in Grand Teton National Park in respect to climate change. Additional information regarding pika and warming climate may also be found at the *Exit Stage Right Extinction News Service* and *World Wildlife* Web sites.

If pika were to be listed under the Endangered Species Act, they would be the first animal in the lower-48 states to be placed under protection for reasons related to climate change. It would join polar bears that have been declared "threatened" because of rising temperatures.

However, in early February 2010, the U.S. Fish and Wildlife Service determined while some pika populations are declining, others are not. They said, "pikas will have enough high-elevation habitat to survive." The agency concluded protection under the Endangered Species Act was not warranted. (see Salt Lake City AP story: "Tiny pika overlooked for federal protection," in *Jackson Hole Daily*, February 5, 2010).

*A Pika's Tail* by Sally Plumb (1994) is a beautifully illustrated children's book about pika and mountain wildlife that can be enjoyed by all ages.

## IV-7
## Mountain Monarchs Help Save a Town

The history of the National Bighorn Sheep Center's origin goes back to the late 1970s, when a small group of activists were opposing any and all proposed timber harvest on the national forests surrounding Dubois, Wyoming. It was an era when environmental protest and activism was popular and effective. Through demonstrations, appeals, and litigation they contested any and all timber management activities. Their ultimate goal became closing down Dubois's Louisiana-Pacific sawmill in order to shut off local demand for timber sales.

They were finally successful. But in retrospect, declaring the shutting down of this mill an environmental victory may be debatable today. With the vast amount of dead and dying forest in the area and no means to utilize it, the mill closure might well become a pyrrhic victory.

The clear-cuts in lodgepole pine that were opposed back then are today all naturally reforested. At the time, there's no question the timber harvest areas were visually objectionable. And the roads required for timber harvest impacted roadless areas and wildlife habitat security. But thirty years later, it takes a trained eye to detect those same places. Most people viewing the areas where timber harvest occurred on the Shoshone and

Bridger-Teton National Forests back then, are today unaware there was even any cutting.

In recent years, there has been a large buildup of beetle-killed timber in the same and surrounding area with no means to utilize it. A brown forest exists. The inevitable result of the incredibly huge fuel loading caused by the dead and dying trees will be catastrophic fire—a replay of the 1988 Yellowstone conflagration or worse. Will the tens of thousands of acres of timber resources and wildlife habitat that potentially stand to be consumed by wildfire be less objectionable than the existence of a local mill that would have allowed processing some of the dead and dying material? I leave it up to readers to decide, I suppose it depends on one's point of reference and value system.

When the Louisiana-Pacific sawmill was shut down, the town of Dubois was literally put out of work. It was an example of what can happen when a local economy is pretty much based on a single resource or employer. The town leaders were left searching for a way to keep their economy viable. One thing they attempted to do was increase ecotourism by publicizing the area's abundant wildlife resources. Something positive that came out of it all, which I believe everyone can agree upon, was the idea for and subsequent establishment of the National Bighorn Sheep Interpretive Center.

In writing this story, I relied upon my research and field trips for three earlier articles I published on the Whiskey Mountain bighorn sheep herd and the Bighorn Sheep Center: "Counting Sheep in Dubois, Wyoming," *Teton Valley* magazine, Winter 1999-2000; "*Ewe* and Me in Dubois," *Persimmon Hill* magazine, Autumn 1999; and "The Dubois Wild Sheep Show," *Yellowstone-Teton Country* magazine, Summer/Fall 2004.

There have also been a number of other popular stories written about the Whiskey Mountain herd, including one that appeared in *Open Lands* magazine, Fall-Winter 2008; "The

Legendary Herd of Whiskey Mountain" by the Jackson Hole Land
Trust; and another by Johanna Love, "Rams to Rut, Butt Heads
in Dubois," *Jackson Hole News and Guide*, November 20, 2002.

Other works I consulted were, *The Wild Sheep of North
America*, proceedings of a Missoula, Montana workshop
sponsored by the Boone and Crockett, National Audubon
Society and the Wildlife Management Institute (1975); Michael
Whitfield's "Bighorn sheep *are* the Teton Range" in the Jackson
Hole Conservation Alliance newsletter (2004); and, professor
Harold Picton's "Chapter 11, The Rocky Mountain Bighorn
Sheep" in his *Large Mammal Ecology Syllabus*, Montana State
University, Bozeman (2007). Picton comprehensively describes
the ecology, history, and status of wild sheep populations within
the Greater Yellowstone region.

A very useful overview of the Teton Range bighorns was
also given in Cory Hatch's "Teton Range herd of bighorns
at risk of extinction," *Jackson Hole News and Guide*, February
17, 2010.

The natural history of bighorn sheep can be found at a
number of Web sites, two that I utilized were www.enature.com
and www.wikipedia.com.

A starting point for information on the potential genetic
effects of bighorn sheep trophy hunting is Robert R. Britt's
"Trophy Hunting Causes 'Reverse Evolution'" in *Live Science* at
www.livescience.com; and also Canadian biologist Marco Festa-
Blanchet's research which I cited in the story's text.

A report and analysis of the petroglyphs in Torrey Valley
can be found in Sharon Kahin and Larry Loendorf's "The Torrey
Valley, Wyoming, Petroglyph Recording Project," *La Pintura*, Vol.
24(1), Summer 1997.

Excerpts from historical journals that describe the
abundance of wildlife, including bighorns, in Teton Valley,
Idaho, may be found in my essay "The Original Natural Setting

of Pierre's Hole—A Changed and Changing Landscape." An essay alluding to and describing early day poaching by local residents of wild sheep in the northern Teton Range is "Bright-eyed Gneiss" by Michael Whitfield. Both essays are found in *Spindrift: Stories of Teton Basin* (2000).

An overview of the Sheep Eaters in the Yellowstone region can be found in Thomas Turiano's outstanding book, *Select Peaks of Greater Yellowstone* (2003), and also the displays and materials at the Dubois Bighorn Sheep Center.

## IV-8
## Rocky the Great Northern Logo

I have never visited Glacier National Park without viewing the iconic mountain goat in the wild. Still, seeing "Rocky," the Great Northern Railway mountain goat logo on trains crossing the northern prairies might cause some people to be curious about what the story is behind it.

If you visit Glacier Park, there are sure to be goats at Logan Pass or along the hiking trails that radiate out from there. The goats allow close-up observation and sometimes delight tourists by wandering through the parking lots. Because they mostly ignore people, and are habituated in that sense, does not mean they aren't wild animals. They are totally on their own to survive in some of the most awesome and vertical alpine terrain in the country.

Over the years, I have observed mountain goats in the Bitterroot Mountains in Montana, in Hell's Canyon below the Seven Devils, Yellowstone National Park near Cooke City, Glacier National Park, and once had one actually contest me face-to-face on a narrow ledge while I was climbing on the cliffs above the Pend Oreille River at Metaline Falls, Washington. I was the one who backed up and gave way, not the mountain goat.

In the 1970s, I had some field experience with mountain goats when I participated in helicopter surveys for them in Idaho's Hells Canyon below the Seven Devils Mountains. Mountain goats don't exactly run from approaching helicopters, instead they try to take cover or refuge among boulders, hiding beneath ledges and in rock recesses or caves. They are terrified of helicopters or airplanes flying low over them.

Some states, whose Game Departments have mountain goat hunting seasons, such as Montana and Alaska, have posted detailed information on the Web on the goat's natural history to help educate hunters; so has Glacier National Park to assist public education. An article, "Clinging to Existence," by Chrissy Koeth, *Montana Outdoors Magazine*, September-October 2008, provides an overview of the current status of the mountain goat in Montana.

The above natural history sources combined with two other works, "The Great Northern Railway Goat," in the *National Editorial Association Outing on Board the Great Northern Railway's N.E.A. Special,* July 27, 1922; and, C.W. Gutherie's excellent history, *All aboard for Glacier: The Great Northern Railway and Glacier National Park*, Far Country Press (2004), served as my major sources for this piece.

The question of how northeastern and north-central Montana towns along the Great Northern route got their names has two different versions: Spinning the globe comes from C.W. Gurthie's history; the other, Hill's daughter's European travels, is found in a *Big Sky* magazine article entitled "Exploring New Territory" by Rick and Susie Graetz, Winter 2009, pp 40-47.

For railroad buffs, there is a Great Northern Railway historical website at www.greatnorthern.net/GneGreatNorthernHistory. The history of the Blackfoot Winter of Starvation can be found at www.motherjones.com/politics/2005/09/accounting-coup

## IV-9
## The Miller Butte Mountain Lion: A Wild Emissary

I consider myself fortunate to be one of the few to have seen a mountain lion in the wild. It was at dawn on the lower Lamar River in Yellowstone National Park. Other than that, I have come upon two separate fresh kills by lions; and still other times, only their tracks. The ghost cat, like for most people, has generally always been one jump ahead of me. Jackson Hole's Miller Butte mountain lions were a unique and extraordinary wildlife event that allowed people to safely photograph and observe the big cats interacting with their native habitat.

However, I have come to realize, too, not everyone was thrilled by this wildlife event. Call me naive, but before the research for this book, I was not fully aware of the existence and extent of organized anti-predator activism and sentiment, such as that of the Abundant Wildlife Society of North America, Idaho Anti-Wolf Coalition, the Wyoming Wolf Coalition, and state-wide predator hunting associations and networks.

The early history surrounding Miller Butte was taken from my previous research and published works on the history of Jackson Hole.

For information on early-day attitudes towards predators and bounty hunting in Jackson Hole and the surrounding area, I referred to Doris Platts, *Wolftimes in the Jackson Hole Country: A Chronicle,* Bearprint Press (1989); pertinent excerpts from Edward Preple's, "Report on Condition of Elk in Jackson Hole, Wyoming," U.S. Biological Survey (c1912); and the April 1924 Jackson Hole stockman's meeting records. The *Jackson's Hole Courier* and *Pinedale Roundup* newspapers stories I cited were obtained from Platts' detailed research.

An insightful source of information into the government's predatory animal campaign in the western United States was

J. Earle Miller, "Hunting Wild Animals for Uncle Sam," *Popular Mechanics*, June 1925.

Numbers of cougar killed in Yellowstone National Park from 1904 to 1925, and "reliable" cougar reports (totaling 105) from 1970 to 1978 in Yellowstone, may be found in D.B. Houston's "YNP Research Note No. 5" (1978).

From 1998 to date, I followed the many newspaper stories and editorials published in the *Jackson Hole News and Guide,* and other Wyoming newspapers, concerning cougars. My files contain more than twenty-two stories, many of which I drew upon for this article. The reporters and writers for those included: Robert Aland, Cara Blessley, Cory Hatch, Rebecca Huntington, Tom Mangelsen, Rachel Odell, Whitney Royster, Karen and Rick Shea, and Angus Thuermer. At this writing, the most recent reporting of cougar incidents in Teton Valley is by Hope Strong, "Troubled cat harvested, more emerge," *Valley Citizen*, January 20, 2010.

Brigid Mander's *JH Weekly* story, "Population: 5000: State of the elk refuge," December 23-29, 2009, provided recent general information and overview on the refuge's management plans.

I owe Jackson Hole's Cougar Fund a great deal of gratitude for their freely given assistance, particularly Director Sara Carlson and renowned photographer Tom Mangelsen for copies of their Winter 2007-08 and Summer 2008 newsletters, informative pamphlets, Mangelsen's and Clara Blessley's admirable book, *Spirit of the Rockies,* and the photograph kindly contributed by Mangelsen. Sara Carlson also kindly reviewed and provided comment on an early draft of this story.

I referred to Ted Kerasote's June-July 1999 *Sports Afield* article, "Too Close for Comfort," regarding concern for the habituation of cougars, and to Sam Curtis and Tom Dickson's article, "A Close Look at Mountain Lions," in *Montana*

*Outdoors,* July-August 2008, for what is happening to the lions in Montana.

There are a number of recent excellent reference books and essays available on mountain lions, those that I consulted in the preparation of this essay were:

Bolgiano, C., "Concepts of Cougar" in: *The World of Wilderness: Essays on the Power and Purpose of Wild Country.* Edited by T.H. Watkins and P. Byrnes. Roberts Reinhart Publications in cooperation with The Wilderness Society, Niwot, CO (1991), pp 85-106.

Busch, R.H., *The Cougar Almanac: A Complete Natural History of the Mountain Lion.* Lyons and Buford. NY (1996), 144 p.

Mangelsen, T.D. with story by Clara Shea Blessley, *Spirit of the Rockies: The Mountain_Lions of Jackson Hole.* Quality Books, Inc. & Images of Nature, Omaha, NE (1999), 64 p.

Matthiessen, P., *Wildlife in America.* Penguin Books, NY (1987), 347 p.

Shaw, H.G., *Soul Among Lions: The Cougar as a Peaceful Adversary.* Johnson Books, Boulder, CO (1989), 140 p.

World Wide Web sites were also researched: "More Jackson Hole Wildlife: Cougars on Refuge (2-25-99)" at www.forwolves. org and "Cougar" at www.wilipedia.org. In addition, the Web was also a source for information on Buffalo Jones and Ben Lilly. Additional materials on Buffalo Jones are on file at the Yellowstone National Park museum archives at Gardiner, Montana and Robert Easton and Mackenzie Brown's book, *Lord of Beasts* (1961). Additional information on Lilly was also found in Robinson's *Predatory Bureaucracy* cited below.

Robinson, M.J., *Predatory Bureaucracy: The Extermination of Wolves and the Transformation of the West,* University Press of Colorado (2005) chronicles a comprehensive history of predator control practices in the western United States, and many of the individual personalities involved, including a comprehensive history of the Bureau of Biological Survey.

William Stolzenburg's *Where the Wild Things Were: Life, Death, and Ecological Wreckage in a Land of Vanishing Predators* (2008), which I cited in the story text, provides information and research findings on the regulatory role of top predators and resulting ecosystem simplification from their absence.

In *Of Wolves and Men* (1978), Barry Lopez gives a profound analysis of the history of man's relationship and interactions with predators. I recommend it for anyone who ponders these things. Lopez addresses the question of why man continues destroying wild things even when the need to do so no longer exists. He decides, that "it is a symbolic act." Essentially, Lopez concludes, predators are scapegoats for European man's fear and hatred of wild things, and their destruction is a way of expressing antipathy towards them and wilderness. Similar sobering analysis on the subject can be found in Steve Nicholls' *Paradise Found: Nature In America at the Time of Discovery* (2009). Obviously, the eighteenth-century exhortations of Puritan minister Cotton Mather to make the "howling wilderness" into a "fruitful field" continues to have a following.

I also studied the Wyoming Game and Fish Commission's 19-page mountain lion hunting regulations booklet and the Wyoming Game and Fish Department's state-of-the-art/ science, September 7, 2006, *Mountain Lion Management Plan*, available online. The plan itself is a good piece of work; the concern remains how it is actually applied locally and elsewhere throughout the state. I also consulted Montana Fish, Wildlife and Park's 2009 mountain lion hunting regulations, a 16-page booklet. Lion hunting in both states is highly regulated. I did not review Idaho's regulations to see how they compare.

It is known that five cougars have died of plague in the

Greater Yellowstone in recent years, others have been killed for livestock depredation, and there have been road kills, too. One of the lions that died of plague in 2010 was a female with kittens. A cougar was road killed on Ski Hill Road near Alta in 2009, and another was shot along State-Line Road in Alta after it killed a pet llama in 2009 (see below). It's uncertain to me how this unplanned mortality figures into the state's quota systems.

An overview of Beringia South's ongoing cougar research project in Jackson Hole and Grand Teton National Park is given in Cory Hatch's article, "A Lion's Tale, *Jackson Hole* magazine," Winter 2009-10, pp 42-48. In nine years of research, they have captured and collared more than seventy individual cougars. The study currently has two more years to run.

As a postscript to this story, in December 2009, a 120 pound mountain lion killed a llama near a residence in Alta, Wyoming. The llama owner claimed to have shot and killed the lion only "reluctantly." Some might say the reluctance was New West; shooting it was Old West. But it was another example where rural residential development had occurred within historic big game winter range. Wintering big game animals attract predators, and if livestock, dogs, or other pets are allowed to run free within those habitats, they can be at risk.

This is not to lay blame. There are many of us that enjoy living close to nature, but to *coexist* with minimal conflict, especially with mega-fauna and predators, people must be aware of the potential human-wildlife interactions they are setting up between the animals and themselves. In such cases, people need to take reasonable actions to minimize or avoid undesirable consequences. With more people and developments encroaching on wildlife habitat, it would appear to be a desirable and positive thing to learn to do. Charles Craighead's book, *Who Ate the Backyard: Living with Wildlife on Private Land* (1997) can be a starting point.

If people and wildlife are going to learn to *coexist* local governments also need to become more proactive and play a positive role in education and incorporating appropriate requirements or protocols into planning and zoning. In many rural areas or places where urban areas and wildlands interface, coexistence has not traditionally been a *modus operandi* or *modus vivendi* (an arrangement for coexistence under which matters of dispute can reasonably be settled). Historically, the value of wildlife has not always been recognized, nor potential interactions with wild creatures fully appreciated; but in truth, sharing the land with wildlife can contribute much to the quality of our lives and to our sense of place.

## IV-10
## North America's Last Great Wildlife Migration

In summer 2001, my wife, Pattie, and I traveled to the Alaska's Arctic National Wildlife Refuge to witness the Porcupine Caribou Herd migration. We feared for the worst: it might be a last opportunity to observe it still intact. The incoming presidential administration and a Republican-controlled House and Senate gave much to worry about for the future of the unprotected "1002 lands" (coastal plains) within the refuge. Subsurface, the "1002" land has been identified to contain oil reserves.

Over the years, Pattie and I have traveled worldwide to many wildernesses to observe endangered wildlands and wildlife—Alaska's McNeil River Bear Sanctuary, the Ecuadorian Amazon, Central America, Uganda and Tanzania in East Africa, the Galapagos Islands, Madagascar and Zanzibar. Our trip to the Arctic Refuge stands out as one of the highlights among those wilderness journeys.

In writing this essay, I drew upon our firsthand experiences and observations while visiting the Arctic Refuge, and the research for articles that Pattie and I separately authored and published in *Teton Valley* magazine entitled "Almost off the Map" (Winter 2001-2002).

The references cited in the story text were adopted from my research for those earlier published stories. In addition, in 2000, we had visited the Serengeti in Tanzania and observed close-up on the ground, as well as from the air, the great wildebeest migration. It allowed comparisons with the Porcupine Herd migration that were useful in preparing this piece. The wildebeest migration is frequently cited in popular journals as the last great animal migration on Earth, overlooking the caribou of America's Far North.

For material on terrestrial migrations in general, and more specifically Jackson Hole's antelope migration, I referred to David Wilcove's *No Way Home: The Decline of the World's Great Animal Migrations*, Island Press/Shearwater Books (2008); Joel Berger's "The Last Mile: How to Sustain Long Distance Migration in Mammals," *Journal of Conservation Biology* 18:320-31 (2004); and, also the biological and political insights on the Arctic Refuge and the Porcupine herd migration in Chapter 10 of Joel Berger's *The Better to Eat You With: Fear in the Animal World* (2008).

For general information on the conservation easements protecting the Jackson Hole/Grand Teton National Park to Green River antelope migration corridor, the reader is referred to Angus M. Thuermer's "Deal helps pronghorn," *Jackson Hole Daily*, February 2, 2010.

A computer-generated map of the Porcupine caribou herd calving areas for 1983 to 1999 was published online by the U.S. Fish and Wildlife Service in 2001. It was viewed by the author at www.maperuzin.com. The maps were originally posted online by the U. S. Fish and Wildlife Service under the title *Potential Impacts of Proposed Oil and Gas Development on the Arctic Refuge's Coastal Plain: Historic Overview and Issues of*

*Concern* at the Web page for the Arctic National Wildlife Refuge, Fairbanks, Alaska. Soon afterward, when the new political administration took office, the map was removed from the Web site. Although the data were scientifically derived, it conflicted with the administration's ideology and political agenda.

I also utilized a number of other Web sites for additional information and verification. These included, but were not necessarily limited to EnviroZine: *Arctic Refuge Treasures* at www.ec.gc.ca, *Caribou in the Artic Refuge* at www.arcticcirle.uconn.edu, and www.beingcaribou.com

I highly recommend conservationist Leanne Allison's and biologist's Karsten Heuer's 2004 inspirational documentary film, *being caribou*. Allison and Heuer followed the caribou migration on foot through all seasons, experiencing firsthand the conditions the caribou endure. Tracking the caribou in extreme arctic conditions was less daunting for them, perhaps, then afterwards, when they tried to present their story and show their film to antagonistic and indifferent congressmen.

The United State's Prudhoe Bay oil discovery and development in the 1960s raised the Canadian government's hope for similar riches in the Yukon and Northwest territories. Canada's Justice Thomas Berger was sent to the Northwest and Yukon territories to hold hearings. Amazingly, and apparently totally unexpectedly, he concluded "the native cultures and the integrity of the land must not be sacrificed for resource development." Instead, the Canadian Ivvavik and Vuntut National Parks were created on the heels of Berger's report. Both Canadian parks are contiguous to the United States' Arctic National Wildlife Refuge. One only need visit Prudhoe Bay today to see the wisdom in Canada's decisions.

Finally, while I do not say it in the story, it should be stated here: As one way to put an end to the continual efforts by development interests within the United States to undo the Arctic Refuge, some have suggested establishing an International Park combining Vuntut and Ivvavik Parks with the Arctic Refuge, similar to the Waterton-Glacier International Peace Park. The establishment of an international park would include designating the controversial "1002 lands" wilderness. This would bring decades of Canadian and American conservation efforts to a lasting and successful conclusion, and protect the priceless biological treasures, among which is one of Earth's last great terrestrial animal migrations.

## IV-11
## The Great Escape: Free-Ranging Bison Return to the Hole

One cold, predawn, autumn morning in the mid-1990s, I was making my way off-trail to the river north of Schwabacher Landing in Grand Teton National Park. I had only a small penlight that barely illuminated the ground in front of me. Suddenly a dark form heaved up out of the tall sagebrush directly in my path. It was only a few steps in front of me. The dull light cast by my flashlight revealed a bull bison standing facing me head-on. It seemed almost close enough to touch. The short hair on the back of my neck began to quiver. I swear steam blew out of the bison's nostrils! I do not know who was the most startled, him or me. I gingerly backed up, and he allowed me to go around him peacefully. I will always remember the adrenaline surge from that unintended close encounter.

I spent a good amount of time in Teton Park in the late 1970s and early 1980s, but I can not recall ever seeing a bison, although I now realize they were there. Since that time, the bison herd has grown and the woolly beasts are readily viewable and immensely enjoyed by many.

I always assumed Teton Park's bison had made their way south from Yellowstone National Park on their own. When I learned of their true origin, I thought it was a compelling story and a generally little known part of Jackson Hole's and Grand Teton National Park's history. It is also an important part of the story of the overall history and conservation of the American bison.

It turns out, too, Teton Park's herd has particularly important conservation value in that, thus far, sampling has shown it to be a genetically pure population—no cattle gene introgression, based on the limited sampling to date. If that's the case, it is significant biologically, and a relative rarity in bison herds today.

There are a large number of encyclopedic and scholarly works on the history of the American bison. The history of the mass murder of the great herds has been a morbidly compelling subject for nature writers and historians alike. The American bison slaughter, which has no equal in ferocity and wastefulness in world history, remains a moral issue shamefully weighing upon the nation's character and conscience.

The primary reference works that I relied on in researching and crafting this story were:

Barness, L., *Heads, Hides and Horns: The Complete Buffalo Book.* Texas Christian University Press, Fort Worth (1985), 233 p.

Danz, H.P., *Of Bison and Man.* University Press of Colorado. Niwot, CO (1997), 231 p.

Dary, D.A., *The Buffalo Book: The Full Saga of the American Animal.* Sage Books, Swallow Press, Chicago (1974), 374 p.

Easton, R. and M. Brown, *Lord of Beasts: The Saga of Buffalo Jones.* The University of Arizona Press (1961), 287p.

Nicholls, S., *Paradise Found: Nature in America at the Time of*

*Discovery.* University of Chicago Press (2009).

Punke, M., *Last Stand: George Bird Grinnell, the Battle to Save the Buffalo, and the Birth of the New West.* Smithsonian Books. HarperCollins, NY (2007), 286 p.

Rinella, S. *American Buffalo: In Search of a Lost Icon.* Spiegel & Green, NY (2008), 277 p.

Robinson, M.J., *Predatory Bureaucracy: The Extermination of Wolves and the Transformation of the West*, University Press of Colorado, Boulder (2005), pp 4-45.

Sandoz, M., *The Buffalo Hunters.* Bison Book ed., Hastings House, NY (1978), 372 p.

For additional and local material on buffalo poaching in early day Yellowstone National Park, I also consulted Diem, Kenneth and Lenore, *A Community of Scalawags, Renegades, Discharged Soldiers and Predestined Stinkers: A History of Northern Jackson Hole and Yellowstone's Influence,* Grand Teton Natural History Association, Moose, WY (1998), 198p.

The early restoration methods for bison in Yellowstone Park are described in the above works and other sources, such as the park's newsletter *Yellowstone's Buffalo Ranch Turns 100.* August 15, 2007.

The detailed history and biology of *The Bison of Yellowstone National Park* by Margaret M. Meagher, NPS Scientific Monograph No. 1, 1972, is available online at www.nps.gov/history/history/onlinebooks/bison It was also the source, in part, for the story on Old Tex, along with personal communication with Yellowstone National Park Museum Curator Colleen Curry, and the 2005 *Boone and Crocket Club's Record Book.*

For material on the Jackson Hole Wildlife Park, I researched the Harold and Jane Fabian Collection, Grand Teton National

Park Archives Historic Collection: Accession No. GRTE-00487 and Catalog No. GRTE 48024, inclusive dates 1930-53. I am indebted to archivist Alice Hurt's kind assistance in providing access to the collection.

The Jackson Hole Historical Society and Museum has a photograph in their collection (image 2005.0018.001) that shows a cow bison being released at the Wildlife Park.

I referred to R.W.Righter's *Crucible for Conservation: The Struggle for Grand Teton National Park,* Colorado Associated University Press (1982), for the history of the establishment of Grand Teton National Park. Righter also contains valuable insights and commentary on the Jackson Hole Wildlife Park.

The 1963 report on the National Park Service by the committee of scientists led by A. Starker Leopold, that I cited, is available on the World Wide Web.

History of the Jackson Hole bison herd was also gleaned from senior park biologist Steve Cain's commentary "Jackson Bison: The Good, the Bad and the (not so) Ugly," in *Grand Teton National Park Report* (2007); and, "History of Bison in Jackson Hole" in the *Draft Bison and Elk Management Plan and Environmental Assessment* prepared by the U.S. Fish and Wildlife Service National Elk Refuge and Grand Teton National Park, June 2005, pp 148-150. The environmental statement also contains some history regarding the Jackson Hole Wildlife Park.

I owe additional thanks to Teton Park biologist Steven Cain, who kindly offered helpful information and updated me on aspects of the current status of the park's bison herd, and also to Yellowstone National Park biologist Rick Wallen, who provided me with valuable insights on the importance of the genetics of Yellowstone's bison and the "conservation value" of genetically pure populations.

The *Boone and Crockett Club's Records of North American Big Game* (12th Edition, 2005) was consulted for the number of record book bison taken in Teton County, Wyoming, from 1990 to 2001. The Boone and Crockett version of Old Tex's demise states the bull was killed in "a herd reduction program." That was not the case, unless you consider Old Tex to have been a herd of one.

I also consulted Web sites, such as www.wikipedia.org/wiki/American Bison and www.answers.goggle.com for additional natural history and general information on the American bison. A starting point for information on white buffalo can be found at the Jamestown Buffalo Museum Web site.

An summary overview of the problem of genetic pollution in bison can be found on the World Wide Web at www.nature.org/magazine/winter 2008/features. For additional and detailed information on bison genetics, the reader is referred to Halbert, N.D and J. N. Derr "A Comprehensive Evaluation of Cattle Introgression into U.S. Federal Bison Herds," *Journal of Heredity* (December 2006), pp 1-12.

My files contain a stack of newspaper clippings, *Buffalo Field Campaign* newsletters, and other conservation organization materials on bison in relation to the recent and ongoing brucellosis controversy and what many consider the inhumane handling and slaughter of those bison that migrate out of Yellowstone National Park. In May 2008, after Yellowstone's bison population had been reduced by half, two ranchers and a statewide ranching group followed up by filing suit against the Montana Department of Livestock insisting that it remove all bison from Horse Butte [on national forest land] near West Yellowstone, even though the Forest Service had retired the grazing permits there. Killing off half the park's bison and separation of cattle and bison was not good enough for them; agricultural producers simply do not want bison outside the park.

My files also contain news articles on the continuing and ongoing reduction program for the Jackson Hole/Teton Park herd. The bison goring hunter story may be found in the *Jackson Hole Daily*, September 29, 2009.

An article in the March 28-29, 2009 *Jackson Hole Daily* describes the attempted efforts to ship genetically pure, brucellosis-free bison that wander out of Yellowstone Park to Indian reservation lands, rather than to slaughter. An editorial "Shipping of Bison to Wyoming a Milestone" in *The Bozeman Daily Chronicle*, April 3, 2009, describes this as a step forward, recognizing Yellowstone bison as an important "last wild bison" genetic repository.

At this time, though, seventy-four or more bison are caught in limbo. Wyoming's Wind River Reservation Arapahoe Tribal Council for some reason voted down the transfer to their reservation. And, while the Fort Belknap Reservation expressed interest, "it wasn't ready" to take the animals in a timely manner. Meanwhile, Montana Governor Brian Schweitzer asked Ted Turner to adopt the bison for five years and then return them to the state. As compensation, Turner asked to keep 90 percent of the calf crop. Some people are opposed to that, saying wild bison shouldn't be "commercialized." Stephany Seay, with the Buffalo Field Campaign, has pointed out, "There's [public] land in Montana, the alternatives are not just slaughter or Turner." While another person asked, "Why can't the captured bison just be returned to Yellowstone Park? They are Yellowstone bison, so let them be Yellowstone bison." Indeed, why not?

Some of the sources for the above are: "Turner's bison bid draws ire," *Jackson Hole Daily*, January 8, 2019; and, "Activists call for bison on state land," *Bozeman Daily Chronicle*, January 8, 2010; and also the Web at http://bozemandailychronicle.com/articles/2010/01/08/000bison.txt

The livestock industry's uncompromising slaughter of bison, ostensibly as a means to control brucellosis, especially when you consider that elk also carry the disease, reeks of red herring. There does not even appear to be a protocol or method for brucellosis testing that is acceptable to livestock producers and state officials. Bison held in quarantine are reportedly sometimes "tested for the disease dozens of times."

In January 2010, Wyoming ranchers opposed a proposal to move fourteen wild bison from Yellowstone National Park to Wyoming's Guernsey State Park. The bison had been repeatedly tested for brucellosis and certified free of the bacteria by the Wyoming state veterinarian. The eastern Wyoming ranching community was reported to be "skeptical about introducing bison into an area that's free of brucellosis." The Wyoming ranching community's opposition to moving bison onto the Wind River Reservation and Guernsey State Park is summarized in the AP story, "Wyoming Ranchers wary of moving bison to park" *Idaho Falls Post Register*, January 24, 2010. Ironically, the bison is Wyoming's state animal, but state politicians and ranchers in Wyoming do not want bison on state land.

I recognize the importance of disease control, but because it appears to be dogmatic and overdone with bison it raises the question: Is it possible publicly unmentionable issues are involved, too? Could it be the severe measures that have been applied to bison reflect a type of atavism, a throwback? Given the Old West history with bison, how much of the overdone reactions reflect a fear of market competition from bison products, the practice of eliminating wild animals that compete for domestic livestock forage (a bison on the average eats twenty-four pounds of forage a day), and simply an ancestral throw back to the nineteenth-century practice of clearing wild animals from the land? Do the biopolitics that destroyed the great herds still lurk beneath it all?

In answer to the above, in a January 17, 2009, *Bozeman Chronicle* article entitled "Bison after brucellosis" by Daniel Person, Errol Rice, executive vice president of the Montana Stock Grower's Association confirms the issue goes deeper than disease control. He is quoted saying: "I think the rancher's No. 1 fear is brucellosis. But yeah, I can honestly say there is fear for competition for grass. But it is more than competition for grass, it is fear of being pushed off the land entirely."

Others might also say the deep-seated reluctance to allow bison to reoccupy parts of their historic habitat is similar that for the wolf: "it lets the wild back into Western lands."

Some may criticize my raising these issues as unconstructive, but in truth, the bison issue is deeply representative of our society's attitudes towards wildlife, especially the western ranching community's. And how we resolve it, will be reflective of our culture's enlightenment. How far have we progressed beyond "shooting with impunity" and "clearing wild animals from the land"?

A 2009 federal General Accountability Office report criticized the bison brucellosis control program, asking for more transparency. The GAO intervention story is summarized in Cory Hatch's story, "Bison group becomes more open to public: Federal report asked for increased transparency," *Jackson Hole News and Guide,* November 25, 2009. At this writing, the most recent report on the issue is Daniel Person's "FWP generating new bison plan," in the *Bozeman Daily Chronicle,* January 15, 2010, in which the Montana Fish, Wildlife and Parks Director Dave Risley, stated his department "wants to be more active [involved] in bison management ...and take the lead on the issue." To their credit, the department is initiating a plan to manage and restore bison on lands within the state.

Finally, I should mention, about a decade ago, I was contracted by the U.S. Forest Service and The Church Universal and Triumphant in cooperation with the Rocky Mountain Elk foundation and the U.S. Department of Interior to prepare a *Devil's Slide Purchased Conservation Easement Baseline Study, Royal Teton Ranch Conservation Project*, January 2001. The purpose of the project was to mitigate conflicts and protect historic winter ranges and migration corridors for wildlife (bison were among the wildlife specifically mentioned) migrating out of the northern part of Yellowstone National Park. The federal government spent tens of million of dollars to purchase easements and conduct a number of significant land exchanges in order to protect the identified "nationally significant wildlife resources." The project was dedicated in an onsite ceremony attended by high-ranking government officials, including the Secretary of Interior Babbitt. However, it has not served its intended purpose for the bison that migrate out of the park. The Montana Department of Livestock has continued to operate *carte blanche* across all jurisdictional boundaries, including the national forest and the adjoining easement lands that were intended to protect wildlife. Only the national park has remained inviolate. Today, few people appear to be aware or remember that the easements were purchased by the government through donations and taxpayer money to provide habitat for wildlife migrating out of the north-end of Yellowstone Park. The Forest Service, caught in the middle, has not brought attention to it either.

Meanwhile, bison continue to be a main draw for tourists. In the *Wyoming 2010 Official Travelers Journal*, bison are pictured in no less than eleven advertisements, more than any other animal.

When Grand Teton National Park was established, compromises were made to be able to move the legislation forward. These included allowing continuation of elk hunting and domestic livestock grazing in the park. For decades, cattle, elk, and bison have quietly intermingled and grazed together on the same ranges in Teton Park without any known brucellosis transmission or occurrence. Now, today, it is potentially an issue. Why should it now become an issue, when for decades it has been *de facto* proven not to be a problem? Brucellosis is without a doubt something to closely monitor, but drastic preemptive actions seem to be overkill.

Interspecies hybridization is a significant threat to species conservation worldwide. It is only relatively recent that America's greatest conservation success story—bison restoration—has been recognized to be threatened by domestic cattle gene introgression. This finding gives genetically pure populations, such as represented by Yellowstone National Park's bison, inordinate conservation and biological value. Genetically pure populations are being identified and, where they exist, designated and managed as "conservation herds." According to Halbert and Derr (op.cit.), of the fourteen public bison herds that occur in North America, cattle introgression has been identified in all but six.

The world's largest private bison owner is Ted Turner, he has nearly fifty thousand. His Castle Rock herd, at the Vermejo Park Ranch in New Mexico, is descendant of animals obtained from Yellowstone in the 1950s. They have been tested and found to be genetically pure bison. Contrary to some, and in all fairness, Turner's interest in conserving the bison has not been strictly "commercial." We should remember also, in the history of bison conservation, it was the foresight of private individuals that originally, and in large part, made the restoration of bison possible.

## IV-12
## Wolveranne: The Alta 4-H Skunk Bear Project

A great deal of my life has been spent outdoors, but I must confess, I have never seen a wolverine in the wild, nor do I ever expect I will. Yet I am thrilled to know that the skunk bear roams the mountains only a few miles from my home in Alta, Wyoming. When I look out at the mountains, it contributes sublimely to the grandeur of the scene knowing wolverines are out there.

There was a paucity of literature and studies on the wolverine for the conterminous United States up until only a decade or so ago. In the mid-1990s, the Biodiversity Legal Foundation's attempt to have the wolverine listed under the Endangered Species Act failed, partially because of inadequate information. This, combined with sightings and incidents around the time, resulted in biologists and conservationists spotlighting attention and research on the species.

The results of the scientifically designed and conducted Alta 4-H wolverine study project were a catalyst encouraging additional research. Today, there are ongoing studies by the Wolverine Foundation, the Hornocker Institute, The Wildlife Conservation Society, the U.S. Forest Service research branch, and State Game and Fish Departments. But it was the 4-H'ers project in the Teton Mountains that had pretty much led the way.

Unfortunately, wildlife studies involving trapping, transplanting, anesthetizing, collaring with transmitters, surgically implanting transmitters, and handling, involves very real risk of injury or death for the animals. Wolveranne was recaptured several times in the years after the 4-H'ers handed the study off to The Wildlife Conservation Society. The last time Anne trigged a log box trap, she was not fully inside it. When the heavy lid dropped, it crushed her. You can observe Wolveranne as a mounted taxidermist specimen at the Wyoming Game and Fish regional office in Jackson, Wyoming.

There are also noninvasive ways to study rare animals that are being used that put them at less risk. These involve motion sensory cameras, hair and feces analyses, tracking, and visual observation. "Hair traps" can be as simple as a strand of barbwire surrounding a bait site. Collected hairs are then analyzed for their DNA patterns which can be used to identify individuals and estimate population status.

Over the past decade, a great deal of research has been conducted and information gathered on wolverines. A summary of this research can be found in the *Wildlife Conservation Society North American Program Newsletter*, Fall-Winter 2009.

Latest findings from ongoing studies are also available on the World Wide Web. One Web source for the Teton Mountains is "Wolverine Ecology and Habitat Use in the Teton Range of Western Wyoming" at www.wolverinefoundation.org/research/teton98.htm.

A number of other Web sites have posted information on the natural history of wolverine, those I consulted, in no particular order, include:

www.defenders.org/wildlife_and_habitat/wildlife/wolverine.php,

www.gi.alaska.edu/scienceforum/ASF14/1436.html,

www.earthscape.org/t2/scr01/scr01gg.html,

www.nps.gov/dena/naturescience/wolverine.htm,

www.wikipedia.org/wiki/Wolverine,

www.wolverinefoundation.org/kids/kids sa.htm,

www.adfg.state.ak.us/pubs/notebook/furbear/wolverin.php,

www.hww.ca/hww2.asp?id=108.

A recent report on the status of the proposal to list the wolverine under the Endangered Species Act, entitled "Groups Plan Wolverine Lawsuit" can be found at www.casperstartribune.net/articles/2008/07/09/news/wyoming/ and www.jhguide.

com/article.php?art_id=3289.

A starting point for information on the wolverine's occurrence in the Sierra Nevada Range, California, is www.allheadlinenews. com/articles/7010254009.

Additional information on the Fossil Butte road kill wolverine can be found at www.casperstartribune.net/articles/2004/04/14/ news/wyomingcbeb62f81650072687.

Articles and reports documenting wandering or dispersing wolverines can be found at

www.mtexpress.com/index2.php?ID=2005124687,

www.msnbc.msn.com/id/6180672,

www.dailycamera.com/news/2009/jun/19/young-wolverine-makes-500-mile-trip-to-co.

Concerns for the potential impacts of winter recreation on wolverines can be found at www.wildwyo.org/NationalForest/ BridgerTetonNF/helicopterskiing

For the Alta 4-H Club wolverine project, some additional pertinent references are:

The "Teton Wolverine Project Progress Report" by Jeff Copeland, Idaho Game and Fish, Idaho Falls, 8 p + map. Bound Mimeo (December 1999).

Inman, R. et al., "Wolverine Makes Extensive Movements in the Greater Yellowstone Ecosystem," *Northwest Science* Vol. 78, No. 3 (2004), pp 261-266.

Schmidt, T., "Wolveranne and the West Slope Mountain Ramblers," *Wyoming Wildlife* (January 1999), pp 32-35.

Strong, H., "Around the Grand – Wolverine," *Teton Valley News* (Feb. 17, 2005), p B1.

In addition, I interviewed Andy Heffron and Dick Staiger, Alta 4-H wolverine study leaders and participants. They also made available their files of newspaper articles, journal articles, reports, study plans, photographs, daily diaries and findings.

Information on the wolverine as a symbol is given at www.amos.indiana.edu/libray/scripts/wolverine.html

www.earthscape.org/t2/scr01/scr01gg.html

www.wikipedia.org/wiki/Wolverine.

Stories of the wolverine in the Dene tradition were obtained from the Dene Wodih Society in *Wolverine Myths and Visions,* edited by Patrick Moore and Angela Wheelock, University of Nebraska Press (1990), 259 p.

An article published in the *Christine Science Monitor* expressing concern over the potential biological impact from trapping wolverines in Montana can be found at www.features. csmonitor.com/environment/2008/05/20/a-husband-and-wife-team-in-mont.

For a summary of recent findings regarding current and historic distribution and habitat use by wolverines, I also reviewed the publication by Parks, N. "On The Track of the Elusive Wolverine," *USDA Pacific Northwest Science Findings,* No. 114 (July 2009), 5 pp.

The most recent information on ongoing wolverine research and findings for Glacier National Park, Greater Yellowstone, the Absoroka-Beartooth, and elsewhere, can be found at the Wolverine Foundation Web site at www.wolverinefoundation. org/research.

Robinson, M.J. *Predatory Bureaucracy* (2005) was the source for information on the last Colorado wolverines.

## IV-13
## The Pack's Memoirs

Not all that long ago, there was little scientific-based information available for wolves. Adolph Murie's *The Wolves of Mount McKinley* (1944) was groundbreaking research. It represented the first time wolves were studied objectively. Murie's published findings, along with L. David Mech's *The Wolf* (1970), and Barry Lopez's *Of Wolves and Men* (1978), were the only reference works available until relatively recently. The passage of the 1973 Endangered Species Act and the 1995 reintroduction of wolves made a huge difference. Today, library shelves groan under the weight of research papers, books, and magazine articles on wolves that were produced over the past ten to fifteen years. But we as a society are still struggling with defining the place and role of wolves in our wildlands.

My limited field experience with wolves includes researching and publishing a 1971 report on anecdotal wolf sightings for Pend Oreille County, Washington. At the time, wolves appeared to be making occasional winter forays into the northern part of the county adjoining British Columbia. My report, entitled "Wolf Sightings and Reports, Sullivan Lake Ranger District," was published by the Washington State Fish and Game Department in their *1974-75 Big Game Status Report*.

Today, it is recognized the area, particularly northern Idaho, had "an unbroken history of wolf sightings in the 1950-1970s" (Robinson, M.J., 2005, op.cit.), but that information was not readily available back then.

After the reintroduction of wolves into Yellowstone National Park, my wife, Pattie, and I participated in "wolf watching" activities for a number of seasons (still do) in the Lamar Valley. As author Laurie Thurston chronicles in *A Story in a Valley*: "On a ridge above Lamar Valley, the Druid Pack makes their entrance. I watch them... against the backdrop of dawn; they walk single file as if they are aware of how captivated they hold their audience below."

On one occasion, we spent several days in the field with biologist Jim Halfpenny, and another occasion we met wolf expert David Mech, who had a group of students with him. And also like anyone who watches wolves in Yellowstone, we had fascinating conversations in Lamar Valley with park biologist Rick McIntyre. We also attended lectures and seminars on wolves. Three in particular stand out: conservationist Renee Askins, and biologists Nathan Varley and Joel Berger. I also attended a seminar by Barry Lopez where the question was posed: "What is *just* treatment for wolves." It's a relevant and timely, but deceptively complex, question.

In April 1997, my wife and I were cycling in Grand Teton National Park. The road had just been plowed open, and only non-motorized use was allowed. I was about a hundred yards ahead of Pattie, when, unseen by me, two wolves crossed the road between us, just ahead of her. It turned out to be the first sighting of wolves in Teton Park. Pattie filed the *first* official sighting report with the park and later published "A Chance Encounter" in the anthology *Stories of the Wild* (2001) about her sighting. It was an experience that, nearly ten years later, she is still thrilled to recount. Later, on another occasion, I also observed wolves in Teton Park while cross-country skiing.

Today, Teton Park is territory for three different wolf packs. A friend recently told me that while he was cross-country skiing at Jenny Lake, a pack of eight wolves appeared and crossed the lake on the ice in single file nose-to-tail. Smiling broadly, he said: "It was a sight I'll remember for the rest of my life."

In winter 2002, I published a story on "Wolf Watching" in *Yellowstone-Teton Country* magazine. Watching the Druid pack travel single file nose-to-tail across the snow and then suddenly, like in a military maneuver, fan out into a skirmish line and sweep down the valley was drum-rolling drama for me.

In 2001, Pattie and I traveled to the Arctic National Wildlife Refuge, where we saw wolves while rafting and camped along the Kongakut River. In one instance, while we were hiking down a draw, other members of our party told us that with binoculars they had observed a lone wolf following along some forty yards behind us. I certainly didn't feel alarmed by that, I imagined the wolf was curious. It's possible it may never have encountered people before.

The principal reference works and source materials I consulted in writing The Pack's Memoirs were:

Askins, R., *Shadow Mountain: A Memoir of Wolves, a Woman, and the Wild.* Doubleday, NY (2002), 321 p.

Busch, R., *The Wolf Almanac,* Lyons & Buford, NY (1995), 226 p.

Coleman, J., *Vicious: Wolves and Men in America*, Yale University Press, New Haven, CT. (2004), 270 p.

Grooms, S., *The Return of the Wolf,* North Word Press, Minocqua, WI (1993), 192 p.

Leopold, A., *A Sand County Almanac,* Oxford University Press (1949), 295 p.

Lopez, B., *Of Wolves and Men,* Charles Scribner's Sons, NY (1978), 309 p.

Nicholls, S., *Paradise Found: Nature in America at the Time of Discovery,* University of Chicago Press (2009), pp 426-449.

Robinson, M.J., *Predatory Bureaucracy: The Extermination of Wolves and the Transformation of the West,* University Press of Colorado, Boulder (2005), 473p.

Smith, D. and G. Ferguson, *Decade of the Wolf: Returning the Wild to Yellowstone,* The Lyon Press, Guilford, CT (2005), 212 p.

Williams, T., "The War on Varmints" in *Speaking for Nature,* The National Audubon Society, NY (1999), pp 62-87.

An additional source that gave insight into the early twentieth century federal and state government's predatory animal and pest campaigns that I utilized was: J. Earle Miller, "Hunting Wild Animals for Uncle Sam," *Popular Mechanics*, June 1925.

There is a great deal of information on wolves posted on the World Wide Web. Some sites that I consulted, in no particular order, included:

"The Eradication of the Wolf" at www.wildrockiesalliance.org/issues/wolves/index.html,

"Wolf Wars: America's Campaign to Eradicate the Wolf" at www.pbs.org/wnet/episodes/the-wolf-that-changed-america,

"Wolves and Wolf Lore" at www.geocities.com?AthensForum/3897/features/wolves,

"Origin of the Domestic Dog" at www.wikipedia.org/wiki/Orgin_of_the_domestic

"Wolf Restoration to Yellowstone" at www.nps.gov/yell/nature/animals/wolf/wolfrest.

The story of Wolf 527's demise, "One of Yellowstone's beloved wolves killed," was posted on the National Resources Defense Council Web site, November 16, 2009. Another side of 527's story can be found in "Outdoors with Ken Hunter 'No.527,'" April 28, 2010, *Webb Weekly*, Williamsport, PA.

There are a large number of journal, magazine, and newsletter articles available on Yellowstone wolves, some of those that I researched and refer to included:

Madson, C., "Wolves at the Doorstep" *Wyoming Wildlife Magazine* (June 1995).

Huntington, R., "How Will the Wolf Survive." *Jackson Hole Magazine* (Summer/Fall 2009).

Weaver, J., "The wolves of Yellowstone, history ecology and status." Natural Resources Report No. 14, National Park Service (1978), 38 p.

*Bugle Magazine* (September-October 2009), "Wolves," pp 55-83, contained data on the status of wolves in the northern Rocky Mountains as of that date, and also that of elk populations overtime in relation to the wolves' recovery.

A well-written piece by editor Anthony Licata and writer Keith McCafferty, "Predator and Prey" in *Field and Stream* magazine, March 2010, more or less contradicts *Bugle's* generalized statement that "wolves are having a major impact on elk populations across the Northern Rockies." That can be shown to be true for selected localized situations, but overall state-wide elk populations are reported as stable.

The abuse and notoriety hunter Robert Millage suffered from anti-hunters by being the first to legally kill a wolf in Idaho is described in the *Field and Stream* article, as well as the widespread hunter frustration and anger with alleged declining elk and deer populations attributed to wolves. Millage is quoted saying, "Anti-hunters threaten ... violence toward hunters but talk out the other side of their mouths in proclaiming 'coexistence.'" Millage created a blogsite where he posts the offensive messages he receives: www.wolfcomments.blogspot.com.

For information on state-of-the-art predator hunting methods, readers should peruse periodicals on the subject, such as: *Predator Hunting* and *The Trapper and Predator Caller* magazines.

The *Northern Rockies Conservation Cooperative*, 2009 annual newsletter, issue 22(1), contains a summary of pilot projects underway designed for reducing human-carnivore conflicts.

The Wildlife Conservation Society's Spring-Summer 2010 *North American Program Newsletter* provides an overview of some of the current Crown of the Continent programs in "Wild Jewels in the Crown of the Continent." Biologist's John Weaver's report documenting the wildlife values associated with the program can be found at www.wcscanada.org/publications.

To begin to learn about numbers of people, livestock, and wildlife killed by feral dogs vs. coyotes and wolves see: Anderson, T., "Rural West going to the dogs," *High Country News,* May 26, 2008, p9.

Volker Radeloff, et al., "Housing growth in and near United States protected area limits their conservation value." *Proceedings of the National Academy of Sciences* 107(2): 940-945 (2010) is an important study measuring the threats of residential development on conservation areas over time. A summary can be found at www.news.wisc.edu/17496.

Not all academics agree that it was the removal of predators that caused the explosion of the Kaibab deer population. For a differing viewpoint see: C. John Burke, 1973, "The Kaibab Deer Incident: A Long Persisting Myth," Bioscience 23(2): 113-114.

The case for declaring the wolf reintroduction illegal under the Endangered Species Act is presented in depth by Pinedale, Wyoming, author and sheep rancher Cat Urbigkit in *Yellowstone Wolves: A Chronicle of the Animals, the People, and the Politics* (2008), 350p. In additional, the *Pinedale Roundup* newspaper and Cat Urbigkit maintain a "Wolf Watch" website that provides detailed and current information on wolf happenings and events.

A legal analysis that finds in favor of the wolf restoration is Elizabeth C. Brown's "The 'Wholly Separate' Truth: Did the Yellowstone Wolf Reintroduction Violate Section 10 (J) of the Endangered Species Act?" Boston College of Environmental Affairs Law Review (2000), pp 425-466. Also on the Web at: www.bc.edu/bc_org/avp/law/wsch

Wyoming Wolf Coalition news releases and testimony in support of Wyoming's wolf management at the January 2010 Cheyenne hearings may be found on the Web. Their organization's stated goal is to "delist the introduced non-native Canadian gray wolf."

In addition to the above sources, for Part II, I also drew upon a large number of what were the latest and ongoing regional news stories at the time. Events shaping the tone and timbre of the "modern wolf wars" were being chronicled in the media almost daily. I've listed some of those that I referred to below:

Timothy Egan, "Wolf hunt reveals dark feelings in the changing West." *New York Times News Service* in *Jackson Hole Daily*, September 3, 2009.

*Jackson Hole Daily* (AP), "Idaho hunter target of anger after wolf kill," September 4, 2009.

*Jackson Hole Daily* (AP), "Wyoming steps up wolf fight," November 10, 2009.

*Jackson Hole Daily* (AP), "Montana ends wolf hunt early," November 17, 2009.

*Jackson Hole Daily* (AP), "Southwest gray wolf recovery act a failure," December 7, 2009.

*Jackson Hole Daily* (AP), "Montana: Wolf hunt works, but suit looms," December 10, 2009.*Jackson Hole Daily*, State/Regional, "Record wolf deaths in Rockies after delisting," December 23, 2009.

*Jackson Hole Daily* (AP), "Wyo. Disputes lack of good faith over wolves." January 1/16-17/2010.

*Idaho Falls Post Register* (AP), "Utah bill proposes wolf captures, kills," January 24, 2010.

*Jackson Hole Daily* (AP), "Tally: Despite hunts, wolves holding steady," January 29, 2010.

*Jackson Hole Daily* (AP), "Wyoming continues wolf fight," January 30-31, 2010.

*Jackson Hole Daily* (AP), "Famed YNP wolf pack down to 1 member," March 8, 2010.

*Jackson Hole Daily* (AP), "Wolf population rose last year in N. Rockies," March 13-14, 2010.

Colligan, C., "Wolves add to mystique of hunting," *Jackson Hole News and Guide*, March 17, 2010.

Hatch, C., "Hunters rally to disperse wolves," *Jackson Hole News and Guide*, March 17, 2010.

Hatch, C., "Wolf protest draws 200 to downtown Jackson," *Jackson Hole Daily*, March 22, 2010.

Strong, H., "Wolf rally considers moot point for many," *Valley Citizen*, March 24, 2010.

Cannon, B., "Wolf protest may spark more," *JH Weekly*, March 24-30, 2010.

*Jackson Hole Daily*, Boise AP, Idaho hunters bag 185 wolves as season ends," April 1, 2010.

Wilkinson, T. "Wolf rhetoric makes some folks look silly," *The New West, Jackson Hole News and Guide*, March 31, 2010.

"RMEF Turns Up Heat on Pro-Wolf Groups," e-mail advertisement sent to Rocky Mountain Elk Foundation members April 11, 2010.

Wuerthner, G. "If we want healthy elk, we need wolves," *Jackson Hole News and Guide*, June 16, 2010.

# V

## QUESTIONS FOR THE READER
## DISCUSSION GROUPS

These questions are intended to be conversation guides for readers and book discussion groups. They are proposed to assist the sharing of conversation and discussion of issues and topics. They are not to be judged as comprehensive, there arc many more unasked and unanswered questions and topics to explore than what are listed here. These represent only a sampling or primer.

1. How important is the natural world in your life? Does wildlife contribute to your quality of life? Do wild animals contribute to a sense of place for you? How close do you live from protected or conserved lands (national forest, Wilderness, national Park, wildlife refuge, etc.), i.e., less than fifty kilometers (~31 miles)?

2. Assuming you feel that wildlife does contribute to your quality of life and sense of place, what animals does that include, and which, if any, large predators?  Do you value some species more than others? Why? Do you feel unduly threatened by the presence or existence of large predators in the wild or near your home?  Why?

3.  Have you or your family ever had an experience with a wild animal that is unforgettable or life altering? What was it? Why was it unforgettable? If you were to pick a favorite animal to serve as your talisman or guardian what would it be?

4. What animals do you consider the most iconic, symbolic or emblematic of the American West?   What animals best symbolize wilderness or wild America? What  is the status of those animals today? What, if anything, can or must we do in order to better coexist with those creatures?

5. What are some of the attitudes, beliefs, and practices that led to the decimation and decline of wildlife in the settlement of this country? Were those attitudes and practices necessary for settlement and the advancement of civilization? Do you believe people growing up in rural areas, farms, and ranches a generation or two ago, could have had their attitudes towards wildlife influenced by government sponsored anti-predator and pest programs and propaganda and the monies local and state governments received for those programs?

6. Do you believe that the animosity and strongly negative feelings and beliefs directed towards certain animals today are vestigial holdovers from earlier times? If so, why do they often appear most strongly directed toward nongame species, predatory animals, and wilderness habitat?

7. Do you agree some attitudes and practices towards wildlife and wildlands have been passed down through generations? Do you think those mindsets color or influence wildlife and resource management decisions through state and local politics and officials yet today, and if so, in what ways?

8. Sport hunter groups frequently claim they were responsible for the restoration of wildlife in North America. Conversely, they led the fight against predators, and in many cases still do. Why is that? What are the agencies, groups or organizations today that are more apt to lead the fight to restore and protect ecosystems, nongame wildlife, and endangered species? What role does science play?

9. What constitutes the differences between sport hunting and simply killing? What does "fair chase" mean to you? Given our general populace's separation from the natural world, use of technology, and the economics of sport hunting, do you think the differences between hunting and killing are sometimes blurred and not well understood or appreciated? Have you ever personally discovered that raising the issue of hunting ethics can risk being labeled "anti-hunting?"

10. Do you feel large predatory animals are too dangerous to allow to roam free in our world today? Who is in charge of managing them? Who in your opinion really makes the decisions for their existence, management, and control? Do you think the management techniques and methods are appropriate, or are they sometimes too heavy handed? Do you believe it is constructive to pose rhetorical questions such as: "must we control what was otherwise intended to be wild?"

11. Given the financial costs for a species recovery, state and local politics, disparate agendas, different ways to interpret data, and the uncontrolled variables involved, do you think maybe quotas or bag limits, recovery efforts, and recovery population goals, should try to err on the conservative side, or should maximum or minimum limits be imposed as dictated by local and state officials and trial and error methods to compensate and mitigate be employed? In your opinion, does it matter? What about public transparency in such methods, do you think it is adequate?

12. Do you feel that a dichotomy or divide between the natural world and contemporary society exists? Is the divide growing or narrowing locally? Nationally? What, in your opinion, might be responsible for fostering the divergence; or on-the-other-hand, improvement? What can be done, or is being done, to establish that we are a part of nature and that we share the Earth with other living creatures? Do you feel it matters and why?

13. Do you think bison are emblematic of the American West? Do you believe bison are still being persecuted? If so, what are the attitudes contributing to their treatment? Where do those attitudes originate? Do you think there could be other issues underlying or contributing to the recent slaughtering of bison that leave the park besides brucellosis disease control?

14. Can you name some wildlife habitats in the Rocky Mountain west that currently appear to be undergoing modification? What wildlife species are being affected? Can you name some habitats that have been impacted over the past century? How about in the recent past? Are you aware of any animals in North America that might be affected by climate

change? Do you think wildfire may eventually play a role in the West's beetle-killed forests, whether we want it to or not?

15. What do you think has made the restoration of big game animals and their attendant predators possible in the western United States, as compared to in the eastern states which once supported the same animals? What more might be done, while opportunity still remains? Where are those opportunities? What are the potential conflicts?

16. Do you believe we can learn to better coexist with wildlife? What does coexistence mean to you? What is meant by "rewilding"? What are "core areas, corridors, and connectivity" and how do they function in helping to maintain ecosystems? Do you think there is value in restoring ecosystems? Is applying the rewilding concept realistic in the United States today?

17. What do you feel have been some of the key components—animals, habitats, etc.— involved in ecosystem restoration in Yellowstone and the northern Rocky Mountains to date? Can you give example(s) of places where in the United States the full pre-settlement assemblage of wildlife species currently exists and/or has been restored? How do you think this may play out in the future as human populations and associated development continues to grow—will maintaining and restoring wildlands and wildlife be recognized as more important, less important, an impossibility, or as conflicting with economic progress?

18. The stories in this book different in style and approach, "from whimsical to the informed scientific," but there are repeated and underlying similar messages throughout most of them. Can you identify some of those? For example, did you find that attitudes towards even widely different animals like

bison, mountain lions, wolverine, grizzly bears, and wolves may have similar historical origins? Do you also find it significant that those are all "flagship species" currently representing major wildlife conservation efforts in the United States? What is it about water ouzels, rock rabbits,  beavers, and whitebark pine that might inspire stories to be told about them; and at least in part, in a whimsical and anthropomorphized manner? In the popularized nature writings, did blending folklore, history, and current issues with scientific facts lessen the veracity and significance of the stories for you, or did it help to make it more interesting,  entertaining, and readable?

# VI
## ABOUT THE AUTHOR

The author, Earle F. Layser, grew up in the 1940s-50s on a farm in a rural and mountainous setting near the small and picturesque village of Cedar Run located in north-central Pennsylvania. It was a different time and place with outdoor privies, no indoor water, and woodstoves. The local populace traditionally relied on hunting, fishing, and other outdoor activities for entertainment and subsistence. The author fished, hunted and ran traplines; from an early age, his destiny was determined by the outdoors and wildlands. He experienced a boyhood freedom of roaming the mountains and forests, which were populated with wildlife; something he admittedly didn't fully appreciate until later in life. After completing an enlistment in the military, at age twenty-one the author matriculated in forestry at the University of Montana and was a smokejumper. He next earned a Master of Science degree in botany and plant ecology at

New York State College of Environmental Sciences at Syracuse and later completed additional graduate studies in biosystematics and ecology at Washington State University and Colorado State University, working his way through school as a teaching and research assistant, herbarium curator, sawmill laborer, and in seasonal forestry positions. He achieved certification as a wildlife biologist by The Wildlife Society, a professional ecologist by The Ecological Society of America, and as a forester by the Society of American Foresters. In 1977, he was the recipient of the prestigious national American Motors Conservation Award. The author's career took him throughout the western United States and Alaska in various resource management and administrative positions with the U.S. Forest Service and Department of Interior, and later, as a private consultant. In 1976, his career brought him to the Greater Yellowstone in Jackson Hole, Wyoming, which he had first visited as child with his parents in 1947, camping out of the back of a wood-paneled station wagon. The author discovered a strong connection to the area, especially its abundant wildlife and backcountry. In 1990, he retired from government service and returned to the Tetons as a natural resources consultant, photographer, and writer. He has published scientific research papers and monographs on land-use planning, botany, plant ecology, and wildlife, and also a number and variety of popular articles in periodicals on natural history, travel and history. He is the author of two other books, *Flora of Pend Oreille County, Washington,* and the award winning biography, *I Always Did Like Horses and Women: Enoch Cal Carrington's Life Story.* He and his wife, Pattie, currently live with their dog, Benji, on the west slope of the Tetons in Alta, Wyoming. Benji provided comfort and support by sleeping on the author's foot throughout the writing of this book.

# NOTES